HARDPRESS.NET
HOME OF HARD-TO-FIND BOOKS

Transactions of the Bombay Geographical Society ...
by Bombay Geographical Society

The Transactions of the Bombay Geographical Society

Bombay Geographical Society

THE

TRANSACTIONS

OF THE

BOMBAY GEOGRAPHICAL SOCIETY.

FROM MAY 1858 TO MAY 1860.

(EDITED BY THE SECRETARY.)

VOLUME XV.

BOMBAY:

SMITH, TAYLOR, & CO.

MDCCCLX.

CONTENTS OF VOL. XV.

CONTENTS OF PROCEEDINGS.

SESSION 1858-59.

OCTOBER MEETING.

NOVEMBER MEETING.

JANUARY MEETING.

FEBRUARY MEETING.

CONTENTS.

CONTENTS.

CONTENTS.

[*N. B.*—The Authors are alone responsible for the contents of their respective papers.]

ILLUSTRATIONS.

RULES AND REGULATIONS.

1st. This Society, established for the purpose of encouraging and instituting Geographical researches in Western Asia, and the countries contiguous, is denominated the Bombay Geographical Society.

2nd. The Society shall consist of Honorary and Ordinary Members.

3rd. Every candidate for admission, whether as an Ordinary or Honorary Member, must be proposed and seconded at one Meeting of the Society, and balloted for at the next.

4th. No person shall be considered duly elected, unless he unite in his favour the votes of three-fourths of the Members present.

5th. An annual Subscription, amounting to Rs. 15, to be paid by all Members in advance, on the 1st of April of each year.

6th. Members may compromise, by a single payment of Rs. 100, instead of a payment of Rs. 15 annually.

7th. *Of the Office-Bearers and Committee.*—The Office-Bearers shall consist of a President, a Secretary, and Treasurer,—permanent ; three Vice-Presidents, and a General Committee of Management (consisting of 20 Members), to be chosen annually.

8th. That the Committee of Management and other Office-Bearers of the Society, eligible annually, shall be chosen by general vote of the Ordinary Members, to whom voting lists shall be forwarded three months previous to the Anniversary Meeting, at which the returns shall be scrutinised and announced.

9th. Two Sub-Committees, consisting of six Members each, shall be annually selected from among the Resident Members of the General Committee, at the first meeting after the annual election of the latter. The Sub-Committee having the superintendence of all the internal management, account, &c. of the Society, shall be denominated the " Sub-Committee of Accounts :" the other shall conduct the correspondence of the Society, and suggest plans for attaining its scientific objects—to be called " The Sub-Committee of Correspondence."

10th. The Secretary shall be a Member of the Committee of Management *ex-officio.*

11th. Each Sub-Committee can meet independently of the other for the purpose of discharging the business especially entrusted to it ; and the meeting shall be summoned by a circular from the Secretary.

p 1

12th.   The Sub-Committee of Accounts shall lay before the Annual General Meeting, to be held in May or April of each year, the state of the Society's Funds.   The Sub-Committee of Correspondence shall lay before the same Meeting a list of the Scientific Contributions made to the Society during the year.

13th.   Each Sub-Committee shall elect, from among its Members, a President to preside at its meetings.

14th.   The President shall preside at the General Meetings of the Society, to conduct the Proceedings, and give effect to the Resolutions.

15th.   The Vice-Presidents shall preside at the General Meetings in the absence of the President, and in rotation at Meetings of the General Committee of Management.

16th.   The Secretary shall attend the Meetings of the Society and those of the Committee, to record their proceedings and conduct the correspondence.   He shall also superintend the persons employed by the Society, and, under the control of the Committee for managing the accounts, shall superintend the expenditure of the establishment.

17th.   The Treasurer will receive, through the Secretary, all monies due to the Society, and make payments out of the funds of the Society according to the directions of the Secretary.

18th.   The Society shall meet on the third Thursday of every month, at 4.30 p. m.

19th.   Notice shall be given, either at a previous Meeting or to the Secretary, of any motion or subject of discussion intended to be brought before the Meeting, at least one week beforehand ; and all matters of business, &c., intended to be brought before the Society, shall be notified to the Members by printed circulars.

20th.   Each Member may introduce a friend to all ordinary Meetings of the Society.

21st.   The Society shall present copies of its transactions to the principal Public Libraries in India, Europe, and America ; and exchange them with Societies, and with such authors or publishers as may be disposed to bestow works of equivalent value, or nearly so, on the library of the Society.

22nd.   All Members of the Bombay Branch of the Royal Asiatic Society are entitled to be admitted Members of the Geographical Society, on making application to this effect through the Secretary, and paying the prescribed annual subscription.

LIBRARY REGULATIONS.

The following are the Rules in force for the Management of the Library :—

1.   The Books of the Geographical Society's Library may be taken out by Members, subject to the following exceptions and restrictions.

2.   No Book shall be delivered out by the Librarian, unless the Member requiring it shall either sign the entry in the Register, or send a receipt to him.

3.   No Member shall keep any Book longer than fourteen days.

4.   Any Member requiring a Book which has been delivered out, may insert, or cause to be inserted, his name in a Register kept for that purpose ;   and it shall be the duty of the Librarian to apply for it as soon as the period specified in the above rule has expired, and, on receipt, to forward it to the first on the list of applicants if there be more than one.

5.   Not more than three volumes to be taken out at one time by any Member.

6.   The Librarian shall inspect carefully every Book at the time it is returned, and, if damaged, shall report the circumstance to the Secretary.

7.   Any Book lost or damaged, shall be charged to the Member in whose name it stood in the Register, at the invoice price, or such price as shall be fixed by the Committee of Management.

8.   Members leaving Bombay, are required to return, before their departure, to the Library, all Books belonging to it in their possession, — and no Book shall be carried out of Bombay.

9.   No Map, Chart, Atlas, or Book of Reference, shall be taken out, without express permission from the Committee of Management, except Books of Reference (for 48 hours) on the order of the Secretary to that effect.

10.   Any Member may propose Books, Charts, Maps, or Atlases, to be added to the Library, by inserting their names in a Register kept for that purpose, and they will be ordered or not as the Committee may deem expedient.

11.   Every new Work, Map, Chart, &c., shall lie on the table one month before it is taken out.

p 1 ● ←

BOMBAY GEOGRAPHICAL SOCIETY.

(Established in 1832.)

Honorary Patron.

EARL CANNING, Viceroy Governor General of India.

Patron.

His Excellency the Honorable Sir GEORGE R. CLERK, *K.C.B.*, Governor of Bombay.

President.

Commodore G. G. WELLESLEY, *C.B.*, R. N., Commander in Chief Indian Navy.

Vice Presidents.

BARKER, Captain W. C., I. N.
FRERE, Honorable W. E., C. S.
LEITH, A. H., Esq., *M.D.*

Resident Members of the Committee.

BHAWOO DAJEE, Esq.
BIRDWOOD, G. C. M., Esq., *M.D.*
CURSETJEE, Sir JAMSETJEE JEEJEE-
BHOY, Bart.
FERGUSSON, Lieutenant E. F. T., I. N.,
F.R.A.S.
HAINES, R., Esq., *M.D.*
HUNTER, W. F., Esq.

MITCHELL, Rev. J. M., *LL.D.*
NARRAYEN DINANATHJEE, Esq.
PENGELLEY, Lieut. W. M., I. N.
RITCHIE, JOHN, Esq.
SINCLAIR, R. S., Esq., *LL.D.*
WINCHESTER, J. W., Esq., *LL.D.*,
F.R.C.S.

Non-Resident Members.

BROUGHTON, Dr. F., *F.R.C.S.*
BUIST, GEORGE, Esq., *LL.D.*
CONSTABLE, Commander C. G.
FRERE, Sir H. Bartle Edw., *K.C.B.*

JACOB, Brigadier General LeGrand.
JENKINS, Captain G., *C.B.*, I. N.
JONES, Captain J. F., I. N.
KEMBALL, Major A. B.

Sub-Committee of Correspondence.

BIRDWOOD, G. C. M., Esq., *M.D.*
HAINES, R., Esq., *M.D.*
HUNTER, W. F., Esq.

PENGELLEY, Lieut. W. M., I. N.
RITCHIE, John, Esq.
SINCLAIR, R. S., Esq., *LL.D.*

Sub-Committee of Accounts.

BHAWOO DAJEE, Esq.
CURSETJEE, Sir J. JEEJEEBHOY, Bart.
FERGUSSON, Lieut. E. F. T., I. N.

MITCHELL, Rev. J. M., *LL.D.*
NARRAYEN DINANATHJEE, Esq.
WINCHESTER, J. W., Esq., *LL.D.*,
F.R.C.S.

Secretary.

KENNELLY, D. J., Esq., I. N.

Treasurers.

Messrs. REMINGTON & Co.

v

𝔐embers

(To September 1860).

Year of Election.		Year of Election.	
1855	Anderson, H. L., Esq., C. S.	1855	30 † Hamilton, Commander B., I. N.
,,	Anderson, T., Esq., *M.D.*		
1843	* Barker, Captain W. C., I. N.	1848	Harrison, C. M., Esq., C. S.
1855	Berkley, J. J., Esq., *C.E.*	1859	Heycock, E., Esq.
1858	Bin Hamees, Captain Mahomed.	1855	Hunter, W. F., Esq.
1859	Birdwood, G. C. M., Esq., *M.D.*	1848	Impey, Elijah.
1849	Bradley, W. H., Esq., *F.R.C.S.*	1836	Jacob, Brigadier General G. LeGrand, *C.B.*
1859	Broughton, F., Dr., *F.R.C.S.*		
1840	Buist, George, Esq., *LL.D.*, *F.R.S.*	1855	Jamsetjee Sorabjee, Esq.
		1851	† Jeejeebhoy, Sir Cursetjee Jamsetjee, Bart.
1860	10 Carlile, the Rev. J. E.		
1837	*Collier, C. F., Esq.	1838	*† Jenkins, Captain G., *C.B.*, I. N.
1846	Constable, Commander G. C., I. N.	1849	* Jenkins, T. L., Esq.
		1846	40 Jones, Captain James Felix, I. N.
1848	Conybeare, H., Esq.	1849	Jugonath Venaik Rao, Esq.
1840	Cursetjee Manockjee, Esq., *F.R.G.S.*	1846	Kemball, Major A. B., *C.B.*
		1856	Kennelly, D. J., Esq., I. N.
1853	* Dajee Bhawoo, Esq.	,,	Kingcome, C., Esq.
,,	Dajee Narayan, Esq.	1860	Kingstone, Dr. H. C.
1848	Davidass Munmohundass, Esq.	1855	Leggatt, C. D., Esq.
1854	Dinanathjee Narayan, Esq.	1858	Leith, A. H., Esq., *M.D.*
1855	Erskine, J. M., Esq., C. S.	1859	† Lewis, Lieutenant G. L.
1860	20 Faithfull, F. D., Esq.	,,	† Lowndes, John J., Esq.
1848	* Fergusson, Lieut. E. F. T., I. N., *F.R.A.S.*	1850	50 McLeod, D. P., Esq.
		1860	Maclean, J. M., Esq.
,,	Ford, C. G. E., Esq., *M.D.*	1859	Madhowdass Virjeevundass, Esq.
1859	Fletcher, the Rev. W. K., *M.A.*	1845	Mahomed Khan Ali, Esq.
,,	Forster, Lieut. C., I. N.	1860	Mansfield, General Sir William, *K.C.B.*
1849	Framjee Dhunjeebhoy, Esq.		
1860	Fraser, J. A., Esq., *M.D.*	1848	† Malet, A. B., C. S.
1845	Frere, the Hon'ble W. E., C. S., *F.R.G.S.*, *F.R.A.S.*	1860	Mitchell, the Rev. J. Murray, *LL.D.*
1859	Frere, Sir H. Bartle Edward, *K.C.B.*	1858	† Montmorency, Lieut. C. W.
1849	Haines, R., Esq., *M.D.*	1838	*† Morehead, Superintending Surgeon C., *M.D.*

Year of Election.		Year of Election.	
1856	† Mylne, Major Charles D.	1854	Sinclair, R. S., Esq., *LL.D.*
1859	60 Narrayen Wishwanath, Rao Sahib, Esq.	1859	Stiffe, Lieutenant A. W., I. N.
		1850	80 Sunkersett Jugonath, Esq.
,,	Nixon, Lieutenant G. J., I. N.	1859	Sweny, Lieutenant M. A., I. N.
1854	Nowrojee Dadabhoy, Esq.	1860	Sylvester, J. H., Esq., *F.G.S.*
1855	Nuthoobhoy Munguldass, Esq.	1848	Taylor, Lieutenant A. D., I. N.
1859	Pandoorung Atmaram, Esq.	1850	Vaughan, Dr. J., *F.R.C.S.,*
1860	Pelly, W. A., Esq.		*F.R.G.S.*
1859	Pengelley, Lieut. W. M., I. N.	1850	Walker, Captain C. W.
1860	† Philbrick, Lieut. T. M., I. N.	1856	Wassoodewjee Venaik Rao, Esq.
1859	Pryce, J. E. C., Esq.	1859	Watson, Lieutenant R. G.
,,	Punnett, T. F., Esq.	1857	Wellesley, Commodore G. G.,
1850	70 Raverty, Captain H. G.		*C.B.*, R. N.
1849	† Ritchie, John, Esq.	1859	Whish, Lieutenant R. W., I. N.
1855	Robertson, A., Esq.	,,	90 Williams, Lieutenant R., I. N.
1860	Robertson, Colonel G. H., *C.B.*, Aide-de-Camp to the Queen.	1854	† Willis, R., Esq.
		1839	† Winchester, J. W., Esq.,
1859	Robinson, Lieut. G. T., I. N.		*LL.D.*, *F.R.C.S.*
1851	Ross, Dr. J. T. C.	1850	Wray, Major J.
1855	† Scovell, F., Esq.	,,	† Young, H., Esq., C.S.
1859	Seward, G. E., Esq., *M.D.*		

Honorary Members.

The following list contains the names of those who have been elected Honorary Members of the Society from its original institution to the present time :—

Avezac, Monsieur D'.
Bache, Professor A. D., U. S. C. S.
Bergans, Professor Heinrich.
Du Pont, Captain, U. S. Navy.
Greni, H. E. M. La.
Johnston, Alex. Keith, Esq., *F.R.S.E.*
Jomard, Mr. E. F., Mem. Inst. France.
Kupffer, Professor M. A. T., St. Petersburgh.

Lyell, Sir Charles, *M.A.*, *LL.D.*, *F.R.S.*
Maury, Commander M. F., U. S. Navy.
Morreau, Cæsar, Esq.
Oberreit, Major General.
Sabine, Maj. Gen. Edw., R. A.
Shaw, Dr. Norton.
Somerville, Mrs. Mary.
Washington, Captain John, R. N., *F.R.S.* Hydrographer to the Navy.

LIST OF PUBLIC INSTITUTIONS, &c.,

TO WHICH COPIES OF THE TRANSACTIONS ARE PRESENTED.

LONDON.

Athenæum Newspaper.

Chairman of the Court of Directors of the East India Company.

Hakluyt Society.

Hydrographer of H. M.'s Lords of Admiralty.

Keeper of the Library of the British Museum.

Library of the Royal Asiatic Society.

Library of the Royal Geographical Society.

Library of the Royal Institution.

Library of the Royal King's College.

Literary Gazette.

Peninsular and Oriental Steam Navigation Company.

President of the Asiatic Society.

Royal Geological Society.

Royal Naval College.

SCOTLAND.

Advocates' Library Edinburgh.

Free Church College   ditto.

Marshall College   ditto.

Library of Writers to the Signet ditto.

Meteorological Society.

Royal Society Edinburgh.

University   ditto.

University Library, Glasgow.

University Library, Aberdeen.

University Library, St. Andrews.

DUBLIN.
University Library.

OXFORD.
University Library.

CAMBRIDGE.
University Library.

DURHAM.
University Library.

WALES.
St. David's College.

MUNICH.
Royal Academy of Sciences.

PARIS.

Asiatic Society.
Ethnological Society.
Geographical Society.

Oriental Society.
University Library.

CAIRO.

Library of the Literary Society.

INDIA.—CALCUTTA.

Asiatic Society.
Bengal Hurkaru.
Calcutta Review.
Director of Public Education.

Englishman.
Friend of India.
Office of the Surveyor General.
Saint Andrew's Library.

MADRAS.

Athenæum Newspaper.
Literary Society.

Madras Observatory.
Trevandrum Observatory.

MAURITIUS.

Meteorological Society.

Royal Observatory.

CEYLON.

The Asiatic Society.

AMERICA.

National Observatory.

Smithsonian Institution, Washington.

BOMBAY.

Ahmednuggur Establishment for the
  Bombay Artillery.
Ahmednuggur Native Library.
Bombay Branch Royal Asiatic Society.
Bombay Mechanics' Institution.
Byculla Boys' School.
Chamber of Commerce.
Colaba Observatory.
Editor of the Bombay Times and
  Standard.
Editor of the Bombay Gazette.
Editor of the Telegraph and Courier.
Editor of the Bombay Guardian.
Elphinstone College.

Fort Improvement Library.
Grant Medical College.
Kurrachee Native Library.
Medical and Physical Society.
Naval Institution.
Naval Sanitarium.
Native Book Club.
Native General Library.
Poonah Library.
Students' Literary and Scientific
  Society's Library.
Surat Native Library.
Tannah Library.

ALPHABETICAL LIST OF DONORS.

INDIVIDUALS.

Avezac, M. D., Esq.
Balfour, Edward, Esq.
Barker, Captain W. C., I. N.
Barth, J. A., Esq.
Berkley, J. J., Esq.
Bhawoo Dajee, Esq.
Birdwood, G. C. M., Esq., *M.D.*
Brown, L., Esq.
Buist, Geo., Esq., *LL.D.*
Constable, Commander G. C., I. N.
Dalzell, A. N., Esq.
Dawson, J., Esq.
Dempsey, G. D., Esq.
De Sa', Mr.
Du Pont, Captain S. F., U. S. N.
Farish, Captain.
Faulkner, A., Esq.
Fergusson, Lieut. E. F. T., I. N., *F.R.A.S.*
Forster, Lieut. C., I. N.
Frere, Honorable W. E.
Frere, Sir H. B. E., *K.C.B.*
Giraud, Dr. H.
Heycock, E., Esq.
Kennelly, D. J., Esq., I. N.
Lange, D. A., Esq.

Leeman, J., Commanding "*Ambrosine.*"
Logan, J. R., Esq., *F.G.S.*
Macgowan, D. J., Esq.
Marriott, Captain W. F.
Morehead, Dr. C. Principal Grant Medical College.
Morris, Captain H., "*Balcarras.*"
Murchison, Sir R. J.
Philbrick, Lieut. T. M., I. N.
Pullen, Captain, R. N.
Quaritch, B., Esq.
Rigby, Lieut. Col. C. P.
Ritchie, John, Esq.
Robinson, Lieut. G. T., I. N.
Sinclair, R. S., Esq., *LL.D.*
Smith, Messrs., Taylor & Co.
Speke, Captain J. H.
Spooner, R., Esq.
Stiffe, Lieutenant A. W., I. N.
Taylor, Lieutenant A. D., I. N.
Thompson, J. G., Esq.
Wales, D., Esq.
Welsh, Captain.
Whish, Lieut. R. W., I. N.
Williams, Lieutenant R., I. N.
Young, H., Esq., C. S.

SOCIETIES AND INSTITUTIONS.

Asiatic Society of France.

Asiatic Society of Great Britain and Ireland.

Bombay (The) Branch Royal Asiatic Society.

Bombay (The) Mechanics' Institution.

Ceylon Branch Royal Asiatic Society.

Chamber of Commerce.

Geographical (Royal) Society of London.

Geographical Society of Paris.

German Geological Society.

Government of Bombay.

Government of British Guiana.

Hakluyt Society.

Hemabae Institute.

Madras Exhibition Society.

Medical and Physical Society of Bombay.

Royal Institution of Great Britain and Ireland.

Smithsonian Institution, Washington.

Society of Antiquaries of Scotland.

Superintendent of the Geological Survey of India.

Superintendent of the U. S. Coast Survey.

PROCEEDINGS

OF THE

BOMBAY GEOGRAPHICAL SOCIETY.

SESSION 1858-59.

FIRST MEETING.—*Thursday, October 21st, 4½ P. M.*

Present.—Commodore G. G. Wellesley, *President*, in the Chair ; W. E. Frere, Esq., C. S., *Vice-President ;* Brigadier General LeGrand Jacob ; Commander Barker ; Dr. Leith ; Jugonath Sunkersett, Esq. ; Cursetjee Jamsetjee, Esq. ; Venayekrao Jugonathjee, Esq. ; Dr. Bhawoo Dajee ; D. J. Kennelly, Esq. ; F. Scovell, Esq. ; Ali Mahomed Khan, Esq. ; Captain Mahomed bin Hamees.

The Minutes of the last Meeting were read and confirmed.

Presents to the Library.

1. Report of the External Commerce of Bombay for the year 1857-58. By R. Spooner, Esq.
2. Journal of the Royal Geographical Society, Vol. XXVII. By the Society.
3. Bulletin de la Société de Géographie, Tome XV. By the Society.
4. Annual Report of the Grant Medical College, Bombay, Session 1857-58. By the Principal of the College.
5. A Lecture on the Laws of Motion, by R. S. Sinclair, Esq. By the Bombay Mechanics' Institution.
6. A Sketch for a Map of Knowledge, by G. D. Dempsey, Esq. By the Author.
7. Government Central Museum (Madras) Catalogue. By E. Balfour, Esq.
8. Paper on the Bhore Ghaut Railway Incline, by J. J. Berkley, Esq. By the Mechanics' Institution.
9. Lecture on Combustion, by Dr. Giraud. By the Author.

The Secretary then stated that a recent change in his occupation began to stand in the way of the discharge of his duties ; that he was still not without leisure enough occasionally to contribute to their Transactions.   Time was no longer at his command, at fixed and definite periods, permitting preparations to be made for or attendance given at Meetings occurring at stated dates, such as was indispensable for an Office-bearer ; and he was, therefore, compelled to tender his resignation of an office for sixteen years held by him.   To avoid occasioning inconvenience to the Society, he should continue, if so desired, to act till his successor assumed office.

After some remarks on the subject, it was suggested that the tender of the resignation had better be submitted to the Committee in writing, to enable Members to put their sentiments on the subject on record.

A discourse was then delivered by the Secretary on the Earthquakes which had occurred in India from 1842 to 1848, in continuation of Colonel Baird Smith's list of Earthquakes from that date backwards, published in the Journal of the Bengal Asiatic Society.

SESSION 1858-59.

SECOND MEETING.—*Thursday, November 18th,* 4½ P. M.

Present.—Commodore G. G. Wellesley, Commander-in-Chief of the Indian Navy, *President,* in the Chair ; the Honorable W. E. Frere ; H. B. E. Frere, Esq., Commissioner of Sind ; Dr. Winchester ; Commander Barker; D. J. Kennelly, Esq., I. N.; F. Scovell, Esq.; Venayekrao Jugonathjee, Esq.; Captain Mahomed bin Hamees.

Letters read.—No. 134 of 1858, from J. A. Crowe, Esq., Acting Secretary to the Chamber of Commerce, Bombay; from Dr. E. Impey, Dr. G. Buist, and from Lieutenant Constable.

Presents to the Library.—Report of the Bombay Chamber of Commerce for the last year.   Presented by the Chamber.

The only matter of business was the election of a Secretary in room of Dr. Buist, resigned.

With reference to Dr. Buist's letter to the General Committee, tendering his resignation of the office of Secretary, it was resolved that the President should address to him a letter on the subject.

The following extracts from letters from Lieutenant Constable, on the Physical Geography of the Persian Gulf, were then read by the President :—

" We have already made some important discoveries, and seen some old places of great interest.   The most curious place was at Tarie, where we explored the ruins of an early Mahomedan city, called Siraf. This was a considerable port and seat of commerce during the ninth and tenth centuries, and even in that early age carried on a trade with China.   It appears that the inhabitants of this town were at last compelled to abandon it, to escape from the oppression of the natives of the interior, and that they removed to this island.   This we learn from the Arabian Geographers; and also·that this island became the seat of Government.   Sir William Ouseley says that the Persian manuscripts state that this became a great commercial place in the tenth century, and that all the islands in the Gulf belonged to the sovereigns of this island.   Therefore, this was a flourishing place long before Ormuz came into notice, or probably long before Ormuz Island was even inhabited.   It appears, however, that there had been a place called Hormuz on the main land (where Gomberoon, afterwards called Bunder Abass, stands) from a very early period; and that these people, like those at Siraf, were compelled to resort to an island, in order to escape the oppression of the natives of the interior.   They, therefore, applied to the king of this island (Ghaise, or Khais, or, as the English call it, Kenn), and having obtained a grant of a desert island, lying opposite to their territory, they removed thither, and gave it the name of the country they had quitted.   These settlers on the new Ormuz, or Island of Ormuz, became rich and powerful to such an extent, that in 1320 they conquered Khais. Thus did Khais fall into decay as Ormuz rose into consequence. The Kings of Ormuz were Arabs, and for 200 years it enjoyed a course of high prosperity, in the acquisition of power as well as of riches, for it extended its sway from Ras-el-ad nearly to Basra. The Portuguese attacked it in 1507, but it was not until eight years afterwards that the Portuguese succeeded in obtaining possession. From this period, the wealthy and powerful kingdom of Ormuz declined. In 1622, the Persians, with the assistance of the English, took it from the Portuguese. I was naturally led to speak so much of Ormuz owing to its relation with this island, but this is the island we are interested in just at present. We have been so long now at Khais, that I have had an opportunity of exploring the island, and have found the ruins of the early Arab city on the north shore of the island. The mounds of stones, the débris of broken, ruined buildings, cover a very great extent of ground. Many of the buildings must have been large and lofty, judging by the size and height of the mounds of stones. The reservoirs for water are numerous, and some very large, and constructed in a superior manner. One was 120 feet long, 24 feet wide, by 30 feet deep ; it had been covered with an arched roof, and the sides had been cemented. Another reservoir near to this was 145 feet long! But the most remarkable was a subterraneous reservoir, which was from $\frac{1}{4}$ to $\frac{1}{2}$ a mile long, with shafts sunk at every twenty yards for the purpose of giving light and air, and also for receiving the rain water. There were thirty-eight of these shafts ; there were also four staircases cut through the rock to descend to it by. This, I felt sure, was the ruins of the commercial city built by the Moslems from Siraf, and which flourished in the twelfth century. The trade which Siraf carried on with China was continued between this place and China no doubt, and what would appear to prove this, is the vast quantity of broken China-ware to be picked up now among the mounds, all small fragments it is true, but some pieces are of superior quality,—of an ornamental pattern not met with commonly.

This island might be made a very valuable possession, barren as it now appears ; the soil is not bad, and if the Natives could afford to irrigate the soil, anything would grow. It might be a garden. Fresh water is obtainable along the shore wherever you please to dig a little hole."   *   *   *

" It is to be regretted that, although Karrak has been twice in the possession of the British, our Government are still without a marine survey of it and the neighbouring island of the Korgo with its outlying reefs.   The Persian Government is so jealous, that to survey those islands, whilst in their hands, is out of the question."

" We left Bushire on our cruise for fixing the positions on 27th September 1857, and returned last Friday, having been absent nearly seven months. We have taken observations on two points of the coast of Arabia, one 67 miles N. W. of El Katif, the other at Cape Moosendom, and fixed the position of Biddulph's Islands, which lie on the Arabian side of the Gulf: with the above exceptions, our attention has been devoted to the Persian shore, considering it the wisest course to proceed systematically, and finish one side at a time. The Persian coast, from Bushire down to the entrance of the Gulf, is nearly done, it remaining only to take observations at three or four more points.   The positions of all the islands on this side have been determined, also those named Surdy, Bomosa, and the Great Quoin. I had long known that the coast line near Linga on our charts was very erroneous ; I therefore triangulated the coast from Mogo Bay to Basadore.   This has proved that Cape Bostana is not the southern or most projecting point, as it is represented on the chart, but Shenas Point, nine miles to the eastward of it ; and the coast, instead of running west from Linga proceeds S.W.

" From every island, hill, or point on which we have landed, I have collected geological specimens, and have now a large collection packed in boxes. I have, moreover, some bricks, which I dug out of a mound about six miles south of Bushire ; they are covered with inscriptions in the cuneiform, or arrow-headed character ; and, therefore, according to Mr. Layard, the buried building from which I took them, belonged to an age preceding the conquest of Alexander.   I have before regretted, as a surveyor, that the opportunity of surveying Karrak was thrown away.   Now, as an antiquary, I must regret that the opportunity which presented when the British occupied the peninsula of Bushire was not seized upon to open this mound.   I was at work upon it with a crow-bar, &c., and a few lascars once ; and, from what I saw, I believe the mound encloses an ancient building.   The very little that I did towards uncovering it, showed the bricks beautifully placed, in perfect order—it was the top of a wall ; no doubt if the sand were carefully removed, a most interesting building would be brought to light."   *   *   *   *

The Acting Secretary said :—" That, though one of these letters had already been published, and formed the subject of a very valuable paper from Dr. Carter in the Asiatic Society, he thought that this was so entirely within the compass of the pursuits of the Geographical Society, that they ought to be embodied in its Reports." He continued :—" This Society, nearly a twelvemonth ago, addressed Government on the subject of collecting information in the Persian Gulf and the Arabian Sea. To these letters they have not hitherto been favoured with a reply. We specially called attention to the information deemed desirable in reference to the supposed volcanic nature of the Islands of Ormuz and Kishim. In one point their nomenclature seems to have fallen greatly short of the wants of Geology. While the terms ' Plutonic' and ' Volcanic' admirably indicate and distinguish two great classes of igneous rocks according to their age and character, 'Granitic' —or ' Primitive,' as they were wont to be called in the Wernerian vocabulary,—and ' Schistose,' the ' Trappean' or ' Volcanic' fails to indicate the difference betwixt the last and true recent volcanoes, whether active or inactive. Our impressions hitherto have been, that many of the islands of the Persian Gulf were true recent volcanoes, like Aden and the islands in the Red Sea from Gibbel Teer to the Straits. The appearance of sulphur bore out this view of the matter. But there is nothing in the letters of Mr. Constable, or paper of Dr. Carter, to show whether the idea be erroneous or correct. On examining the specimens themselves, I find that there is only one—a piece of red cemented mud—that can with any positiveness be pronounced the product of a recent volcano. The Asiatic Society has several specimens, collected twenty years ago by Commodore Brooks, several others presented in 1841 by Dr. R. Woosnam,—at that time on board the *Sesostris*—that have all the appearance of lava ; but the whole are so imperfect as specimens, as to lead us to speak with deference on the subject, and in reference to a fact so very easily determinable and of such very great interest—as to whether these be true recent volcanoes like those of Aden or the lower part of the Red Sea,—we are still in a state of incertitude. During the Persian Gulf expedition in 1856, some very excellent mill-stones were found at Bushire, said to have been brought from Bagdad ; they are about $2\frac{1}{4}$ feet in diameter and 8 to 9 inches thick ; they probably weigh about a hundred-weight, and must be driven —like those of the corn-mills in Egypt, when wind is not employed,— by bullock or horse power. On examining them, I found them composed of a variety of lava called Leucite—identical with that imported for mill-stones into Malta from Vesuvius—a specimen of which is now in the Central Museum, brought by me to Bombay in 1846. This again is identical with much of the lava of which Aden is composed. On inquiry, I found that Bagdad had been long famous for the manufacture and sale of mill-stones, and here are some dozen of those just described now in Bombay for the use of the Government flour-mills about to be established in the Deccan. Millstones will not bear the charge of long carriage, and the conclusion I arrive at from this is, that they must be from a recently extinct volcano in the neighbourhood of Bagdad, of which we know nothing. I make these remarks mainly in the hope of this meeting the eye of some one who may inquire into the matter. Any manufacturer of mill-stones would very readily show where the raw material came from, and a drawing and tolerable description of the mountain, with a collection of specimens, would furnish the bulk of the information we desire.

" It continues still necessary to direct the attention of collectors to the importance of obtaining, fresh and fair, specimens which they may send in ; they should be at least 5 inches square and $1\frac{1}{2}$ inch thick, and no portion of them weathered, decomposed, or decayed. Three-fourths of the specimens of the harder rocks sent to the Presidency are utterly worthless for the purposes of science, from want of attention to these indispensable and not very intricate or difficult provisions."

The Secretary then asked and obtained permission to postpone the paper on the Meteorological and Geological peculiarities of the Matheran and Bhow-Mullen masses of mountain, as he had not been able to prepare the model he proposed to exhibit, or make such a set of drawings as he considered satisfactory, and to substitute in its place some remarks on the views of Professor Owen, as laid before the British Association, on the age of man upon the earth. The paper will appear in the next number of the Transactions.

SESSION 1858-59.

THIRD MEETING.—*Thursday, January 20th,* 4½ P. M.

Present.—W. E. Frere, Esq., *Vice-President,* in the Chair.

Members.—D. J. Kennelly, Esq.; T. H. Bentley, Esq.; Dr. Birdwood; Dr. Bhawoo Dajee; and Juggonath Sunkersett, Esq.

The President and Secretary had both been absent from the Presidency on the 14th December, and there had not been a sufficient number of Members in attendance to constitute a meeting. The Minutes of the November Meeting having been read, the following letters were laid on the table.*

"To the General Committee of the Bombay Geographical Society.

Gentlemen,—A wish having been expressed at the last meeting of the Society, that my resignation of the office of Secretary, then tendered, should be submitted in form to the Committee, I now, in compliance with this, have the honour to intimate that it will no longer be in my power to hold the office, the duties of which I have, for sixteen years, used my humble endeavours to perform.

2. Looking back to the demise of your first Secretary, Dr. Heddle, whom I succeeded in March 1842, I feel fully satisfied of my many shortcomings, and of the kindness and consideration experienced in the midst of these at your hands.

3. If, of late years, our meetings have been less numerous than they were wont to be, and papers have flowed in on us in a scanty and interrupted stream, compared to the never-ceasing torrent in which they were wont to pour, our misfortune in these matters has not been peculiar; and, I trust, is not to be ascribed to any neglect on the part of your Secretary.

4. Though unable longer to attend with that punctuality which is indispensable for an official, I am not so utterly without leisure as to be compelled to forego the hope of sometimes contributing to your Transactions; and if my services in preparing and passing any portion of these through the printer's hands should be deemed desirable by the Society, they are at your command.

---

* We have given the whole correspondence on the subject of the resignation of the Secretary; in reality, the last two letters alone were read, the other had been disposed of at previous meetings, the reports of which have only in part been published.

5. I shall, meanwhile, if so wished, do my utmost to carry on the business of the Society until my successor be appointed and initiated in his duties ; and shall, in an especial manner, deem it a privilege to be permitted to bring to a state of completion the number of your Transactions sometime due, the printing of which is already in a considerable state of advancement.

I have the honour to be,
Gentlemen,
Your obedient Servant,

October 28th, 1858.　　　(Signed)　GEORGE BUIST."

"To GEORGE BUIST, Esq., LL.D.,
Secretary to the Geographical Society.

SIR,—At a meeting of the Geographical Society held on the 20th instant, your letter of October 28th, to the General Committee of the Society, tendering your resignation of the office of Secretary, and to which were appended the minutes made thereon by various Members thereof, was read, and it was unanimously resolved that the President should address to you a suitable letter of acknowledgment, expressing the sentiments which the Society entertain in regard to the services you have rendered, while fulfilling the onerous and responsible duty of Secretary for a period of above sixteen years, and their regret at the necessity which compels you now to relinquish that post.

2. The result of your labours in the paths of science is known and appreciated not only here, but through Great Britain and Europe. Enduring proofs of your efforts for the benefit of Geographical Science, however, in particular, are to be found on the records of this Society ; and any sketch that I could make of your exertions for the extension of the interests of it, must be most imperfect ; I shall, therefore, not attempt a recapitulation of them, but content myself with performing the pleasing duty with which I am entrusted.

3. In tendering to you the warmest thanks of the Bombay Geographical Society, for the zeal and faithfulness with which you have conducted the duties of its Secretary, I am happy to be assured that, as Member, you will still feel a deep interest in the objects of the Society,

and will continue to devote any leisure time to the subject in which its Members are so much interested.

I have the honour to be,

Sir,

Your most obedient Servant,

(Signed)   GEORGE G. WELLESLEY,

President, Geographical Society."

Bombay, 24th November 1858.

"To COMMODORE G. G. WELLESLEY,

President of the Bombay Geographical Society.

SIR,—I have the honour to request that you will convey to the Members of the Bombay Geographical Society my very grateful sense of the most kindly terms in which my name has been mentioned, on receiving my resignation, in your letter of the 24th November.

2. When, soon after the commencement of my connection with the Society, the Surveys of the Indian Navy, which had so richly stored our Reports with matter of interest, came to a close, and our wars beyond the North-West frontier shut against us countries, until then, so fertile in matter of description, it seemed to me expedient that we should betake ourselves to the department of Physical Geography, on which one precluded from the power of travelling by professional avocations at the Presidency might be still able to write.

3. On this ground, and to fill the blank with which our Transactions were threatened, I commenced, rather as a duty than a matter on which I felt competency or call, to contribute more largely to your journals than I should otherwise have ventured on ; and these contributions having been received in Europe in a manner for which I was not prepared, I continued to extend them here, and to transmit others occasionally to other quarters.

4. If, through these means, the Society has become more extensively known than it otherwise might have continued to be, after its supplies of Geographical information, strictly so called, had become dried up, the circumstance is due to accident much more than to any merit of mine ; and if, through the same cause, I have become known to many illustrious men who otherwise might never have heard of me, I owe my good fortune in a great measure to my connection with the

Society,—the merit, if any there be, is much more theirs than mine.

I have the honour to be,

Sir,

Your obedient Servant,

(Signed)   GEO. BUIST."

Bombay, 10th December 1858.

The Society having then proceeded to the election of a Secretary, Mr. Kennelly, I. N., was unanimously chosen.

Letters Read.—Nos. 78 and 80 of 1858, from the Secretary to Government, General Department ; and from the Secretary to the Ceylon Branch of the Royal Asiatic Society.

Presents to the Library.

1. The Journal of the Indian Archipelago and Eastern Asia, Nos. II. and III.   Presented by Government.
2. Reports of the Juries of the Madras Exhibition of 1857.   Presented by Government.
3. Journal of the Ceylon Branch of the Royal Asiatic Society for the years 1856-58.   Presented by the Secretary.
4. Proceedings of the Royal Geographical Society of London, No. VI., Vol. II.   Presented by the Society.

The Acting Secretary said that, in compliance with a wish expressed by the Smithsonian Institution, Washington, in 1857, the Society had forwarded copies of its reports to that body, along with a very large collection of published papers forwarded through them by the Bombay Government.   The approaching departure of the U. S. Frigate *Minnesota* affords the hope of a quicker communication than they had hitherto enjoyed with the United States, and the Secretary had no doubt that Captain Du Pont would readily undertake to assist in promoting the intercourse which had for many years now prevailed betwixt the literary men and institutions of America and India.   He, therefore, proposed that Government be once more on this ground applied to for a continuation of their publications issued since last despatch, and for those of them,—such as the Custom House Returns, the Observatory Reports, &c.,—that had then been omitted.   In the present might be included the publications of any other body which might think fit to make the Society the medium of communication with Washington.

The proposal having been agreed to, the Secretary was directed to write to the officer in command of the *Minnesota*, and to address Government on the subject.

Dr. Buist said, in reference to the paper he had formerly promised on the Meteorological and Geological peculiarities of the Matheran, Bhow-Mullen and Parbull group of mountains :—" I have not as yet got anything like the collection of drawings requisite for illustration, and I have not been able to commence the model map I desired to form part of the illustrations, and fear I must postpone all thoughts of it for the present. I had hoped that, before now, a successor to me might have been appointed, to have taken up the task of providing a paper for each meeting, which the Society, in September 1854, ordered to be seen to by their Secretary. In want of illustrations— for these only are wanting,—I have taken up a subject which has before now occupied our attention, and which has been several times before our brethren upstairs. Two months since, I received from some unknown friend the collection of specimens now before you. They were simply described as ' from the carboniferous bed of Cochin,' and I hope the donor, who has deprived me of the opportunity of thanking him personally, will accept my published acknowledgments. Specimens of lignite, copalite, and blue clay, such as those now before you, had, from time to time, reached me from General Cullen, and now adorn the shelves of various museums at home as well as that of our sister Society. The rarity is the laterite which accompanies them. The doubt, which had long attended the origin of this rock, was at length supposed to have been disposed of by the papers of Major Wingate, Lieutenant Aytoun, Dr. Carter, and Dr. Broughton, when Mr. Brown, the eminent magnetist and meteorologist, revived the theory of Captain Newbold, a name revered in the annals of Indian Geology, that laterite was not decomposed trap,—as Drs. Vesey and Turnbull had first suggested, and as the great bulk of geologists had long believed,—but a Neptunian rock, which, if not itself containing organic remains, as indeed highly ferruginous rocks rarely do, was intersected with beds abounding in vegetables such as those now before you. Captain Newbold had given his ideas at length in his account of the Geology of Southern India, laid before the Royal Asiatic Society of London in 1846, and reproduced in the *Calcutta Review* of 1848. General Cullen, entertaining the same views as Captain Newbold, with that industry and exactitude of inquiry which characterises all his numerous investigations, had dug several wells through the upper beds of laterite, and among the cliffs, found the rock almost always overlying, near the sea shore, the lignite beds of Cochin and Quilon. The present specimens seem to reconcile all these discrepancies of opinion. They consist of laterite in the ordinary form, but in this is embedded recent fresh-water shells and rounded pebbles, confirming the views I have long entertained, that the Cochin and Quilon laterite was not in the position in which it had been formed, but had been transported by the action of running water and recemented in its new bed. The specimens meet the whole difficulty; they show at once the grounds of the misapprehension of the Travancore geologists, and bring us back at once to the more orthodox and intelligible view of things all but universally entertained. Half the conflicts of Indian naturalists arise from the limited locality to which the experiences of each are restricted, and the difficulty of getting abroad to compare one district with another. Those who have seen the laterite cliffs at Vingorla, formed from decomposing granite and hornblende rock, with the quartz minerals, and veins of the latter extending through the former up to the surface of the soil, or examined the wells on Matheran, or the transformation of greenstone into laterite, disclosed in a cutting in the road betwixt Louisa and Porcupine Point—wonder that there can be any doubt on the subject of its genesis. The Travancore observer, again, has always seen it overlying organic remains, and marvels that any one should suppose it other than a Neptunian rock." The lecturer then made a number of observations on the periodic depressions and upheavals of the crust of the earth, stating that, often as this had been discussed, it could never be too frequently urged on the attention of geologists. One of the latest and ablest writers on the silicified woods of India and Egypt accepted the old doctrine that the last-named was probably due to drift brought down by the Nile; the Sind and Perim wood to the floods of the Indus, or those of the four great rivers debouching into Cambay Gulf; the Travancore wood to the Cauvery. That these fossils were very much of the same age, and probably owed their origin to kindred causes, was most probable;—to assume that these, whatever they were, had anything whatever to do with the physical conformation of the globe, as now exhibited, was most unreasonable. The formations referred to for the most part rest immediately on nummulite—a rock of the Miocene, or older Pleiocene age. Dr. Carter informs us that since this, with the rocks resting conformably over it, was laid down, it has, in Southern Arabia, been lifted up 4,000 feet. But we have seen of late that long after the Pleiocene period had closed, and when the animals existing were all identical with those now in being, those of Gibraltar, and probably along the south-east of Spain inland, had risen at least 1,200 feet. Recent shells were found at this elevation in the south-west of Scotland, and at half this they are abundant everywhere. We had no right whatever to assume that, at the period the silicified woods enumerated assumed their present position, there were any such rivers as the Nile, the Indus, the Nurbudda, or Cauvery, in existence; change the levels of our dryland by 4,000 or even by 1,000 feet, and the whole features of the country are altered. The point requires to be constantly urged on geologists, that they must dismiss from their mind existing arrangements as having anything to do with formations other than the most recent—or their speculations might become as unsound as those of a Horner or an Owen, men of the highest order of talent, misled by an assumption or a dream. The great movements, the multitude and magnitude of which were so conspicuous in the earlier periods of the earth's history, were still going on, though somewhat more languidly than in remoter times, and we must ever remember the verses of Dr. Beattie, as sweet in poetry as sound in science :—

" Earthquakes have raised to heaven the humble vale,
And gulfs the mountain's mighty mass entombed ;
And where the Atlantic flows, fair Continents have bloomed."

Some discussion having followed, the Society adjourned to the third Thursday of February, its ordinary day of meeting.

SESSION 1858-59.

FOURTH MEETING.—*Thursday, February 17th,* 4½ P. M.

Present.—Commodore G. G. Wellesley, C.B., R. N., *President,* in the chair ; W. E. Frere, Esq., *Vice President. Members.*—Commander W. C. Barker, I. N. ; T. H. Bentley, Esq. ; G. Buist, Esq., LL.D ; Dr. A. H. Leith, and D. J. Kennelly, Esq., I. N., *Secretary. Visitors.*—The Rev. J. S. S. Robertson, M. A. ; Lieut. Brooman, I. N. ; P. Jones, Esq., I. N. ; E. Heycock, Esq. ; and H. Williams, Esq., I. N.

The minutes of the last Meeting were read and confirmed.

Letters read.—No. 351 of 1859, General Department, from H. Young, Esq., Chief Secretary to Government ; No. 554 of 1859, Territorial Department Revenue, from B. H. Ellis, Esq., Acting Secretary to Government ; No. 399 of 1859, General Department, from H. Young, Esq., Chief Secretary to Government ; No. 232 of 1859, from Richard Spooner, Esq., Commissioner of Customs, Salt, and Opium ; from the Superintendent of the Geological Survey of India ; from Captain Du Pont, U. S. N. ; from E. Heycock, Esq. ; from the Acting Secretary Bombay Chamber of Commerce ; from D. Wales, Esq., Harbour Master, Port Louis, Mauritius, enclosing a Bottle Log.

Presents to the Library.

1. Report of the Superintendent of the U. S. Coast Survey, showing the progress of the Survey, during the years 1852, 1853, 1854, 1855, in four volumes.
2. Sketches accompanying the Annual Report of the Superintendent of the U. S. Coast Survey, 1851.
3. Maps and views to accompany the message from the President of the United States to the Two Houses of Congress, 1855-56.
4. U. S. Light-House Establishment, Rules, Regulations, and General Instructions.
5. Instructions and Directions to Light-keepers.
6. List of Light-Houses, &c. of the United States, 1857.
7. Cruise of the Dolphin, Lieutenant S. P. Lee, U. S. N.
8. Map of Central America, 1856. Presented by Capt. S. F. Du Pont, U. S. N.
9. Journal of the Indian Archipelago and Eastern Asia, No. IV. Vol. II. By J. R. Logan, Esq., F. G. S.
10. A Short Review of Mr. Plowden's Report on the Salt Excise of Bombay, by Nicholas A. Dalzell, A. M., F. B. S. E., being a selection from the Records of the Bombay Government. Presented by Government.
11. Memoirs of the Geological Survey of India, Vol. I., Part II. Presented by the Superintendent of the Geological Survey of India, under instructions from the Governor General in Council.

p 4

12. The Exodus of the Israelites out of Egypt explained, and the place where they passed through the Red Sea determined. Presented by E. Heycock, Esq.

Also several Selections from the Records of the Bombay Government. Presented by the Government, for transmission to the Smithsonian Institution, Washington, United States.

The best thanks of the Society were voted to the donors for these presents to the Library. The Secretary then stated to the Society that he had communicated with Captain Du Pont, U. S. N., in reference to the conveyance of the books and papers which the Society were desirous to present to the Smithsonian Institution, Washington, and then in course of preparation for despatch when opportunity should offer.

Captain Du Pont responded most warmly to the application, stating that it would afford him the greatest pleasure, if, by his assistance, he could in any manner contribute to the extension of the scientific views and interests of both Societies.

It was further stated that, through the liberal grant of Government of its publications, a large and valuable collection of books, &c. had now been transmitted to America, and it was only to be regretted that the early departure of the U. S. F. *Minnesota* from Bombay prevented the despatch of other important publications, which had reached the Society too late for transmission by that opportunity.

In addition to a letter addressed, by the Président of the Society, to Captain Du Pont, for his very handsome gift of valuable books, the Secretary was directed to convey to him the thanks of the Society for the very kind manner in which he had met its wishes, and to forward, for his acceptance, a set of their Transactions.

The Bottle Log, referred to in letter 9 above, bears the following account :—

"No. 20. This Bottle, with its enclosure, was thrown from on board the H. C. Brig *Tigris*, on her way from Bombay to Muscat, at noon on the 19th day of June 1858, in Lat. 4.46 South, and Long. 57.33 East.

(Signed) G. T. ROBINSON,
Lieutenant, Commanding."

Mr. Wales, who forwarded the above, states :—"Picked up at the Point of Coetivy, on shore, Lat. 7.9 South, Long 56.13 East, on the 27th day of August 1858. No particulars forwarded."

It appears, from the data faced on the Bottle Log, that it has drifted in a direction S. 29° W., or a little more than south, two and half points westerly. A period of sixty-nine days had elapsed from the date of immersion to the date of recovery on the Island of Coetivy, one of the Amirants, which form the South-western group of the Seychelles ; and, if it be supposed that the Log had been recovered immediately on its touching the island, the rate of drift amounts only to 2.37 miles a day. The currents about this part of the Indian Ocean are known to be irregular.   The indication in this case seems to be more southerly than usual.

At this stage of the proceedings, the Society, in reference to the subject contained in letter No. 3, proceeded to inspect the new room allotted to them by Government, and which, under the new arrangement, adjoins the rooms of the Asiatic Society.

On resuming the business of the meeting, the Secretary was directed to take advantage of the opportunity, which the forthcoming change of rooms would present, for the construction of a Catalogue of the Society's Books, Maps, and Papers, to be printed with as little delay as possible.

Lieutenant W. M. Pengelley, I. N., and S. Barker, Esq., I. N., were proposed as Members, to be ballotted for at the next Meeting.

Commander W. C. Barker, I. N., read the following Paper :—

Remarks on the Navigation between Bombay and Suez, with reference to the proposed Suez Canal of Monsieur Ferdinand de Lesseps.

1. It has been a matter of great surprise to me that England alone, of all the civilized nations of the earth, should be opposed to the proposed scheme of Monsieur Ferdinand de Lesseps, namely, that of uniting the Red Sea with the Mediterranean, by means of a navigable ship canal.

2. Surely, after all our declarations in favour of free trade, and the development of the commercial resources of the world, it is very inconsistent to let it be said that "Great Britain stops the way" in a matter of such deep interest to all nations, merely on account of its supposed political inexpediency : but this is too delicate a point for me to venture on ; further than to state that, in my opinion, such a canal as that proposed would be productive of more advantage to England than any other nation, even on political grounds, considering her mighty Empire

in the East, and her vast colonial possessions in the South, which would thus be brought so much more within the influence of the mother country. Another objection is, that the navigation of the Red Sea would be attended with so much delay and risk, particularly to sailing vessels. This objection we may fairly deal with.

3. If this Canal be completed, Bombay will then, from its geographical position and magnificent harbour, become the great commercial capital of the East : it is proposed, therefore, in the following pages, to consider the nature of the navigation between that port and Suez, dwelling more particularly upon the Red Sea portion thereof.

4. It is now near a quarter of a century since the so-called Overland Route has been established. During this period, only one steam-vessel has been lost while thus engaged in the conveyance of mails and passengers between Bombay and Suez, and *vice versâ ;* that vessel was lost under very peculiar circumstances, not in the Red Sea, but on Ras Asscir, the N. E. Cape of Africa, and south side of the entrance to the Gulf of Aden.

5. When we consider that, up to the present period, there is not one single lighthouse from Aden to Suez, a distance of 1,306 miles, we can only come to the following conclusions : first, that there are excellent charts of this locality ; and, secondly, that the Red Sea is not so dangerous as it is supposed to be. It is, however, highly desirable that lighthouses should be erected on the following sites :—viz. 1st, at Suez, on the small reef situated almost in the middle of the Harbour ; 2nd, on the extreme northern end of the Ashruffie Reefs, to the northward of Jubal Island ; 3rd, on Abdool Keesan or the Dædalus Reef ; 4th, on the eastern end of Perim Island, Straits of Babel Mandeb ; 5th, on Jezeerat Sulliel, at the entrance to Aden Back Bay.

6. I will now take a view of the dangers to be met with by steamers plying direct between Suez and the Straits of Babel Mandeb.

7. In the Sea of Suez there are no dangers but such as can be avoided with common prudence, except in the Straits of Jubal. The navigation of this part is attended with some risk (particularly at night-time), owing to the coral reefs and sunken rocks forming the north-western, north-eastern, and eastern boundaries thereof, lying out in deep water, so that the lead gives no warning of approach to their vicinity. Should the erection of a lighthouse on the Ashruffie Reefs be found to be attended with too great an outlay, then I would propose that a light-

house be erected on the N. E. end of Jubal Island, of sufficient elevation and brilliancy to be seen from the deck of a ship in ordinary
weather (20) twenty miles. The safe navigation of these Straits will
thus be ensured at all seasons of the year, whether by night or day.
Jubal Island is high, so that there will be no difficulty as to elevation.

8. Having passed through the Straits of Jubal, the next danger
met with in the " Outward Voyage" is the Brothers, or " El Fena-
deeah," two small Coral Islets opposite to Cosire, rising abruptly from
the sea to an elevation of about (60) sixty feet, having no bottom at
(100) one hundred fathoms close to. They are, therefore, not very
dangerous, as they may be avoided in any weather with but ordinary
prudence. Not so, however, the next danger, Abdool Keesan, or the
Dædalus, which is a coral reef but slightly elevated above the sea,
having no bottom at (300) three hundred fathoms close to it, and situated directly in the track of ships, being nearly in mid-channel (45)
forty-five miles from the nearest danger off the Nubian Coast, and (50)
fifty miles from the reefs off the Arabian Coast. This is, in fact, the
most dangerous spot throughout the Sea, and is directly in the track
of ships, as will be seen by the following :—

9. With the south-east end of Shadwan Island (which is situated
at the entrance of the Sea of Suez to southward of Jubal Island) bearing true west, distant (3) three miles, the direct course down the middle
of the sea to Jibble Teer is true . . . . S. 30° 49' East, 833 miles.
South-east end of Shadwan (3) three miles

    as above to Abdool Keesan . . . . S. 31° 57' East, 179 miles.
    Ditto to "Northern Brother" . . . . S. 31° 18' East, 77 miles.
" Southern Brother" to Abdool Keesan . . S. 32° 30' East, 101 miles.

As observed before, the " Brothers," from their elevation above the
sea, and being steep too, may be avoided with common prudence in any
weather. A lighthouse is, therefore, not essentially required thereon ;
but it is absolutely necessary that a lighthouse should be erected on the
" Dædalus," of sufficient elevation and brilliancy to be seen from the
deck of a ship (10) ten or (12) twelve miles. I am aware that this
will be attended with some difficulty and expense, but when the great
advantage to be derived therefrom is considered, the difficulty is
not so great but that it can be overcome, and the expense will be
more than compensated for by the increased safety thus afforded to
navigation.

10. From Abdool Keesan, or the Dædalus, to Jibble Teer, a distance of (654) six hundred and fifty-four miles, there is a clear, wide channel down the centre of the sea, the dangers on either side of which are all distinctly and correctly laid down on the Charts of the Survey of the Red Sea, by the late Captain Moresby and Officers of the Indian Navy.

11. Jibble Teer is a volcanic island, situated in mid-channel ; steep to all round, rising precipitately from the sea, and attaining an elevation of (900) nine hundred feet. It is, therefore, not at all dangerous ; on the contrary, it is a very valuable guide to the navigator, it being visible from the deck of a ship (20) twenty miles in moderately clear weather ; hence, towards the Straits of Babel Mandeb, a distance of (196) one hundred and ninety-six miles, are the Zebayr, Zoogur, and Hhaneish Islands, all of volcanic origin, generally well elevated above the sea, and steep too. There is one exception,—the eastern boundary of the Zebayr Group is formed by a dangerous rock awash. I know not whether the error has been rectified, but in the early printed charts of the Red Sea this rock is represented as an island. It is advisable for vessels to pass to the westward of the Zebayr Group, and to the eastward of the Zoogur and Hhaneish Islands, particularly at night-time.

12. With the island of Jibble Teer true East (1) one mile, a course true S. 33.40 East, or S.S.E. ¼ E. per compass, will carry a vessel at (25) twenty-five miles, (2½) two and a half miles to westward of the Quoin Rocks, the northernmost of the Zebayr Group ; at (38) thirty-eight miles, (1) one mile to the westward of the southernmost island of that group ; and at (103) one hundred and three miles close to the eastward of Aboo Eyle, the north-eastern of the Zoogur Islands.

13. From Aboo Eyle, to the east end of Perim Island, passing to the eastward of all the Zoogur and Hhaneish Islands, and at (52) fifty-two miles close to the westward of the shoals off Mocha, the true course is S. 22.40 East, or S. by E. ½ E. per compass, (93) ninety-three miles. The lead is a good guide in passing the shoals off Mocha, taking care not to come under (12) twelve fathoms during the day, or (16) sixteen fathoms at night-time.

14. A lighthouse, erected on the eastern end of Perim Island, Straits of Babel Mandeb, of sufficient elevation and brilliancy to be seen (10)

ten or (12) twelve miles from a ship's deck, will ensure the safe passage of these Straits.

15. From the anchorage at Suez to Perim Island, the distance is (1,202) one thousand two hundred and two miles, steering as directly as possible ; and by deviating slightly to avoid unnecessary risk by passing too close to dangers, the distance is (1,208) one thousand two hundred and eight miles. By the erection of lighthouses, as stated above, I am confident that this sea will be as successfully navigated by sailing vessels as it has hitherto been by steam-vessels. The only danger hence towards Aden is the foul ground off Cape St. Anthony, for clearing which the lead is a good guide.

16. There is sufficient evidence on record, from the numerous voyages made by the mail steamers, to warrant my stating that the voyage either way between Bombay and Suez may be performed by powerful steamers in from (12) twelve to (17) seventeen days throughout the year.

17. For sailing vessels, the outward voyage, or that from Suez to Bombay, the most favourable period is from the middle of May to the early part of September. During this period, N. N. W. winds prevail from Suez to Babel Mandeb; thence to the Meridian of Ras Asseir (the N. E. Cape of Africa), westerly winds, with occasional squalls from the northward ; off the coast of Arabia, occasional strong S. W. breezes out of the Gulf of Tajoorah, and calms. By keeping on the Arabian Coast, favourable currents will be experienced, at the rate of twent to forty miles a day. On approaching the meridian of Ras Asseir, and opening the channel between that Cape and Socotra Island, the South-west Monsoon will be met with (setting in from the southward, and hauling round to south-west and westward, as a vessel advances eastward), which will carry a vessel to Bombay at the rate of two hundred to two hundred and fifty miles a day.

18. It is by no means a rare occurrence for a vessel to carry a continued fair wind the whole way from Suez to Bombay at this season. Under such circumstances, a vessel of but ordinary sailing qualities ought to make the passage in fifteen or sixteen days ; but supposing in that portion of the voyage between Babel Mandeb and Meridian of Ras Asseir an interval of light winds is experienced, still the voyage ought to be made in twenty or twenty-five days at the utmost. One or two steam-tugs stationed either at Perim Island (which possesses an

excellent harbour), or at Aden, would, by towing the vessels thence, to the limits of the South-west Monsoon, remove this uncertainty, so that we may safely reckon that a moiety of the entire voyage from England to Bombay could be performed at this season of the year in about a fortnight.   The distance from Perim Island to Bombay is one thousand seven hundred and forty-five miles, or the total distance between Bombay and Suez, two thousand and nine hundred and fifty-three miles.   I am not competent, from personal experience, to form any opinion as to what time would be required, at this season of the year, for the voyage from England to Suez, but should suppose not more than six or eight weeks, so that the entire outward voyage would only require two to two and a half months.

19.   That portion of the homeward voyage, comprised between Bombay and Suez, cannot be performed by sailing-vessels (unless in exceptional cases) with the same celerity as the outward voyage, owing to the prevalence of N. N. West winds throughout the year in the upper part of the Red Sea.   The most favourable period is during the months of November, December, January, and February.   A vessel quitting Bombay at this season will experience N. E. and Easterly winds as far as the Straits of Babel Mandeb ; thence the wind, following the direction of the coast, veers round gradually to S. S. Eastward, on passing through the Straits, extending to Jibble Teer, occasionally as far North as Jedda, and sometimes, but very rarely, even to Suez. However, a vessel is sure of a fair wind for at least two-thirds of the way, and this portion ought to be performed in twelve or fifteen days.

20.   On meeting with the wind at N. N. W., the Arabian side of the channel is to be preferred for working up till a vessel can fetch St. John's Island on the Nubian Coast ; thence, towards the Straits of Jubal, keep that coast on board.   In making this part of the voyage, viz. from Jibble Teer to Suez, more will depend upon the skill of the navigator than on the sailing qualities of the ship (provided she is but ordinary weatherly), for, although the coast cannot be approached in many parts to within sixty or seventy miles, on account of the coral reefs, yet it is necessary to be on the inshore tack at the right time, for even when blowing strong the wind veers and hauls two points during the twenty-four hours, inclining from the land during the night, and from seaward during the day.   The reefs do not extend far off the shore on the Nubian and Egyptian coasts above St. John's Island, and

therefore greater advantage may be derived from "slants of wind" by being able to approach so much closer to the shore.

21.   The coral reefs and islands which bound the Channel on either side show well during the day, except in calm or cloudy weather.   Great care must be taken, however, never to approach the reefs at night-time too closely, nor even during the day, without great caution and a good look-out from the mast-head ; for it must be borne in mind that, except in some parts of the Sea of Suez, and the lower part of the Red Sea, the lead does not give the slightest warning of approach to danger.   In a word, the navigator must be guided by the eye, not by the lead.

22.   On an average (supposing a N. N. W. wind is met with), the passage from Jibble Teer to Suez ought not to occupy more than twenty or twenty-five days, or a total of about five weeks from Bombay,—oftener less time than-more,—so that, by allowing a similar time for the voyage from Suez to England, less than three months for the homeward voyage for a ship propelled by sails alone.

23.   Clipper-built or fast sailing ships of one to two thousand tons, with auxiliary steam (screw), and facilities for raising the screw entirely out of the water when using sail alone, will be the best class of vessels for this route, for the general purposes of commerce.   They ought to perform the outward voyage, or a moiety thereof rather,—that is from Suez to Bombay—during the favourable season, in from twelve to fifteen days, and during the unfavourable season, in about six or seven weeks ; homewards during the favourable season in about one month, and during the unfavourable season or S. W. Monsoon in six or seven weeks.

24.   The upper portion of the Red Sea is, at present, but little known to European navigators,—indeed unknown to, and unvisited by, any ship but those of the Indian Navy, and Peninsula and Oriental Company, except a solitary vessel now and then, with coal for the steamers of the latter Company.   The navigation, therefore, is generally considered difficult and dangerous, but the difficulty and danger will rapidly disappear when it becomes better known and frequented.

25.   At the risk of being thought tedious, I will again repeat that N. N. W. winds prevail throughout the Red Sea during the mouths of May, June, July, August, and September, the same wind prevailing during the remainder of the year in the upper or northern portion

thereof, frequently extending as far south as Jibble Teer, or about five-sixths of the entire distance from Suez to Babel Mandeb.

26. Southerly or S. S. E. winds commence at the Straits of Babel Mandeb about the middle or towards the end of October, and continue till May, with slight interruptions, extending as far north as Jibble Teer, at times as far as Jeddah, and sometimes, though very rarely, as far as Suez. Occasionally N. N. W. winds are experienced in the lower part of the Red Sea, about the end of January or early in February, but very light, and never continuing more than a day or two.

27. Between Bombay and the Straits of Babel Mandeb, north-easterly and easterly winds prevail from the middle or towards the end of October till April ; south-west and westerly winds for the remainder of the year ; light winds and calms about the change of the monsoons or seasons.

28. The season most favourable for rapid communication between Suez and Bombay, and *vice versâ*, are also the most favourable for all the ports of our vast Indian Empire, as well as for China and the Australian Colonies.

29. Kurrachee, the seaport of the Indus, already of some importance as a commercial port, is considerably retarded in its advancement, by being placed so far beyond the immediate reach of European enterprize. When the canal is completed, then we shall possess, by means of steam-vessels, a rapid and almost direct route between Europe and the N. W. Provinces of our Indian Empire, by way of this port and the Indus.

30. Aden, prior to the discovery of the passage to India, *viâ* the Cape of Good Hope, was a great emporium of commerce, and the seaport of the once fertile Hadramaut, whose capital, "Mareb," was described by an ancient writer " as a diadem in the brow of the universe." Aden already bids fair far to exceed its former grandeur, but how much will its commercial importance be increased when, by the opening of the canal, commerce is again restored to its ancient route.

31. The larger islands of the Red Sea, the Pharsan and Dhalac Islands, were once densely populated by a by no means uncivilized people, judging from the ruins of the very extensive tanks or reservoirs for water to be found thereon (particularly on the latter island), and from the very extensive burial grounds. These islands, as well as the ports of Berbera, Zeyla, Tajoorah, Amphilah, Massowah, Suakin, and

Cosire, on the western shore; Mocha, Hodeidah, Lohire, Gongidah, Jiddah, Yembo, on the eastern shore,—and many other minor ports will once more resume their commercial character,—now at its last gasp,—and afford means for penetrating to the " far interior" on either side. In fact, both shores of the Red Sea abound in natural and well sheltered harbours (particularly well adapted for coasting craft), that no doubt were once crowded with shipping of the earlier times,—alas ! for ages past almost deserted, but soon again, I trust, to resound with the busy hum of civilized man, the cheerful voices of the mariner and the trader.

32.   At present the mail steamers, as they pass to and fro, voyage after voyage, scarce ever encounter a single sail between Suez and the Straits of Babel Mandeb.   When the canal is completed, the surface of the sea will, I doubt not, be dotted from one end to the other with vessels from every maritime nation of Europe, eagerly engaged in commerce, and carrying civilization to nations long sunk in ignorance and barbarism.   In fact, the successful completion of this grand undertaking, " Du Canal Maritime de Suez," will open out vast fields for commercial enterprize, as well as for the labours of the philanthropist and the missionary.

33.   In conclusion, while vessels have at present to traverse a distance of twelve or fifteen thousand miles between England and Bombay, by way of the Cape of Good Hope, when this canal is completed, they will have to traverse but six thousand miles.   Powerful steam-vessels can proceed direct outwards from Suez to Bombay throughout the year, and homewards from Bombay to Suez direct, for nine months out of the year, the remaining three months distance is increased from four to five hundred miles to avoid unnecessary wear and tear to ship and engines, by driving direct against the south-west monsoon.   Sailing vessels are sure of a fair wind for the entire portion of a moiety of the voyage outwards, for two-thirds of the said moiety for a similar period.

Finally, it is difficult sufficiently to appreciate the vast benefits to commerce and civilization that will accrue from the "piercing the Isthmus of Suez" by a navigable ship canal, such as that proposed by Monsieur Ferdinand de Lesseps.

Bombay, 15*th February* 1859.   W. C. BARKER.

After the thanks of the Society had been voted to Commander Barker for his valuable paper, the meeting adjourned.

SESSION 1858-59.

Fifth Meeting.—*Thursday, March 24th,* 4½ p. m.

Present.—Commodore G. G. Wellesley, C.B., R. N., *President*, in the Chair ; the Honorable W. E. Frere, *Vice-President.*

Members.—Commander W. C. Barker, I. N. ; J. W. Winchester, Esq., LL.D. ; G. Buist, Esq., LL.D. ; J. H. Bentley, Esq. ; Venayekrao Juggonath, Esq. ; Juggonath Sunkersett, Esq. ; Captain Mahomed Bin Haimees ; and D. J. Kennelly, Esq., *Secretary.*

Visitors.—Captain Pullen, R. N., and Drs. H. V. Carter, and G. C. M. Birdwood.

The Minutes of the last Meeting were read and confirmed.

Presents to the Library.

1. Further Correspondence relative to the introduction of a Rough Survey and Revenue Settlement in the Province of Sind. Presented by Government.
2. Observations Meteorologiques Anno 1855.
3. Ditto   ditto   Anno 1856.
4. Journal Asiatique, Tome XI.   Presented by the Asiatic Society of France.
5. Les Voyages d'Americ Vespuce au Compte de l'Espagne et les Mesures Itineraires.   Par M. D'Avezac.
6. A List of the Members, Officers, &c. &c., with the Report of the Royal Institution of Great Britain.
7. Notices of the Proceedings at the Meetings of the Royal Institution of Great Britain, Part VIII., November 1857—July 1858.   Presented by the Institution.
8. Allen's Index, containing the Names and Geographical Positions of all Places on the Maps of India.   Presented by the Secretary.
9. Magnetical and Meteorological Observations made at Toronto, in Canada, Vol. III., 1846-47-48.   By Col. Sabine.   Presented by Government.

Charts.

10. Track Survey of the River Paraguay (sheets) Nos. 10, 11, 12, 13, 14, 15, from the Department of States, Washington. Presented by Government.

Members elected.—Lieut. W. M. Pengelly, I. N., and S. Barker, Esq., I. N., were balloted for, and unanimously elected Members of the Society.

Members proposed.—By Dr. George Buist,—E. Heycock, Esq.

By Commander Barker,—Lieutenant Whish, I. N., to be balloted for at the next Monthly Meeting.

Letters read.—From the Secretary, Royal Geographical Society ; from Dr. Giraud ; from Lieutenant Whish, presenting a descriptive Sketch of the Island of Jibbleea, Kooria Mooria Bay, also specimens of Guano from that Island, together with two Drawings.

The Paper read by Captain Barker, I. N., before the last Meeting of the Society, underwent a discussion, in which Captain Pullen, R. N., took a part. Captain Pullen also was good enough to present to the Society, Sections, &c. of the Soundings of the Red Sea and to the Coast of India, taken by him lately in H. M. Steamer *Cyclops*, in connection with the projected Red Sea Telegraph, for which the thanks of the Society were unanimously voted.

The following Paper, by Lieutenant Whish, I. N., on the Island of Jibbleea (Kooria Mooria Islands), was read by the Secretary. The specimens of Guano accompanying the paper were considered to be of so great value, as to cause regret that larger specimens had not been obtained. His drawings were also much admired.

Descriptive Sketch of the Island of Jibbleea, Kooria Mooria Bay, to accompany some Specimens of Guano from that Island, as also two Drawings in explanation.

As considerable interest appears to be entertained on the subject of the Guano Island of the Kooria Mooria, I took the opportunity, during our stay as Guard Vessel at Jibbleea, in January, of dotting down a few general remarks, and now place them before the Bombay Geographical Society, to accompany some specimens of the guano, and a sketch giving a view of the Island from S. E., hoping the brief description will not be deemed superfluous. I have only to regret that I did not bring away more of the material, and that I am not able to furnish a more elaborate account.

The Kooria Mooria group consists of four islands :—Haski (or the laughing island), Soda (or black island), Helaneea (or life and death island), Jibbleea (or mountain island), and, five and a half miles N. E. from Helaneea, is Rodondo (or booth island), which is only a high rock.

The specimens were taken from the summit of two of the highest peaks of the island of Jibbleea, as it is found coating nearly the whole of the island.   It is very white and polished ; and in some places so slippery, as hardly to be able to retain one's footing ; and in showing them to Mr. McCalmont, Agent for the Lessees of the Island, and Analytical Chemist, they were declared to be the best he had seen.   The ships, twelve in number (last season there were fifty-two I believe, anchored all round the island), were loading with guano, separated from the soil by sifting ; and from a cave in the bluff, forming the eastern extreme of the island (which we called "Flett's Cave," from the Captain who secured the cargo), no less than 400 tons of guano were shipped.

The following description of the cave is submitted by one of a party who visited it :—

" Entering by an opening, twelve or fourteen feet high, and twenty feet wide, you proceed for a short distance till you come to a narrow gut of eight feet high, and one and a half foot wide, but not upright ; passing through which, and descending about four feet sudden drop, you find yourself in a chamber forty to fifty feet high, and sixty feet long, but only ten feet broad,—in this the guano was perfectly pure and moist, and required no sifting.   Push on, and squeezing through a still more narrow and intricate passage, a second chamber is observed, not so large as the first, and from which we were assured that the noise of the workmen outside was distinctly audible through the crust of the hill."

Some cargoes of the solid guano had been shipped, which were, of course, very valuable ; the great difficulty being separating the guano from the rocks, which materially protracted the process of loading, —this, however, was absolutely necessary to avoid shipping a cargo of rock.

We found the vessels at anchor with the highest peak of the island (800 feet) bearing from N.N.W. to N.N.E., and from half a mile to one mile off shore, in from twelve to eighteen and twenty fathoms ; bottom very uneven and rocky, exactly where no soundings are recorded on the chart.   The weather was very boisterous during the month of January, blowing in heavy "Belâats" from N. and N.N.W., at times cutting off all communication with the shore, and so hazy, as to be unable to see the island two miles off.

A heavy breaking sea and swell sets round the east end of the island, rendering the "holding on" very doubtful, and causing a great strain on the ground tackle : the ships for the most part lay with their yards braced-by, and with reefs in their topsails.

In the bay, however, formed between the southern extreme of the Island and the Well Rock, it is perfectly sheltered and smooth, during the prevalence of these winds, and there is tolerable landing.

When we left the island in February, the ships were shifting round to the N. E. side, where, I understand, the guano is of a better quality and more plentiful. The appearance of some portions of the rock on the N. E. side of the island is best represented by the broad guttering of a candle, the solid guano hanging in perfect stalactytes from the projecting rocks ;—many rocks on being struck gave a musical sound ! Several attempts were made to procure fresh water,—which is possible almost anywhere, I believe, on Helaneea, by digging,—but although they bored down several feet, they were doomed to be disappointed, for they only came to salt water. I heard afterwards that they had not gone below the sea level.

The nearest watering place is Helaneea, which is (13) thirteen miles distant, but the best is Morbât, 90 miles to the westward, on the coast. In the N. E. monsoon it is perfectly sheltered, as any ship can anchor, as we did, with the cape bearing S. by W., centre of town E. S. E. (or on with Jibbul Jingen) in seven fathoms. The natives are very civil, for I know them of old, and would only be glad to be patronized by vessels frequenting their port.

The island also offers a very fair field for the Naturalist. The birds, which appear to be a kind of gannet, are extremely numerous, and very noisy. They invariably inhabit the weather side of the island, according to season ; and, after returning from a cruise, or fishing expedition, which they generally do surfeited with fish, they became an easy prey to those who would wantonly shoot them. The eggs are, I believe, wholesome, though I can hardly think, from the diet of the parent, delicate or well flavoured. There are sundry kinds of fish, amongst which we caught a curious snake-like fish, five feet three inches long, and weighing thirty pounds. Its general colour was brown ; but, to enter into more detail, I would say that it was covered with angular and irregular brown spots, with a yellow ground between them, running in a narrow line between. It had extremely powerful jaws ; and whilst on board, reared r: more than once, as we thought, to make an attack on the by-standers. It had no dorsal fin, but something like a crest or mane, commencing from eight to ten inches from the head, and tapering off towards the tail. On opening it, we found it full of large fish bones : we succeeded in skinning it without a flaw (being entirely devoid of scales, and as thick as the skin of a young heifer, or about a quarter inch ; it had a fearful array of sharp teeth set inwards) : but our stay on the station extending over a longer space of time than we had at first anticipated, we were obliged, I am sorry to say, having no means of preserving it, to relinquish our project and intention of introducing it to the Society. I have made a sketch from memory of this extraordinary animal, which, although not perhaps quite correct, cannot be much in error, as it conveys to me a good idea of the brute as it lay upon the deck.

The specimens of sea anemones, and sea weeds, are very beautiful and rare, and some fine sponges may be procured in from five to seven fathoms water ; indeed, to a person anxious to fit a vivarium, a trip to Jibbleea would be most satisfactory and interesting.

The Agent's house is on the southern side of the island, and there are a few small guns placed near it on an elevation ; and a little below it are two natural creeks, where boats can load clear of the swell. Outside, at the head of these creeks, regular jetties are built and sheers rigged for hoisting up heavy stores, machinery &c., for the use of the establishment. They have a distilling, or rather a condensing apparatus ; but the quantity of fresh water made is something very small, say four to five hundred gallons a day, which falls far short of an adequate supply for the consumption on the island. They depend entirely upon the supply from Helaneea, and may be a merchant vessel or two bringing a cargo of it from Bombay. In conclusion, I may premise that ere very long the erection of an Electric Telegraphic Station on Helaneea will bring these islands and their diggings to a more familiar acquaintance ; and trusting these few lines may lead to a further investigation on the subject, I beg to subscribe myself,

R. W. WHISH, Lieutenant, I. N.

The best thanks of the Society were voted to Lieut. Whish, I. N., for his valued and highly interesting contributions.

The meeting adjourned.

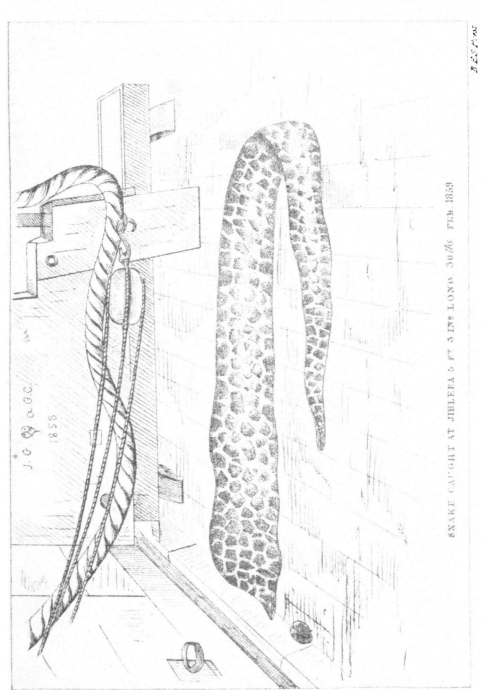

SNAKE CAUGHT AT JIBLEFA 5 FT 3 INS LONG. 30 lbs FEB 1859

J. G. ...a.G.C. W 1858

BENSON

H.P. 880 f^t   Elphinstone   Plotts Cave

SESSION 1858-59.

SIXTH MEETING.—*Thursday, April 21st,* 4½ P.M.

Present.—The Honorable W. E. Frere, *Vice-President,* in the Chair.
Members.—Dr. A. H. Leith ; C. Leggatt, Esq. ; Lieut. W. M.
Pengelley, I. N. ; Commander W. C. Barker, I. N. ; G. Buist, Esq.,
LL. D. ; Juggonath Sunkersett, Esq. ; Munguldas Nuthoobhai, Esq. ;
and D. J. Kennelly, Esq., *Secretary.*
Visitor.—Capt. J. T. Annesley.
The Minutes of the last Meeting were read and confirmed.
Lieutenant R. Whish, I. N., and E. Heycock, Esq., having been
balloted for, were unanimously elected Members of the Society.

Presents to the Library.

1. Bulletin de la Société de Géographie, Quatrième Série, Tome
    XVI. Presented by the Society.
2. Journal Asiatique, Cinquième Série, Tome XII. Presented by
    the Society.
3. Meteorological Registers kept at Cuddalore, for December 1858
    and January 1859 ; at Cocanada, for January 1859 ; and at
    Pahlunpoor, for October, November, and December 1858.
    Presented by Government.
4. Madras Exhibition of 1859, of the Raw Products of Southern
    India ; Official and Descriptive Catalogue of the Madras
    Exhibition of 1857 ; Report of the Juries of the Madras
    Exhibition of 1857. Presented by the Madras Exhibition.
5. Report of the Heemabhace Institute for the year 1858. Pre-
    sented by the Institution.

A small quantity of prepared Guano from the Island of Jibbleea
(Kooria Mooria Bay), together with several specimens of the sea bottom
at depths varying from 240 to 1,800 fathoms, between Ras-ul-Hadd,
Coast of Arabia, and Kurrachee, were presented to the Society by
Captain Pullen, R. N.

Letters read.

1. From Lieutenant W. M. Pengelley, I. N., acknowledging a
letter from the Society electing him a Member.
2. From J. Dawson, Esq., contributing a Paper, embracing some of
the principal of his observations made while at the Kooria Mooria Islands.

p 6

On the Geography and Meteorology of the Kooria Mooria Islands.

These islands, situated on the S. E. Coast of Arabia, in a mean latitude of about 17° 30′ N., and longitude of 56° 25′ E., are five in number named as follows, in order of their magnitude, viz :— Hallany, Soda, Jibly, Hasky, and Gurzood.

Hallany is about nine miles in length and four in breadth ; Soda about five miles in each direction ; Jibly about three by two miles ; Hasky about one and a half by half a mile ; and Gurzood (or Rodonda, as it is sometimes called), is a rock about two miles in circumference. The islands form a group, having a general direction E. and W., and good navigable passages exist between them.

There is a reef, distant four miles, due E., from the easternmost point of Jibly, which reef is mentioned in Captain Haines's survey ; but there are two others, equi-distant between the point of the island and that reef, which are not noticed in the charts of Captain Haines's survey. I do not know the exact depth of water upon them, but they broke water throughout the whole of the last S.W. monsoons.

The highest part of the largest island rises about 1,500 feet above the level of the sea, the smallest of the group is not above 300 feet. There is good water, and a little dwarf vegetation upon the largest two of the group, viz. Hallany and Soda ; the three others are without water or vegetation. The islands are composed of rock of an apparently volcanic origin, — the strata in many places being in a vertical position.

Only two of these islands, viz. Jibly and Hasky, furnish guano ; the former of them having considerably the larger quantity.

The guano is found deposited on the lower and level parts of the islands, covering extensive tracts, and in beds varying from one to six feet in thickness, but generally about two feet. It is mixed with small stones, and requires fine screening before shipment. In various places extensive beds of gypsum are met with below the guano.

I would beg particular attention to the fact that the chemical constitution of the Kooria Mooria guano differs widely from that of the Peruvian and other guanos, although the fertilizing properties exist in nearly an equal total percentage in them all. The Kooria Mooria is composed of about 70 per cent. of phosphates, and only 1 of ammonia, the residue of 29 per cent. consisting of silica and moisture. The Peruvian has about an equal complement of silica and moisture, but the ammonia exceeds the phosphates as two to one.

The weather in these islands is uniformly fine during the N. E. monsoons, with an occasional stiff breeze from the N. W. The S. W. winds commence lightly early in April, and continue so, with little variation, until the middle of May, when the regular monsoon sets in, and increases in strength, until it becomes a moderate gale, occasionally blowing a strong gale, with a heavy sea. The monsoon begins to moderate about the end of August ; but the wind from the S. W. continues till the latter part of September, when the fine weather sets in. During the two monsoons of 1858 rain fell only twice, and then, for only about two hours on each occasion,—once early in January, and once in the middle of July.

The temperature during the S. W. monsoons never rose above 89° fahr. On the 3rd of August 1858, the sun being vertical, cocoanut-oil congealed, while the thermometer stood at 55° fahr. The thermometer during the N. E. monsoons ranges rather higher than in Bombay.

I trust these few facts, collected by my own personal observations, regarding a group of islands but little known, although becoming of great commercial importance, may be of some interest to the members of the Geographical Society; and I can only wish that my opportunities and ability had enabled me to present a more detailed account.

The estimated quantity of guano on these islands is 200,000 tons ; the total quantity exported up to this time amounts to 45,000 tons.

These islands were ceded to Her Majesty. by the Imaum of Muscat, through negotiations conducted by Captain Freemantle, R. N., and John Ord, Esquire. They are now held upon lease, for the term of five years, by the firm of Messrs. Ord, Hindson, and Hayes, Merchants of Liverpool.

Joseph Dawson,
Late Principal Resident and Superintendent for the Lessees.

3.   From A. Faulkner, Esq.

4.   Also read a letter from Captain Pullen, R. N., H. M. S. " Cyclops," communicating to the Society, through Commander Barker, I. N., some interesting experiments connected with the temperature of the ocean at great depths, and eliciting a fact in result so contrary to the generally conceived notion of the minimum temperature of the

ocean, as he thought might be sufficient to commend the subject to the Geographical Society, and be considered one worthy of inquiry.

The following is a statement of the experiments above referred to :—

No. of Casts.	Position.		Temperature.		Depth.	No. of Therm.
	Lat.	Long.	At Surface.	Minimum at Bottom.		
			Fahr.		Fathoms.	
1	26° 46′ S	23° 52′ W	75° 0′	35° 0′	2700	10
2	7 12 S	60 48 E	81 5	38 2	2000	6
3	5 37 S	61 29 E	82 0	35 0	2253	6

The barometer stood at 30 inches. The thermometers were most carefully tested, as will be shown, and found correct.

Captain Pullen, not entirely prepared for such a result, took the earliest opportunity to test the instruments by which the thermal measurements were made, proceeding as follows :— Procuring a quantity of ice, he caused it to be placed in a tub with the thermometers, and enveloped the whole in a thick cloth. After the lapse of half an hour, the thermometers were removed, No. 10 showing a minimum 32°, while No. 6 showed 33° 5′. The result of a second experiment showed No. 10 to remain at 32°, while No. 6 stood at 33°.

Captain Pullen then caused the ice to be pounded small, and mixing salt with it, the instruments were again inserted. On removal, they showed a temperature zero, sufficient proof of the correctness of the instruments, at all events, at the low temperatures.

It was then stated by the Secretary that Captain Pullen, having been good enough to permit a copy to be taken of the Track of the " Cyclops," and also of the sections of her deep-sea soundings from Suez to Kurrachee, advantage was taken of the permission, and completed copies are now before the Society. That they are produced, is entirely due to Commander Barker, who, in the absence of the Secretary from the Presidency on duty, with most praiseworthy zeal undertook their execution at a cost of much time and labour. Requested by the Vice-President, Commander Barker proceeded to explain the nature and particulars of the different Red Sea and Ocean sections. Several striking peculiarities present themselves in these sections of deep-sea soundings, those of the Red Sea showing the very irregular formation of the bed thereof, and the precipitous character of its shores and reefs. One peculiarity is also apparent—while, as a general rule, mud will be found at all great depths ; we find that in the central section sand prevails, the deep sounding on either shore being mud. One instance of rock is found at a depth of 800 fathoms.

The sections of that part of the coast from Aden to the Kooria Mooria Islands, also show great irregularities in the bed of the ocean. Seven miles from Haski (one of the Kooria Mooria group), the formation of the bed of the ocean is that of an inverted cone, having in its centre a depth of 1,150 fathoms, rising abruptly on its eastern face to 25 fathoms from the surface, and on its western to 182 fathoms, the distance between these two last being but 25 miles.

It should be observed that, in taking these deep-sea soundings, Captain Pullen was provided with a very ingenious sounding machine, which caused the " sinker" (or, as we would generally term it, the lead, only as on these occasions a hollow iron cylinder is used, we prefer the the other term,) to detach itself as soon as it came in contact with the bottom, so that an iron rod, weighing about (8) eight pounds only, had to be drawn to the surface. At the lower part of the rod was a small hollow tube, so constructed, that while descending, a small valve, kept open by means of a spring, allowed the water to pass freely through, but as the sinker detached itself in passing over the spring it closed it, and it was kept in that position by means of a tight-fitting ring placed over the hollow sinker.

In the Red Sea the greatest depth obtained was 1,054 fathoms, and in the Indian Ocean, crossing the mouth of the Gulf of Oman from Ras-ul-Hadd, the extreme eastern cape of Arabia, to Kurrachee, 2,010 fathoms was found ;—rather more than half way across the depth near Ras-ul-Hadd, very precipitous ;—and at about 60 miles from Kurrachee equally so, rising suddenly from 1,600 to 64 fathoms.

Captain Pullen also sent several specimens of the bottom obtained by means of the instrument before alluded to. One obtained from a depth of 1,900 fathoms, on the Kurrachee section, was fine mud, but it is said on no occasion has it ever been found that any of the specimens thus brought up, possess in them any sign of animal life being found at these great depths.

The members present evinced a most lively interest in the explanation given by Commander Barker, and the thanks of the meeting were voted to that gentleman for the labour and patience evinced by him in drawing up these sections, and for the obliging manner in which he explained them ; and also to Captain Pullen, through whose kindness such valuable and highly interesting matters have been brought before the Society.

Resolved that the geological and other specimens now before the meeting be presented to the Museum of the Bombay Branch Royal Asiatic Society, and that Dr. Carter be requested to favour this Society with an analysis of one or more of the specimens of the sea-bottom found at the greatest depths.

The thanks of the Society having been voted to J. Dawson, Esq., for his interesting paper on the Kooria Mooria Islands, the Meeting adjourned.

SESSION 1858-59.

SEVENTH AND ANNIVERSARY MEETING.—*Thursday, May 19th, 4½ P. M.*

Present.—Commodore G. G. Wellesley, C.B., R. N., *President,* in the chair ; W. E. Frere, Esq., C. S., *Vice-President.*

Members.—Commander W. C. Barker, I. N. ; Dr. Bhawoo Dajee ; C. Leggatt, Esq. ; W. F. Hunter, Esq. ; Jugonnath Sunkersett, Esq. ; and D. J. Kennelly, Esq., *Secretary.*

Visitor.—Lieutenant R. G. Watson, 2nd B. E.

The Minutes of the last Meeting were read and confirmed : —

Members proposed.—Lieutenant G. J. Nixon, I. N. ; F. D. Faithfull, Esq. ; Lieutenant R. G. Watson ; D. J. Vaughan, F.R.C.S. ; Dr. F. Broughton, F.R.C.S. ; Rao Saheb Wiswanath Narrayen, Esq. ; Dr. Atmaram Pandoorung ; Virjeevundass Madowdass, Esq. ; and Kalliandass Mohundass, Esq.

Presents to the Library.

1.—Catalogue of Valuable Books in the Stock of Bookseller Bernard Quaritch. Presented by Mr. Bernard.

2.—Proceedings of the Royal Geographical Society ;—of the Meetings held on the 8th and 22nd November 1858. Presented by the Society.

3.—Abhandlungen der Mathemat-Physikalischen. Presented by the Society.

Letters read.

From Captain R. F. Burton, dated Aden, 20th April 1859.

From Reverend W. Isenberg, C. M. S., communicating information received from Zanzibar to the effect, that the Lake Uniamesi, described in the Map which the Reverend Messrs. Rabman and Erhardt had drawn up, has not been found to be a single one, but a series of lakes, the largest of which is said to be in the north, and is probably a source, or perhaps *the* source of the White River.

Extracts of a letter from Commodore Jenkins, C.B., I. N., to the Secretary, were also communicated to the Society, stating the progress of a Survey of Babylon and the countries on the Euphrates, Tigris, &c., and expressing a hope that, in course of a short time, a complete map of the surveys will be placed before the world.

The business of the Monthly Meeting being concluded, that of the Annual Meeting was entered on.

On examining the Voting lists, the following, in order of votes, were declared the Office Bearers for the ensuing year.

Vice-Presidents.—W. E. Frere, Esq., C. S. ; the Honorable Arthur Malet ; and H. L. Anderson, Esq., C. S.

Resident Members.—R. S. Sinclair, Esq., LL.D. ; Geo. Buist, Esq., LL.D. ; Dr. A. H. Leith ; Captain Barker, I. N. ; Dr. J. Winchester, LL.D. ; Dr. R. Haines ; W. F. Hunter, Esq. ; Dr. Bhawoo Dajee ; John Ritchie, Esq. ; Sir C. Jamsetjee Jejeebhoy, Bart. ; and Lieutenant W. M. Pengelley, I. N.

Non-Resident Members.—Brigadier General LeGrand Jacob ; Captain J. F. Jones, I. N. ; Major A. B. Kemball, C. B. ; Dr. C. Morehead ; Lieut. A. D. Taylor, I. N. ; Commodore G. Jenkins, C. B., I. N. ; Lieut. J. C. Constable, I. N. ; and P. W. LeGeyt, Esq., C. S.

The Secretary read the Annual Report as follows :—

Report for 1858-59.—Since the commencement, in October, of the Session now closing, the Bombay Geographical Society has met six times, when the following papers were read, and business transacted :—

October 21*st.*—On the Earthquakes which have occurred in India betwixt 1840 and 1858, in continuation of Colonel Baird Smith's Catalogue.   By Dr. Buist,—ordered for publication.

November 18.—On the views of Mr. Leonard Horner and Professor Owen on the Age of Man upon the Earth,—printed for the Transactions just about to appear.

January 20.—No Meeting in December, in consequence of the absence of the President and Secretary, with other members, from the Presidency. No paper was on the occasion read.

February 17.—Remarks on the Navigation betwixt Bombay and Suez, in the event of the construction of a Canal across the Isthmus. By Captain Barker, I. N.

March 24.—Discussion on Captain Barker's paper on the Navigation betwixt Bombay and Suez; and a paper on the Kooria Mooria Islands, by Lieutenant Whish, I. N.

On Sea Soundings for the Electric Telegraph from Suez, by Captain Pullen, R. N.

April 21*st*.—Deep Sea Soundings, with Temperatures at great depths, betwixt the Cape of Good Hope and Aden, by Captain Pullen. A paper on the Kooria Mooria Islands, by Mr. Dawson, late Superintendent of Guano export from the Kooria Mooria Islands.

Within the past twelve months four new members have been added to our list, while we have suffered no loss by death, and only two by resignation,—Messrs. W. P. Adam and H. Borrodaile, on their final retirement from India. We have now on our roll sixty-seven paying members, and the number has of late been steadily increasing. There are ten members proposed this day.

The following state of our Accounts shows a balance to our credit :—

In the Treasurer's hands................	Rs.	769	8	3
„ Secretary's „	„	10	11	6
Total	Rs.	780	3	9

and we have already paid the heavier portion of the printing of the forthcoming Number of our Transactions, kept, by the delays of the printer (Mr. D'Souza) nearly twelve months at press beyond its time.

We have, since last May, sold twenty-seven pocket magnifiers, and one small pocket compass; no other instrument has been disposed of; and barometers and thermometers, with which we were wont to provide our friends, can now so easily be had elsewhere, that it will probably be deemed superfluous to continue longer to provide supplies from home. We have at present on hand two by Adie, both in charge of Dr. Buist, one with a beautiful silver scale fitted up with reflectors and magnifiers, and affording much more desirable readings than have ever, heretofore, been thought of. The barometer lent to Captain Burton, in December 1856, is stated by him to have been left at Aden, from which place it will be forwarded by first opportunity ; one barometer and three mountain sympiesometers, sent home for repair, are now on their way out to be added to our supplies. When mountain sympiesometers were first taken up by us in 1850, and a series of comparisons published in our Transactions for last year, betwixt the indications at various elevations of the mercurial barometer by Adie and by Newman, of the aneroid and of the mountain sympiesometer, Sir John Herschel, in reference to a similar paper from the same pen, published in the Transactions of the Royal Geographical Society of London, said that the last-named instrument was one we had never heard of. In the instructions for observation issued in 1856 by the distinguished association named, the instrument just mentioned is specially commended to the attention of travellers.

In speaking of instruments, if I may for a moment be permitted to digress, I might, perhaps, be pardoned for expressing a regret that, while the whole maritime powers of the world have agreed on employing an uniform set of instruments,—that agreed upon by the Brussels Congress of 1853 and 1854, constituted under the direction of the Kew Committee,—the Indian Navy continues to be supplied with the old-fashioned manufactures of Newman ; and while we find around us first class instruments in the ships of the Royal Navy, of the Navies of France, Austria, and America which visit our shores,—in the magnificent steamers of the Peninsular and Oriental Steam Navigation Company, and the best found of our merchantmen,—our own war Navy, yielding to none in the position it holds in the enterprises of war, or pursuits of science, is still provided with instruments the rest of the world have agreed to set aside. If the Society sympathises with such views on these points, its sentiments require only to be made known through the proper channel to secure a remedy.

Since last year's anniversary meeting, the Society has lost the services of the oldest of its office-bearers, Dr. Buist, on being appointed a Municipal Commissioner, having felt himself compelled to resign, after a sixteen years term of zealous and indefatigable servitude in the cause of science and of the Society.

After a somewhat prolonged delay, the room granted to the Society in February last has been vacated, and is now being made ready for occupation, an event which, it is trusted, may take place before the setting in of the approaching monsoon. It may be here stated, that the present room has been occupied by the Society for a period of 23 years. It is also hoped that a catalogue in full, as ordered in February last, will be placed in the hands of the Society on their first meeting of the next session, in September of this year.

The Society's Records of 1836 show that, on application during that year to Government, valuable maps were permitted to be copied, and spare copies of all charts in the Hydrographic stores were granted to the Society. It would seem of late years that such boon had been forgotten by the Society, to its disadvantage ; for, while the Admiralty and United States Congress, continue to forward contributions of their charts from time to time, the more valued Indian contributions have altogether ceased, while contributions of maps and geographical documents are but seldom received, and nothing communicated with reference to surveys in progress or in prospect.

When we look back into this Society's annals, which tell us how much many of our honoured predecessors had, by their labors, added to the cause of geographical science, and not merely to its mathematical divisions only, but also to its other and equally important divisions, physical and political, it behoves us in the present time—a time particularly becoming the age of research and progress—to emulate those good and great men who have passed from us, and also looking to what the great similar Society of England is doing, so aim that we may in no way permit this Society to fall short of that standing and usefulness to which it had, as a scientific body, attained in past years.

The report having been adopted, notice was given that Sub-Committees of Accounts and Correspondence would be selected from among the resident members at the next meeting of the Society. At the close of the proceedings, a few remarks fell from the Secretary, conveying the desire to vacate his post in favor of a more competent successor. The desire was over-ruled.

The meeting adjourned.

SESSION 1858-59.

EIGHTH AND EXTRAORDINARY MEETING.—*Thursday,*
June 16th, 4½ P.M.

Present.—W. E. Frere, Esq., C.S.; F.R.G.S., *Vice-President,* in the Chair.

Members.—Captain Barker, I. N.; Lieut. A. D. Taylor, I. N.; Dr. A. H. Leith; Venayekrao Juggonathjee, Esq.; T. H. Bentley, Esq.; Munguldass Nathoobhai, Esq.; Lieut. W. M. Pengelley, I. N.; E. Heycock, Esq.; and D. J. Kennelly, Esq., I. N., *Secretary.*

Visitors.—Dr. G. C. M. Birdwood and Captain C. Heycock, H. M.'s 89th Regiment.

The Minutes of the Annual Meeting, held on the 19th May, were read and confirmed. It was stated by the Secretary that the special object of the Meeting was to select, from among the Resident Members elected at the Annual Meeting, a Sub-Committee of Accounts, and a Sub-Committee of Correspondence, as per the Society's ninth rule. Opportunity might also be taken to appoint a Special Committee of Survey on old and otherwise damaged books and maps, the Society's property, and to bring to ballot the Members proposed at the last Meeting.

An abstract of the votes of the Members present having been made, there appear to have been chosen—

Sub-Committee of Accounts.

Chairman.—Captain W. C. Barker, I. N.

Members.—Dr. R. Haines; John Ritchie, Esq.; Narayan Dinanathjee, Esq.; Sir Cursetjee Jamsetjee Jejeebhoy, Baronet; Lieut. W. M. Pengelley, I. N.

Sub-Committee of Correspondence.

Chairman.—G. Buist, Esq., LL.D.

Members.—R. S. Sinclair, Esq., LL.D.; Dr. A. H. Leith; J. W. Winchester, Esq., LL.D.; W. F. Hunter, Esq.; Dr. Bhawoo Dajee.

Captain Barker, Lieut. Pengelley, and the Secretary were appointed a Committee of Survey on such property of the Society as would be laid before them at a time convenient to the Secretary.

The following gentlemen, proposed at the last Meeting, were unanimously elected Members of the Society:—Lieut. G. J. Nixon, I. N.; F. D. Faithfull, Esq.; Lieut. R. G. Watson, 2nd B. E.; Dr. J. Vaughan, F.R.C.S., F.R.G.S.; Dr. F. Broughton, F.R.C.S.; Rao Saheb Wiswanath Narayen, Esq.; Dr. Atmaram Pandoorung; and Virjeewundass Madowdass, Esq.

Members proposed.—Lieut. C. Foster, I. N., and Lieut. R. Williams, I. N.

Papers.—Meteorological Observations, for the months of January, February, and March 1859, from Pahlunpore and Bhooj ; and from Baghdad, for October and December 1858, and January and February 1859. Presented by Government.

Sketch Map.—Copy of one drawn up by Captain Speke of the East African Expedition, showing the route travelled by the expedition, and the positions of the newly discovered Lakes Tanganyka and Nyanza.

Presents to the Library.

1. Transactions of the Medical and Physical Society of Bombay. Presented by the Society.

2. Jahrbuch der Kaiserlich Koniglichen Geologischen Reichsanstalt, from January to September 1858.   Presented by the Society.

Letters read.—1 and 2. From C. Gilder, Esq. 3. From H. L. Anderson, Esq., Secretary to Government, Political Department, No. 2014 of 1859.   4. From Major Kendall, Civil Architect, No. 536 of 1859.   5. From H. B. Ellis, Esq., Acting Secretary to Government, No. 1289 of 1859.   6. From the Editor of the 'Bombay Times.' 7. From the Civil Auditor, No. 267 of 1859.   8. From Henry J. Carter, Esq., Secretary B. B. R. A. Society, in answer to a communication addressed to him by the Society, requesting the favor of his analysis of sea-bottom procured from various deep soundings of the Indian Ocean, and from which the following is extracted :—

Microscopical Examination of Sea Bottom from the Southern Coast of Arabia.

Locality.	Latitude.	Longitude.	Depth in fathoms.	Remarks.
	° ′ ″	° ′ ″		
Rasel Hud to Kurrachee ..	22 57 10	61 6 0	1673	Fine plastic clay of a greenish colour, effervesces with acids, contains grains of quartz, but no trace even of organic remains.
Ditto	23 47 0	62 0 0	1900	
Ditto	21 24 10	64 69 0	1780	
Makulla to Curia Muria Islands..	14 3 9	50 4 0	236	Almost entirely made up of minute " Foraminifera " of the kinds found in the seas of Europe. Ditto.
Ditto.	15 6 40	57 52 0	139	
Ditto.	16 36 0	53 40 20	625	
Aden to Makulla.	12 58 35	45 44 50	243	
Ditto.	14 17 20	49 5 8	204	
Ditto.	14 6 40	66 3 0	477	
Ditto.	13 8 20	46 55 35	403	

List of Foraminifera.—Orbulina, Nadoraria, Robulina, Novionina, Rotalina, Globegerina, Vingorina.

From R. S. Sinclair, Esq., LL.D., in answer to a note from the Secretary, having reference to M. Faucault's pendulum experiment for exhibiting the rotation of the earth, and the desirableness of testing the experiment at Bombay as discussed before the Society's meeting of February 1857, from which the following is an extract :—

"If the experiment is to prove of any scientific value for determining, with an approach to accuracy, the inclination of the plumb-line of the place to the axis of the earth, it should be made under favorable circumstances of suspension, of freedom from currents of air, of elevation of the point of suspension, and of observation.

"Some of these conditions seemed to me to be offered by the dome which is above the circular area on which at present stands the statue of Sir Jamsetjee, and I applied to the late General Waddington for permission to make such use of the dome as the experiment might require, but the engrossing nature of my official duties rendered me unable to carry the matter into execution. Still it is desirable that Bombay should be included in the list of places which have contributed experimental facts, which, in addition to their being exemplifications of the laws and phenomena of nature, serve to add accuracy to and to correct statements of geography. If the Geographical Society should wish to pursue the matter, I would beg to suggest that application be made to Paris for the appliances of suspension, &c., and a description of the mode of observation employed there, with the experimental details. Profiting by the results of the best European experience, we, who have so little time and other necessaries at command, would be most likely to arrive at useful results. Should you approve of my suggestion, will you have the goodness to propose it at the next Meeting of the Society."

The following letter was also read, being a copy of one dated Zanzibar, 17th March 1859, from Captain Rigby to the Government, and transmitted for the information of the Society by H. L. Anderson, Esq., Secretary to Government :—

"I have the honor to report, for the information of the Right Honorable the Governor in Council, the safe arrival at this port, on the 5th instant, of Captains Burton and Speke of the East African Expedition. Both these officers were suffering from the effects of exposure and privations, but are already considerably improved in health, and they proceed to Aden in an American vessel which sails in a few days.

" The object contemplated in sending this expedition into East Africa appears to have been most successfully carried out as far as the limited time and means at disposal would admit of the exploration of so vast an extent of country.

" The lake of Tanganika, situated about six hundred miles from the east coast, and never before visited by any white man, has been discovered and partially surveyed. Captain Speke travelled alone through an unknown country for about 5 degrees to the north-east of Lake Tanganica, and discovered the Lake Nyanza, a vast sheet of water extending north and south. The south extremity of this lake is situated in 2° 25' South Latitude, and its length is so great that no native on its shores has any idea where its northern limit terminated, and from its great elevation, 3,700 feet above the sea, and the general slope of the country, Captain Speke is confidently of opinion that the northern end of this great lake will prove to be the source of the White Nile.

" Both Captains Burton and Speke talk in the highest terms of the assistance afforded to the Expedition by His Highness Syud Majid and his officers, and of the friendly reception they everywhere met with from the Arab residents in the interior through being provided with recommendations from His Highness.

" Captain Speke describes the country visited by him as very populous, the natives very friendly and courteous, the land well cultivated, producing a great variety of grains and vegetables, coffee, cotton, sugar-cane, and also abundance of rich iron-stone.

" The Belooch Sepoys and Arabs who accompanied the expedition all talk of Captain Speke with the greatest affection. By his kind and considerate treatment of them, he has acquired their entire confidence, and they were ready to accompany him again to any part of Africa. From his tact in conciliating the natives, his resolution, and scientific acquirements, I am confident he has proved himself eminently qualified for any future African explorations."

The subject of this letter seemed to excite a very lively interest in the minds of all present, but as much time had already been spent upon the business of the evening, and also in examining the newly discovered positions as pencilled on one of the Society's African Sheets, it was found necessary to reserve the further discussion of this very interesting subject until another opportunity.

With the permission of the Vice-President, extracts of letters from Captain Pullen, R. N., dated Cosire, 8th of May, and Aden, 31st May, 1859, addressed to Captain Barker, I. N., were read by that officer as follows :—

From letter dated 8th May, H. M.'s Frigate " Cyclops," from Bombay to Aden.

" To give you an account of my proceedings since leaving Bombay. In the first place, I had most beautiful weather the whole way and made as straight a course as possible, except going out of it a short way at the last in the Gulf of Aden, to get a cast of the lead.

" Mind you, I could not think of attempting a continuous line, but it would hardly have been the thing to go on such a distance without having a try for the depths, and a look at the nature of the bottom, so I only got three casts of the lead in different localities, which I think will give us some idea of the level nature of that bottom between Aden and Bombay. The first cast, of 1,880 fathoms, was in Lat. 16° 59' N., and Long. 64° 27' E. The bottom, brown mud, with a minimum temperature of 44°, the surface at the same time 81° 5'. The next was about half way between Socotra and the Coast of Arabia, 1,500 fathoms, light colored sand, very much less depth than I expected,—however, here is the fact ; the minimum temperature at this depth was 43° 5' ; the surface 82°. The next cast, and last, was 1,200 fathoms, light colored mud with minimum temperature of 45°, surface 81° 5'. Thus I think we see what an even bottom it is between these two ports after getting well off the bank. I did not reach Aden until the evening of the 26th April."

From letter dated 31st May.

" The Red Sea cable is laid, and thus far are we in closer communication with old England than when I left you at Bombay. It is a glorious job, and has been most successfully done ; and whatever credit may reflect on the one whose opinions have thus been so fully proved, those who have thus got it down deserve praise. The course of the cable is very nearly that which I sketched in my last Report on the Red Sea, supposing Massowah was not to be a station ; but to put you in possession of the complete line, we will commence and fancy ourselves at Suez. Although my ideas were, and still are, that running the cable up—not down—the Sea, was the way for least possible risk, I am satisfied now that it is down, and I suppose a cable has never yet been so well laid. The starting point is from the Lime Kiln in that notch of the coast nearly opposite Moses' Wells ; the connection from there to Suez by wires on poles ; down the Gulf (of Suez) nearly about mid-channel, passing close to the northern part of that shoal east of the Ushuruffe ; thence to the westward of Shadwan, and nearly in a straight line to Cosire. Thus they pass rather outside my line of soundings, and likely to get greater depth, but that does not appear to be any objection. We only got away from Cossire after two unsuccessful attempts, but the damage was chiefly occasioned by the great heat of the sun. I accompanied the "Imperador" the third time, for I was anxious to get as much as 100 tons of the coal I found thereon, if possible ; and I believe this coal was stored here in the days of the "Hugh Lindsay," so you may fancy it was not worth much. However, to try back, we left Cosire with the cable this time under very favorable circumstances, and went along cheerily, passing close outside the Fury Shoal, off Ras Benass and the long shoal off Elba Cape. Here "Cyclops" got up, but had not been able to get any soundings. So the first I got, not far off the shoal, was 461 fathoms. We now led, passed through that passage off Ras Roway, Oom-al Grushe, and Shab Bazar, getting 351 fathoms, not a quarter of a mile from the island, and thence on to Suakin, taking all three ships in without any damage to either, nor delay (except for day-light) or stoppages the whole of this No. 2 Section, and it was the one, too, I had not sounded ; even now there is a portion with the cable down where we have not the depth. Still the work went on so well that the conductors, &c., think the bottom very even, and the depths between three and four hundred fathoms.

"Thus far all right, and the part I felt most anxious about so soon completed, getting stations established and other matters, made another start. Success seemed to be the order of the day, or rather a merciful Providence guiding and directing us on this great undertaking.

"The line, after getting a sufficient distance outside Suakin, off to the southward, passing eastward of the Etwid and Gaad Hoggart Shoal, west of Tella-tella Suggeer-Darah Terass and the Shoal Patch off Isle Hadjarah. Thence to the northern part of Dhalac bank, keeping from two to four miles within its edge west of Jibbel Zoogur and the Harnish direct to Perim, and through the small Strait of Babel Mandeb to Aden arriving at the place with at least 200 miles of cable still on board.

From this latter circumstance, you may infer that the loss in laying has not been great—very much under what they had calculated on,—in fact, I do not think throughout more than 10 per cent., when I believe, they calculated on 18. It is possible that I go into the Red Sea again, but I can assure you that the heat has been dreadful. I have never in all my tropical experience felt or suffered so much."

Captain Barker having sat down, the Secretary expressed a regret that the charts of the Red Sea were not on the table to assist in the elucidation of the interesting and valuable matter placed by Captain Barker before the Society. He (the Secretary) further regretted that he was not in a position to lay before the Society the valuable—he might say magnificent—contribution made by Captain Barker in the shape of newly constructed charts copied from the original surveys of the Red Sea and Arabian Coast, and on which were shown the recent deep soundings taken by H. M.'s Steamer "Cyclops," being further delineated by carefully drawn sections of the sea bottoms from Suez to Babel Mandeb and to Kurrachee ; but he trusted that, when out of the hands of the map-binders, these charts would have their merited place to the adornment of the Society's rooms.

Resolved.—That the Secretary be directed to obtain the latest information on the subject of M. Faucualt's pendulum experiment as applicable to its practice at Bombay, and also that an estimate of the expense likely to be incurred by the Society in order to give effect to Professor Sinclair's views be prepared with as little delay as possible.

Resolved.—That an extra clerk on Rs. 20 per month be employed for the purpose of copying a portion of the Society's records much damaged by age and insects.

The best thanks of the Society were directed to be conveyed to Dr. Carter for his valuable analyses of sea bottoms, in which is afforded so much new and interesting information relative to the beds of the Red Sea and Indian Ocean ; and also to the several donors to the Society.

Reference was made to the presence, among the assembled members, of one who had long been absent from the Society's meetings, but who had proved himself a firm supporter of the Society in its many scientific channels, and a hope was expressed that his labors in its cause would be found not to have terminated.

The meeting then adjourned.

p 8

SESSION 1859-60.

First Meeting.—*September 15th*, 1859, 4½ p.m.

Present.—Commodore G. G. Wellesley, C.B., R.N., *President*, in the Chair. W. E. Frere, Esq., C.S., F.R.G.S., *Vice-President*.

Members.—Captain W. C. Barker, I. N.; Lieutenant A. D. Taylor, I. N.; John Ritchie, Esq.; J. W. Winchester, LL.D.; T. H. Bentley; Esq.; Edwin Heycock, Esq.; Ali Mahomed Khan, Esq.; Virjeevundass Madowdass, Esq.; Dr. J. Vaughan, F.R.G.S.; C. D. Leggatt, Esq.; Dr. A. H. Leith; Lieutenant W. M. Pengelley, I. N.; Dr. F. Broughton; Dr. G. C. M. Birdwood; Narrayen Diannathjee, Esq.; Dr. Bhawoo Dajee, and D. J. Kennelly, Esq., *Secretary*.

Elections.—Lieutenants C. Forster and R. Williams, I. N. were elected Members. Dr. G. C. M. Birdwood was declared a Member of the Society under its rule that "All Members of the Bombay Branch of the Royal Asiatic Society are entitled to be admitted Members of the Geographical Society, on making application to this effect through the Secretary, and paying the prescribed annual subscription."

Proposed Members.—The Rev. W. K. Fletcher, M. A.; Lieut. G. T. Robinson, I. N.; Lieut. M. A. Sweny, I. N.; Dr. G. E. Seward; Lieut. A. W. Stiffe, I. N.; T. F. Punnett, Esq.; and Lieut. G. L. Lewis, I. N.

Donations.—The donations presented to the Society since the last Meeting were:—Four copies of the account of the Cyclone in the Andaman Sea on the 9th and 10th April 1858, by G. Von Liebig, M. D., presented by the Government; Register of Meteorological Observations, Malabar Coast, by Lieutenant R. Williams, I. N.; Annual Report of the Grant Medical College, for the Session 1858-59, presented by Dr. C. Morehead; Narrative of a Voyage to the West Indies and Mexico, presented by the Hakluyt Society; Jarbuch der Kaiserlich Konighlichen Geologischen Reichsanstalt, by the Society; Greenwich Magnetical and Meteorological Observations, 1856, presented by the Royal Society; Meteorological Elements, British Guiana, 1854-56, presented by the Government of British Guiana; Memoirs of the Geological Survey of India, Vol. II. part I., and Map of Budelcund, presented by the Superintendent of the Survey; Catalogue of the Library of the Royal Geographical Society, presented by W. E. Frere, Esq., F. R. G. S.; Transactions of various Societies, &c.

Maps.—Seven Sheets of the Track Survey of the River Parana. two Sheets of the Uruguay, one Reference Chart to the Tributaries of La-Plata, and Map of the Basin of La-Plata, from the Smithsonian Institution, Washington, through the Government. There were also received from the Government, printed copies of State Correspondence and Reports, for transmission to the Smithsonian Institution, United States of America.

Exhibitions.—Captain W. C. Barker's Outline Sketch of the South-east Coast of Arabia from Aden to Macula, from Macula to Haski, Kooria Mooria Islands, and from Ras Masseera to Ras El Had, showing the track and deep sea soundings, by Captain Pullen, R.N., and the Officers of H. M. S. "Cyclops," 1858-59 ; also Sections of the deep sea soundings in the Red Sea, H. M. S. "Cyclops," 1858 ; Specimens of the bank of soundings on the Malabar Coast from between Mount Dilly and Cape Comorin, at depths varying from 35 to 100 fathoms, chiefly of detritus, shells, and coral, by Lieutenant C. Forster, I. N. ; Specimens of iron pyrites from the Islands of Larrack, and Ormus, and from the Bostana Hills, Persian Gulf, by Lieutenant C. E. Beddome, I. N., (one specimen in particular, a hexagonal prism of the second order, rhombohedral system, was much admired for its perfect symmetry of form) ; the published sheets of the recent Survey of the Western Coast of India, from Cape Comorin to a short distance south of Bombay, placed on the table by Lieutenant Taylor, I. N. ; Colored Map of Bombay with the country adjacent, by Dr. George Buist.

Letters.—From Dr. G. C. M. Birdwood, Lieutenant C. Forster, I. N., Lieutenant C. E. Beddome, I. N., Atmaram Pandoorung, Esq., Lieut. R. Williams, I. N., J. A. Barth, Esq., S. Barker, Esq. I. N., Dr. C. Morehead, Messrs. Smith, Elder, and Co., Major A. B. Kemball, C. B., D. C. R. Leighton, Esq., Manockjee Cursetjee, Esq., Thomas Oldham, Esq. Supt. of the Geological Survey of India, H. Young, Esq., Chief Secretary to Government, No. 44 of 1859, C. Beyts, Esq. Secretary Bombay Mechanics' Institute, Joseph Henry, Esq. Secretary Smithsonian Institution, Messrs. Herman and Robert Schlagintweit, and from Captain W. F. Marriott, Acting Secretary to Government, Marine Department.

Announcement.—The Secretary announced, by permission, that the President would be prepared to deliver an address to the Society at its next Anniversary Meeting of May 1860. Hitherto it had not been the practice to deliver such address.   The announcement was received by the Members present with marked satisfaction.

Read the following letter from Dr. George Buist :—

" D. J. KENNELLY, Esq.,
      Secretary to the Bombay Geographical Society.

Bombay, 24th August 1859.

SIR,—In forwarding you, for distribution, the 14th number of the Transactions of the Bombay Geographical Society, my editorial labors, by their kind permission surviving those of Secretary, come to a close.

2.   An apology for their frightful delay at Press appears in the Preface, sufficient, I trust, to exonerate me from blame—made purposely as mild as possible to avoid injuring the feelings (of the friends) of a dead and worthy man, though very unskilful tradesman.

3.   In point of fact, there is not a page of the 200 I have not required to read four times over at least, sometimes much oftener than even this, as a third or fourth revise was often sent to me much more full of errors, freshly introduced, than those I had previously corrected.

4.   This, however, had nothing to do with the delay at press.   My work was invariably performed the moment material was supplied me ; but Mr. DeSouza hardly ever managed to get through with so much as eight pages a month, and during my six weeks' absence in May and June, four were all that were submitted to me.

5.   The work has now been transferred to the *Government Gazette* Press, Byculla, and I believe there are already nearly 50 pp. of No. XV. thrown off or ready for press.

6.   I have to request that you will now tender to the Society my resignation of membership of the various Committees to which they have done me the honor to elect me.

7.   Leaving for Bengal on the 16th proximo, I hope I may, while at Allahabad, continue an occasional contributor to your Transactions, as I certainly shall remain a diligent student of them, &c. &c.

GEO. BUIST."

The Secretary stated that, having circulated this letter to the General Committee, he was, at their unanimous desire, directed to present Dr. Buist with an elegantly bound set of their Transactions, accompanied by a letter expressive of the Society's sentiments in connexion with the gift.

The Transactions had been prepared as directed, and were now before the meeting for inspection. They had been bound very elegantly, and to each volume a lithographed page had been added, of which the following is a copy :—

"To Geo. Buist, LL.D., F.R.S., &c.
    Late Secretary to the Bombay Geographical Society.

Sir,—Having circulated your letter, dated 24th August 1859, to the General Committee of the Geographical Society, intimating the close of your editorial labours in the 14th number of the Society's Transactions, and your resignation of the membership of the different Committees of the Society, on your departure from Bombay, I have the honor to communicate to you the gratification of the Society on learning, that your absence from Bombay will not sever the connexion between yourself and them, and also their unanimous resolve as follows :—

Resolved.—That this Society present Dr. Buist with a set of their "Transactions" bound, in order to mark their sense of their obligations to him, for his zealous, long-sustained, and most valuable labours as their Secretary and Editor ; that they select this mark the more particularly, because the volumes stand enriched with many valuable contributions from his own pen, not only on the Geography of Western India, but also on Geography in the most enlarged acceptation of the term.

I have the honor to be, &c.,
                D. J. Kennelly,
        Secretary, Bombay Geographical Society.
Bombay, 14th September 1859."

Also read the following letter from Dr. Buist :—

                        " Bombay, 20th August 1859.

" Sir,—Amongst the stores of the Society will be found 600 Copies of the Reports of the Observations made by Mr. Mayes at Aden, at the suggestion and under the supervision of the Society, betwixt 1846 and 1850.

2. The expense of the establishment, as well as the charges of printing, were defrayed by Government, Government having undertaken to meet the further charge of printing the preface, expected to amount to about 300 pages.

3. Of this about 100 pages have been written and thrown off. It was meant to consist of a history of Meteorological Research in India and an Analysis of the Observations.

4. An amount of imperious occupation, not anticipated when the task was undertaken, two visits to England, with several severe attacks of sickness, and changes of occupation since its commencement, long retarded—and have since suspended—its preparation, and I would now recommend the issue of the Observations as they stand, with a short preface, explanatory and apologetic, which I shall prepare.

5. The intention was to have retained 300 copies for the Members and Correspondents of the Society, and to have made over 300 to Government for distribution. All these arrangements will be found duly set forth in the correspondence and minutes, and I should earnestly recommend them to be carried out as they stand.

6. In recommending immediate issue, I have no idea of the volume permanently remaining in its present mutilated form. I propose devoting the first leisure I can command at Allahabad to the completion both of the Aden observations as originally proposed, and the preparation of a preface on the observations made by me while in charge of the Colaba (since termed the Royal) Observatory, containing a general analysis of the Meteorological Observations already published throughout India, with a description of the climates of our Empire in the East.

7. For these I have great abundance of material prepared and arranged, and which has long been beside me ; a little leisure is all that is required for its elaboration. This I hope to find in Bengal.

I have the honor, &c.,

GEORGE BUIST."

In reference to this letter it was stated that, in accordance with the desire of the General Committee, it had been intimated to Dr. Buist that the Society would be prepared to adopt the recommendation set forth in his letter, on 'the receipt from him of the short preface, explanatory and apologetic, meant to accompany the Meteorological Observations, when issued to the Government. The Secretary also explained that, in addition to publishing the new preface, it would be necessary to reprint the old one on account of its present soiled and torn condition, and as there remained with Government a balance of the grant passed to the Society for the publication and issue of the Observations, he begged to be permitted to carry this arrangement into effect.

Permission granted.

Read a circular letter, addressed by the Secretary to the Sub-Committee of Finance, on the subject of presenting Captain Mahomed bin

Hamees—the Society's only African member—with a set of their Trans-actions on his departure for Zanzibar.

The President then requested that the meeting would proceed to the election of a Chairman Sub-Committee of Correspondence in lieu of Dr. Buist, resigned. On the votes being scanned, Captain W. C. Barker, I. N., Chairman Sub-Committee of Finance was declared to be elected. The Secretary was then directed to issue an election circular to the members of the General Committee, for the purpose of electing from among their number a Chairman of Sub-Committee of Finance in lieu of Captain Barker, elected Chairman of Sub-Committee of Corres-pondence. It was deemed necessary to adopt this measure on account of the large amount of business before the meeting.

The following propositions were then laid before the meeting by the President :—

1. *Proposed*, that, as there exists a pressing necessity for an index to the Society's Transactions, the Secretary be requested to commence the compilation of such a work, so soon as it may be convenient for him to do so.

2. That the form of Appendix contained in the late numbers of the Society's Transactions be continued, in which may be inserted gleanings from the subjects, *Meteorology, Zoology, Botany, Hydrography,* and from other miscellaneous subjects, which, like the above, may not be specifically represented in any Indian journal or periodical.

3. That, as the new rooms of the Society do not afford accommoda-tion necessary for the display, for reference, of their maps and charts, the Secretary be directed to address the Bombay Branch of the Royal Asiatic Society with the view of obtaining in their adjoining room such space as they would grant to the Society for this purpose.

These propositions were agreed to unanimously.

The President having called upon the Secretary to read extracts from Dr. Buist's paper on "The Hurricanes in the Eastern Seas, from 1854 to 1859," the following were read :—

" On receiving from Mr. Hugh Crawford, Allipey, a very valuable series of observations on the hurricane which made its appearance in the lower part of the Bay of Bengal on the 23rd April last, crossed over the southern extremity of the Peninsula, committing violent ravages on the Malabar Coast, and manifesting itself as far west as Aden, I meant to have endeavoured to give a description of the gale, an account of the area it swept, the direction in which it advanced, and rate at which it revolved. This, however, was the only contribution I received ; none of the vessels in our port appear to have crossed its track, and the information contained in the newspapers is so singularly meagre, that my purpose was abandoned.

Since the death of Captain Biden at Madras, and that of Mr. Piddington at Calcutta, and the return of Dr. Liebig to England, there seems no one in India who takes any interest in Cyclonology.   I hope Captain Tennant, on fairly taking up the office of Director of the Madras Observatory, may prove an exception, and supply a want that we ought to have no cause to complain of, considering the extreme importance of the subject to be investigated, and the gigantic dimensions to which our shipping interests have recently grown.

On this side of India, Dr. Thom, of H. M.'s Service, and Captain Carless, of the Indian Navy, from each of whom we have an admirable account of the *Cleopatra's* hurricane of April 1847, are the only parties who have written on hurricanes. I attempted to give an account of our own very remarkable tempest of November 1854 ; more, because there seemed no one else disposed to take up the task, and the material for its performance must have perished with the occasion, than from any feeling of aptitude, or any assumed accomplishment in the science.

In the Appendices to each of the two previous numbers of our Journal, are lists of the hurricanes in the Eastern seas for a century back ; and which, for a quarter of that period, may be considered tolerably complete. To preserve the information scattered about in reference to subsequent hurricanes, and with the view of continuing the abstract at all events, I subjoin the various instances I have from time to time collected, bequeathing these as a legacy to others who may wish so much of a contribution which further additions may extend.

I have no doubt but that there is abundance of information regarding them fully recorded ; and it in general requires merely the industry or enthusiasm of an individual to draw it forth ; so soon as it is seen that it will be turned to account, it makes its appearance. It would surely be a matter of much regret were Bombay with its University, its Royal Observatory, its Hydrographer, and its two millions of tons of outward and inward freight, borne in fourteen thousand vessels departing or arriving annually, its forty millions sterling worth of seaborne commerce—were Bombay, by far the largest shipping port between the tropics, to be the only one where the collection and promulgation of meteorological information, a matter of such moment to the mariner, was neglected.

List of Hurricanes.

1855. April 12th.—Hurryhur, Madras Presidency, Lat. 13° N., Long. 77° E., seems to have been a local squall of unusual violence, but whether or not possessed of the character of a cyclone does not appear.

April 23rd—May 10th.—Indian Ocean, South of the Line.

May 15th—20th.—Bay of Bengal, betwixt Burmah and Madras.

July 21st.—Off Hongkong.

October 29th and 30th.—Arabian Sea, betwixt Cooria Mooria Bay and the Gulf of Aden.

1856. April 18th.—Arabian Sea, betwixt Cooria Mooria Bay and the Gulf of Aden.

May 14th.—Bay of Bengal.

October 18th.—Typhoon in the China Seas.

November 18th—21st.—Bay of Bengal, from 5° to 20° N.

1857. September 4th and 6th.—Off Chusan, and Northern China Seas.

September 30th.—In China Sea.

October 28th.—Off Ceylon, and in the Bay of Bengal.

October 29th, November 5th—12th.—In China Seas.

November 20th.—Ceylon.

1858. April 9th and 10th.—Bay of Bengal and Andaman Sea.

May 15th and 20th.—Bay of Bengal and Malabar Coast.

August 30th—September 20th.—North China Seas.

October 25th.—Calcutta.

November 8th—10th.—China Seas, betwixt Hongkong and Shanghae.

1859. April 21st—27th.—Bay of Bengal and Arabian Sea.

June 3rd.—Arabian Sea, betwixt Cooria Mooria Bay and the Gulf of Aden.

June 12th—17th.—Bay of Bengal, off Akyab.

June 20th.—Violent squall off Jacobabad.

July 25th—27th.—Lower Bengal.

In the Bay of Bengal, betwixt nearly the same parallels, the number of hurricanes being the same, the proportions for each month differ most importantly from those in the China Seas. In the former region, April and May give us five ; and for three years out of five they occur on nearly the same day of the latter month ;—in the latter we have none.   In the China Seas, September is the stormiest month in the year.   In the Bay of Bengal it has, since 1854, furnished us no storms at all.

Turning next to the Arabian Sea betwixt the parallels of 6° and 22° N.—overpeaceful so far as cyclones are concerned—we find that we have only had four within the period under discussion.   One of these (26th April 1859) was in reality a Coromandel storm, crossing over to Malabar.   The other three all occurred betwixt Cooria Mooria Bay and the Gulf of Aden : though of great violence, as they were singularly circumscribed in their field of action, it is needless to classify them. The following extract from the Appendix to the previous number (XIV.) gives an abstract of the hurricanes in the Arabian Seas so far as our records extend.   It is not a little singular that, out of nine, three should have occurred in the first week of November.

1648.   May 27.—" A hellish hurricane," as it is termed by the Portuguese historians, accompanied by an earthquake, shook Western India ; and similar things occurred on 27th May 1848, but on this occasion the gale was not revolving.

1783.   November 3-7.—Violent hurricane from Tellicherry north to Bombay ; great loss of shipping and lives ; proving fatal to almost every ship within its reach.

1799.   November 3-7.—Frightful hurricane from Calicut north. H. M.'s Ship " Resolution" with about 1,000 small craft, and 400 lives, lost in Bombay harbour.

1807.   June 24.—Furious hurricane off Mangalore.—*As. An. Register*, p. 171.

1819.   September 25.—At Kutch and Kattiawar, lasted a day and two nights.—*As. Jl.* 1820, vol. ix., p. 307 (?)

1827.   December 20.—Bombay (?)

1837.   June 15.—A tremendous hurricane swept over Bombay : an immense destruction of property and loss of shipping in the harbour, estimated at nine and a half lakhs (£95,000) ; upwards of 400 native houses destroyed.

1847. April 19.—Terrific hurricane from the Line north to Scinde, in which the H.C.S. " Cleopatra" was lost, with 150 souls on board. The Maldive Islands submerged, and severe want and general famine ensued.

1854. November 2-3.—Hurricane at Bombay ; and a thousand human beings and half a million worth of property supposed to have perished in four hours' time.

In the Appendix to the 12th Number of our Transactions (p. 2) the following classification of the hurricanes of the East and West Indies occurs :—

PROPORTIONS OF HURRICANES OCCURRING IN EACH MONTH.

	West Indies.	East Indies.
January	5	0
February	7	0
March	11	1
April	6	5
May	5	9
June	10	2
July	42	4
August	96	5
September	80	8
October	69	12
November	17	9
December	7	5

The West India list extends over three hundred years, commencing with 1493, giving a table of four hundred hurricanes ; of three hundred and sixty-five of which only are the dates made known. The Bombay list extends over a century ; but as it could only be made anything like correct for the space of twenty-five years, the abstract is deduced from those occurring betwixt 1830 and 1854, to the north of the line and betwixt the meridians of Canton and Kurrachee. We find that in the West Indies, a hundred and eighty-eight hurricanes have occurred within the present century, or at the rate of 3·5 annually : in our seas sixty-one have been recorded during the past twenty-four years, or on an average of 2·5 annually. The space over which our review extends includes the singularly tranquil waters of the Arabian Sea, and excludes the great hurricane track of the Mauritius.

The list I have already given furnishes the means of materially extending this classification ; and I shall subdivide them not only according to the months in which they occur generally, but arrange them under the heads of the places of their occurrence.

CHINA SEAS, LAT. 8° to 22° N.

Hurricanes.	Date.	Hurricanes.	Date.
None.	January.	1	August 30th, 1858.
None.	February.	4	Sept. 6th, 1857 ; 5th,
None.	March.		20th, and 30th, 1858.
None.	April.	2	October 18th, 1856 ;
None.	May.		and 29th, 1857.
None.	June.	None.	November.
2	July 21st, 1856 ;	None.	December.
	and 25th, 1858.		

It will from this be seen that, for the past five years, nine hurricanes in the China Seas have been confined to the months of July, August, September, and October—September showing the most. The cyclone month of November, betwixt the Burmese and African shores, is barren east of the Straits.

BAY OF BENGAL.

Hurricanes.	Date.	Hurricanes.	Date.
None.	January.	None.	June.
None.	February.	1	July 26th, 1859.
None.	March.	None.	August.
2	April 10th, 1858 ;	None.	September.
	and 21st, 1859.	2	October 28th, 1857 ;
3	May 15th, 1855 ;		and 20th, 1858.
	15th, 1856 ; and	1	November 18th, 1856.
	15th, 1858.	None.	December.

The other gales enumerated in the list do not require to be classified ; and I am not sure besides that they were revolving or true hurricanes.

The talent and labour,—or rather the labour, for no talent is required,—in producing this form of classification is insignificant to the pains and experience requisite for analysing the elements of a hurricane. Yet were the system carried out—for which a little industry suffices—there need not be a degree over the surface of the ocean where the mariner was not provided with the means of guessing his chances of encountering a gale at any given date.

The following remarks followed :—

MR. KENNELLY.—I regret that the paper before the meeting should contain the expression of so severe a rebuke to those of this Presidency who, from their official position or professional pursuits, naturally represent the class most interested in the development of cyclonology, and who are, I assume, those principally referred to by Dr. Buist. I beg to state that there are at Bombay, and among the members of this Society, gentlemen who have not lacked industry, and may be, enthusiasm, as alleged against us ; but whose fault at most amounts to this that they have not placed the results of their labours before the public. We however, may hope for better things to come, and I may state that Mr. Ritchie has promised to forward to the Society much valuable data connected with the cyclonology of the China seas. And, further, that Captain Barker, whose opportunities are many, has also promised to interest himself to the full in procuring information on the subject for the Society.

THE PRESIDENT.—Captain Barker's services would be valuable, and I would suggest that the Secretary forward to him printed circulars detailing the particular data required for a system of Indian cyclonology, which he, as opportunity offered, would have filled up and returned to the Secretary. I would remark that the expressions " Royal Observatory" and " Hydrographer," contained in Dr. Buist's paper, as applied to the Observatory at Colaba and to the Indian Naval Draughtsman, are, so far as I am aware, applied incorrectly.

DR. BIRDWOOD.—May I hope that an opportunity will be afforded for deliberately discussing Dr. Buist's paper ?

THE PRESIDENT.—The paper is to be submitted to the Sub-Committee of Correspondence, after which an opportunity of discussing it will be afforded, if desired.

After a vote of thanks had been accorded to the different donors to the Society, the meeting adjourned.

SESSION 1859-60.

SECOND MEETING.—*October 20th*, 1859, 4½ P. M.

Present.—Commodore G. G. Wellesley, C. B., R. N., *President*, in the Chair.

Members.—Dr. Bhawoo Dajee ; Lieut. R. Williams, I. N. ; F. D. Faithfull, Esq. ; Munguldass Nuthoobhoy, Esq. ; Dr. G. C. M. Birdwood ; Dr. Atmaram Pandoorung ; E. Heycock, Esq. ; and D. J. Kennelly Esq., *Secretary*.

Visitors.—Colonel G. Pope, Lieut. Colonel Birdwood, and Captain J. T. Annesley.

Elections.—The Rev. W. K. Fletcher, M. A. ; Lieut. G. T. Robinson, I. N. ; Lieut. M. A. Sweny, I. N. ; G. E. Seward, Esq., M. D. ; Lieut. A. P. Stiffe, I. N. ; T. F. Punnett Esq. ; and Lieut. G. L. Lewis, I. N. ; were elected members. John J. Lowndes, Esq., was declared a member of the Society under its rule that " All members of the Bombay Branch of the Royal Asiatic Society are entitled to be admitted Members of the Geographical Society, on making application to this effect through the Secretary and paying the prescribed Annual Subscription."

Proposed Member.—J. E. C. Pryce, Esq.

Donations.—The donations presented to the Society since the last meeting were :—

Report on the External Commerce, Bombay, for 1858-59, by Richard Spooner, Esq., Commissioner of Customs. Extract from Log of P. & O. Co.'s Steamer *Pekin* having reference to the Hurricanes of the China Seas, by John Ritchie, Esq. Jahrbuch der Kaiserlich Koniglichen Geologischen Reichsanstalt, by the Society. Proceedings of the Royal Geographical Society, Nos. 3 to 5 of Vol. III. of 1859, by the Society. Journal Asiatique, Tome XIII., No. 51, Avril-Mai 1859, by the Society. The Valley of the Amazon, by the Hakluyt Society. Copy of the Log of the Steamer *Cowasjee Family*, having reference to the Hurricanes of the China Seas, by Captain C. W. Barker, I. N. Mortuary Report for 1858, by the Director General Medical Department, &c. &c.

Letters.—From Captain J. S. Kemball, Belgaum ; Captain C. W. Walker, Tannah ; John Peet, Esq. ; John Ritchie, Esq. ; John J. Lowndes, Esq. ; and H. Newton, Esq., Civil Auditor.

Exhibition.—Chart of the Islands of Zanzibar and Pemba, by Captain W. F. W. Owen, R. N., 1823-24, forwarded by Lieut. J. Sedly, I. N.

Lieut. W. M. Pengelley, I. N., was elected Chairman of the Sub-Committee of Finance.

A list of the Institutions in the receipt of printed Copies of the Society's Transactions having been placed on the Table for inspection, the Secretary was directed to submit it to the Sub-Committee of Correspondence for revision.

A paper was read by Dr. Birdwood.

At the conclusion of which, and after the President and several of the Members having made various remarks on the Nile deposit as influenced by the Mediterranean currents, more especially in their journey along the Syrian Coast, an unanimous vote of thanks was accorded to Dr. Birdwood, and to the different donors to the Society.

The President then announced that Dr. Bhawoo Dajee would read a paper on the Geography of India in the 4th century before Christ, and in the 1st and 7th century after Christ, illustrated by maps, before the next Ordinary Meeting of the Society. The Meeting then adjourned.

SESSION 1859-60.

THIRD MEETING.—*November 17th*, 1859, 4½ P.M.

Present.—Commodore G. G. Wellesley, C.B., R. N., *President ;* W. E. Frere, Esq., C.S., F.R.G.S., *Vice-President.*

Members.—Dr. Bhawoo Dajee ; Dr. G. C. M. Birdwood ; Rev. W. K. Fletcher, M.A. ; Dr. Narrayan Dajee ; Lieut. A. D. Taylor, I. N. ; Dr. Vaughan, F.R.G.S. ; J. M. Erskine, Esq., C.S. ; Dr. Haines ; Munguldass Nuthoobhoy, Esq. ; and D. J. Kennelly, Esq., *Secretary.*

The minutes of the last Meeting were read and approved.

Elections.—The President, in announcing the election of Sir Bartle Frere as member under the rule applicable to the admission of members of the Bombay Branch Royal Asiatic Society, expressed the pleasure he had in so doing, which he doubted not would be shared in by all present.

J. E. C. Pryce, Esq., having been proposed by Captain Barker, I. N., and seconded by the Secretary, was declared duly elected.

Donations.—The following donations were laid on the table, for which the best thanks of the Society were directed to be given to the donors :—

1.   Memoirs on the Ruins of Babylon, by Commander W. B. Selby, I.N., with plans.   By the Government.

2.   Isthmus of Suez Canal Question, viewed in its Political Bearings. By D. A. Lange, Esq., F.R.G.S.

3.   A translation of the Law of Storms into the Chinese made by D. J. Macgowan, Esq., M.D.   By John Ritchie, Esq.

4.   Various Meteorological Registers.   By the Government.

Letters.—1.   From the Officiating Secretary Director General Medical Department, No. 1984 of 1859, requesting to be informed whether the " Meteorological Reports" for stations in the Presidency which have been furnished since 1850, are any longer required by the Society, as Dr. Buist, to whom the reports were originally sent, has now left Bombay.

2.   From H. L. Anderson, Esq., Secretary to Government, No. 4702 of 1859, transmitting, for presentation to the Geographical Society, two printed copies of a Memoir on the Ruins of Babylon, by Commander Selby of the Indian Navy, with two lithographed copies of the plan which accompanied the memoir.

3.   From Sir H. Bartle Edward Frere, K.C.B., forwarding a memo. of information by Major Henry Green, Political Agent at Khelat, showing the heights above the sea of the following places as ascertained by the boiling point :—

	Feet.
Jacobabad..	600
Bagh...	650
Dadur	700
Kirta (Bolan)	1,200
Abijoom (Bolan)	3,000
Sir-i-Bolan......................................	4,370
Quetta	5,900
Moostung	5,700
Khelat	7,000
Chekul-Tan, Peak of, between Quetta and Moostung	2,300

4.   From John Ritchie, Esq., sending, as a contribution, a translation of the Law of Storms made by D. J. Macgowan, Esq., M.D., into the Chinese, and forwarding a transcript of a letter by Mr. Browne to Captain Robson, giving an account of a terrific typhoon which visited between Swatow and Amoy, also an extract of log.

5.   From H. Young, Esq., Chief Secretary to Government, forwarding, for information of the Society, the meteorological reports of—

Cuddalore, from Feb. to Sept. 1859.
Cocanada ...... Feb. to May 1859.
Bhooj .... April to Sept. 1859.
Pahlunpore .... April to June 1859.

6.   From H. J. Carter, Esq., Secretary Bombay Branch of the Royal Asiatic Society, acknowledging letter No. 89, applying for space in the Library of the Asiatic Society, and stating that the same had been submitted for the consideration of the Committee of Management, who, before they can come to any decision on the question, request the favor of a conference on the spot of the President and Secretary of the Geographical Society and himself, respecting the required space and its situation in the Library.

Notice of Motion.—The Secretary, at the request of Captain Barker, who was prevented from attending, gave notice that at the next meeting of the Society, he would move the revision of the list of institutions and individuals now in the receipt of printed copies of the Society's Transactions.   Captain Barker's proposed revision having been read, the business of the evening came to a conclusion.

The President then called upon Dr. Bhawoo Dajee, who read the paper advertised for the evening.   A magnificent map of Central Asia and India, illustrative of the Travels of Hionen-Thsang in the 7th century of our era, and measuring sixteen by ten feet, was employed by the learned member to delineate the different periods treated of in his subject.   An unanimous vote of thanks having been passed to Dr. Bhawoo Dajee, the meeting adjourned.

SESSION 1859-60.
FOURTH MEETING.—*December 15th,* 1859.
Present.—W. E. Frere, Esq., C.S., F.R.G.S., *Vice-President.*
Members.—Captain W. C. Barker, I. N. ; Dr. G. C. M. Birdwood ; Sir Cursetjee J. Jejeebhoy, Bart. ; Jugonath Sunkersett, Esq. ;
p 10

Dr. Bhawoo Dajee ; Lieut. G. T. Robinson, I. N. ; Lieut. A. D. Taylor, I. N.; Lieut. W. M. Pengelley, I. N.; C. D. Leggat, Esq.; Dr. Vaughan, F. R. G. S.; J. M. Erskine, Esq., C. S. ; T. H. Bentley, Esq. ; J. E. C. Pryce, Esq. ; Lieut. G. T. Nixon, I. N. ; Venayek Jugonath-jee, Esq. ; and D. J. Kennelly, Esq., *Secretary.*

Visitors.—Captain and Mrs. Grounds, Lieut. Chitty, and H. Williams, Esq., I. N.

In the absence of the President and Vice-Presidents, Captain Barker, the senior member present, took the chair, until the arrival of the Vice-President.

The Secretary having read a note from the President expressive of the regret it gave him to be absent from the Society's meeting, the minutes of the last meeting were read and approved.

Members proposed.—J. A. Fraser, Esq., M. D., and J. H. Sylvester, Esq., F. G. S.

Donations.—The following donations were laid on the table, for which the best thanks of the Society were directed to be given to the donors :—

1. Thompson's complete Phonetic Alphabet. Presented by the Author.
2. Catalogue Raisonné of rare valuable and curious Books. By B. Quaritch.
3. Memoirs of the Geological Survey of India. Part III. Vol. I. By Government.
4. Annual Report of the Superintendent of the Geological Survey of India. By Government.
5. Annual Report on the Sind Forests for the year 1858-59. By Government.
6. Official Correspondence on the system of Revenue Survey and Assessment in the Bombay Presidency. By Government.
7. Winds and Current Charts of the Indian and China Seas, for each month throughout the year laid down from well-kept Logs, by Lieut. Fergusson, I. N. Presented by Lieut. A. D. Taylor, I. N.

Letters read.—From Captain J. H. Speke, having reference to the exploration of Central Africa, and describing the route intended to be taken by him when next he proceeds to that country, also forwarding, for the information of the Society, a paper on the commerce of that part of Africa which has been recently explored.

2. From Captain Barker, I. N., forwarding an account of a Cyclone experienced in the Southern part of the Bay of Bengal.

3. From the Secretary Bombay Benevolent Library, requesting the presentation to their Library of the copies of the Transactions of the Society from its beginning.

In reference to the revision of the Society's list of Institutions to which are presented published copies of Transactions, the following Resolution, proposed by Captain Barker and seconded by Dr. Birdwood, was passed unanimously :—

" That there be added to the Society's list the following Societies and Institutions, to which shall be sent printed copies of Transactions :—

" The Geographical Societies of Berlin, Darmstadt, Frankfort, St. Petersburg, and New York, the Royal Irish Academy, the Libraries of the Queen's Colleges at Cork, Belfast, and Galway, and to the Library of St. Paul's College, Sydney, N. S. Wales ;" and "that the following persons, now in the receipt of printed copies of the Society's Transactions, be elected to the list of Honorary Members :—

Captain Du Pont, U. S. Navy.
A. K. Johnston, Esq., F.R.G.S.
Sir Charles Lyell.
Professor Powell, Oxford.
General Sabine, and
Mrs. Mary Somerville."

Permission having been granted, an extract of a letter from Dr. Buist to the address of the Secretary was read, having reference to the present state of meteorology, as a science, in Western India, and making allusion to certain wind and current charts of the Indian Ocean published in 1854, but of which copies had not been presented to the Society. It was explained by the Secretary, that the charts referred to by Dr. Buist were this evening on the Society's table for the first time ; and although he had given them but a cursory inspection, he regretted to find, among other errors, that the Island of Rodrigue had been omitted from them all—an omission which, he said, was the more grave, on account of this island being in the general track of the hurricanes of the Indian Ocean, and therefore closely connected with their history in these seas.

Lieut. A. D. Taylor, I. N., read a paper, " on the present state and requirements of our Surveys in the Indian Ocean with reference to the existing errors of its Physical Geography." This will appear in the printed papers.

On the proposition of Mr. Frere, Lieutenant Taylor consented to draw up such suggestions, in reference to certain wants shown in his paper, as would enable the Society to act in order to meet them.

A vote of thanks having been passed to Lieutenant Taylor, and to the different donors to the Society, the meeting adjourned at a late hour.

SESSION 1859-60.
FIFTH MEETING.—*January 19th*, 1860, 4½ P.M.

Present.—Commodore G. G. Wellesley, C.B., R. N., *President*, in the Chair.

Members.—Captain W. C. Barker, I. N. ; Dr. J. W. Winchester, LL.D., F.R.C.S. ; Rev. W. K. Fletcher, M.A. ; Dr. G. C. M. Birdwood ; John Ritchie, Esq. ; Dr. Vaughan, F.R.C.S., F.R.G.S. ; T. H. Bentley, Esq. ; Lieut. E. F. T. Fergusson, I. N., F.R.A.S. ; J. M. Erskine, Esq., C. S. ; E. Heycock, Esq. ; C. D. Leggat, Esq. ; J. E. C. Pryce, Esq. ; Dr. Atmaram Pandoorung ; and D. J. Kennelly, Esq., *Secretary.*

Visitor.—John Leggat, Esq.

The minutes of the last meeting were read and approved.

Elections.—J. A. Fraser, Esq., M.D. (having been proposed by the Secretary, and seconded by Dr. Winchester) ; and J. H. Sylvester, Esq., F.R.G.S. (proposed by the Secretary, and seconded by Dr. Birdwood).

Donations.—The following donations were laid on the table, for which the best thanks of the Society were directed to be given to the donors :—

1. Journal of the Royal Geographical Society of London, Vol. XXVIII. Presented by the Society.
2. Catalogue of Charts and Nautical Books, published by the Admiralty E. I. C. By Mr. D'Sá.
3. Account of a Storm experienced by the Ship "Lady Ottawa." By John Ritchie, Esq.
4. An extract from the "Pekin's" Log, during a Cyclone in the China Seas in July 1859. By J. Ritchie, Esq.
5. Correspondence relating to Canal clearances in the Hydrabad Collectorate in 1857-58, with a Map in a separate case. By Government.

6. Catalogue Raisonné of rare valuable and curious books. By B. Quaritch, Esq.
7. Prospectus of Messrs. De Schlagintweit's Collection of Ethnographical Heads from India and High Seas. By J. A. Barth, Esq.
8. Literary Circular of New Publications and Miscellaneous Articles. By Smith, Elder, and Co.
9. Proceedings of the Royal Geographical Society, Vol. III., No. VI. By the Society.
11. Geological Survey of Great Britain (Horizontal Sections), Nos. VII., VIII., IX., X., and XI. By Lieut. A. D. Taylor, I.N.
12. Ditto ditto (Vertical Sections) Nos. II., IV., VI., VII., VIII., IX., and X. By Lieut. A. D. Taylor, I.N.
13. Contoured Index to the Townland Survey of the County of the City Kilkenny (mounted on a model of the ground). By Lieut. A. D. Taylor, I. N.
14. Major's (R. H.) Early Voyages to *Terra Australis*, now called Australia. By the Hakluyt Society.

Letters read.—From Norton Shaw, Esq., Secretary Royal Geographical Society, forwarding, in the name of the Royal Geographical Society, the Vol. XXVIII. of the Journal. 2. From John Ritchie, Esq., Superintendent P. and O. Steam Navigation Company, contributing to the Society an extract from the "Pekin's" log during a cyclone in the China Seas in July 1859 ; also presenting to the Society an account of a Storm experienced by the ship "Lady Ottawa." 3. From R. Thornburn, Esq., Librarian Admiralty Library, acknowledging the receipt of the Transactions of the Bombay Geographical Society, No. XIV., which was presented to the Admiralty Library. 4. From Messrs. Smith, Elder, and Co., of London, acknowledging the receipt of two remittances sent through Messrs. Smith, Taylor, and Co., of Bombay, and informing the Society of their having distributed the copies of its Transactions addressed to several gentlemen, and of being instructed by these gentlemen to distribute their pamphlets on their disbursements, which they have done. 5. From G. T. Robinson, I. N., applying for a set of blank bottle-logs for the use of H. M.'s Ship "Bernice." 6. Memorandum No. 62, from H. Young, Esq., Chief Secretary to Government, forwarding a copy of the Selections from the Records of the Bombay Government. 7. From Joseph Leeman, Commanding the ship " Ambrosine," of London, forwarding the bottle-log picked up at sea on the 23d May 1859, in lat. 30°40′ N. long. 46° 34′ W. The paper was saturated with water owing to the defective state of the cork.   After carefully drying it, he was able to distinguish the ship's name—" Malta" from Bombay to London; and informing the Secretary that, should the Secretary possess the means of ascertaining the part of the ocean in which it was thrown overboard, he should esteem it a favour if he would inform him, as he feels much interest in everything tending to develop the Physical Geography of the sea and its ocean currents.

The Secretary stated to the effect that the existing defects in private Charts, and in Charts sold by private sale to commanders of merchant vessels, called for some measure of reform whereby this great evil could be combated.

It was also stated that the existing Hydrographical system for India was disadvantageous in the extreme, wanting not only unity and system, but also in that wholesome supervision absolutely required to the attainment of success in this branch of science.   This is and has been felt particularly by our President who has expressed a desire to see such a system introduced as shall operate for good, and who is equally ready to forward the laudable views of the Society in this direction.

It was moved by John Ritchie, Esq., and seconded by Dr. Birdwood, that the Secretary submit the subject in form to the Sub-Committee of Correspondence in order that they would lay before the Society such a scheme as would enable them to take steps necessary to meet the question before them.

Captain Speke's paper, published in the Transactions, was then read.

Dr. Birdwood said, he regretted that he had not seen the paper previous to its being read before the Society.   It was very interesting. Indeed any intelligent observations on the resources of the district traversed by Lieut. Speke—districts so important to, and yet so strangely neglected by, British merchants—could not fail to be interesting.   He wished particularly to refer to our reticence in connection with the extension of the electric telegraph to Muscat and Aden, for the purpose of ventilating proposals already made to place British enterprise in those quarters on an equality with the French and American.   The to-and-fro trade between Bombay, the Coast of Africa, the Persian Gulf, and the Red Sea, amounted in round numbers to £2,530,000.   The population of these districts, according to the best authorities, was 36,250,000 (?) distributed as follows ;—

Persia	8,000,000 ?
Arabia.	8,000,000 ?
Abyssinia .... :	6,000,000 ?
Possessions of the Imam of Muscat in Africa ...	10,000,000 ?
Portuguese Settlements in Africa	250,000
The African Archipelago	4,000,000
	36,250,000

Now if the Muscat and Aden telegraph were followed up by regular postal communication with Muscat, Bushire, and Zanzibar, the to-and-fro trade with them now represented by about £2,500,000, would in a few years, at the most moderate computation, rise to from £10,000,000 to £15,000,000. That was a very moderate computation. The extension of the telegraph to Muscat and Aden gives additional importance to the suggestion for the connection of Bombay with Kurrachee by a direct submarine line. Will Bombay consent to be a day or two behind Kurrachee in respect to advices from those parts ? The tendency of such a state of things would be to transfer the emporium of those places from Bombay to Kurrachee. It is thought that the sheer force of circumstances must make Bombay the great store city of the east, but he would venture to state that it will only attain that position, if it be possible at all, with the greatest exertions. But the question forces itself—Why should these districts trade indirectly with Europe ? Why should not their gum resins, gums, ivory, hides, &c., and the manufactures of Europe and America be exchanged direct, instead of through the intervention of either Bombay or Kurrachee ? When that is done, the productions of Europe will be forced on the inhabitants of these districts. To buy them at the best advantage, they will be literally forced to utilize their own raw resources ; and to do this they will be forced to establish orderly governments among themselves, when commerce will be developed beyond calculation, and its channels through Babylon, Tyre, and Alexandria overflow even their ancient limits. The importance of good government on these districts was forcibly brought to my mind in Persia. I will read an extract from my note-book on the subject :   "·April 2nd 1857.—Went on shore (Mohumra) again, and also up to the Karoon, a short distance.

Conversed with all sorts of people—and all are quite fascinated with English justice. They dread that the English will give up the'place after the war. ' Now,' they say, ' we are paid for our supplies and labour, and the date harvest this year will make us all rich. The Persians robbed us of our labour and supplies, and a ryot can barely get enough from his date grove to feed himself. They say, too, it is only this fear which prevents them raising rice along the river banks, and sugar cane more inland. If the English remain, they will do so, &c. &c.,' to the same effect." Rice and sugar could be obtained to an illimitable extent from the Shatal Arab. Now the Persians obtain their sugar from Bombay, returning it in the form of *sherbets*, conserves and *oolwah*. The same remark applies to wool, tragacanth, hides and horns, liquorice, and hams from date-fed boars of the most delicious flavour imaginable, all of which things are wasted at present. For one hundred miles the Tigris and Euphrates are fringed with liquorice, and the fact is not known beyond the district—unknown commercially at least, and by botanists even, so far as I have searched.

Mr. Leggat observed, that the matters referred to by Dr. Birdwood had already been prominently noticed by the " *Bombay Times*."

Dr. Birdwood said, it had escaped him to state that, but he took it for granted that every one understood he was repeating the proposals of the " *Bombay Times*" and he thought they could not be too much discussed. He had extended the application of the measures proposed by the " *Times*" and had adduced the population of certain districts as a basis for calculating the increase of trade with them, when connected with us by the electric telegraph and regular steam communication.

SESSION 1859-60.

SIXTH MEETING.—*February 17th*, 1860, 4½ P.M.

Present.—Commodore G. G. Wellesley, C. B., R. N., *President*, in the chair.

Members.—Captain W. C. Barker, I. N.; W. F. Hunter, Esq.; C. D. Leggatt, Esq.; Dr. Birdwood; Dr. Bhawoo Dajee; Dr. Atmaram Pandoorung; Mirza Ali Mahomed Khan, Esq.; Dr. J. A. Fraser; and D. J. Kennelly, Esq., *Secretary.*

Visitors.—John M. Maclean Esq.; and John Leggat, Esq.

The minutes of the last meeting were read and approved.

Elections.—The Rev. J. Murray Mitchell, LL.D., proposed by the Secretary, and seconded by Dr. Winchester ; and W. A. Pelly, Esq., proposed by C. D. Leggatt, Esq., and seconded by Captain W. C. Barker, I. N.

Donations.—The following donations were laid on the table, for which the best thanks of the Society were directed to be given to the donors :—

1. Catalogue of Charts and Nautical Books. Presented by Mr. D'Sá.
2. Meteorological Register kept at Cuddalore during the months of October and November 1859. By Government.
3. Ditto ditto kept at Cocanada during the months of October and November 1859. By ditto.
4. Barometical Observations made at Bhooj for October, November, and December 1859. By ditto.
5. Ditto ditto at Pahlunpoor for August 1859. By ditto.
6. Bombay Magnetical and Meteorological Observations for 1858. By ditto.
7. Memoir on the Thurr and Parkur Districts of Sind, by Captain Raikes, with a map. By ditto.
8. Catalogue Raisonné of rare, valuable, and curious books. By B. Quaritch, Esq.
9. Literary Circular of New Publications. By Messrs. Smith, Elder, and Co.
10. Proceedings of the Society of Antiquaries of Scotland, Vol. II. Part III. By the Society.
11. Annual Progress Reports of the Executive Engineers in the Southern, Central, and Northern Provinces for 1857-58, with maps, plans, &c. in a separate Book. By Government.

Letters read.—From the Principal Librarian British Museum, acknowledging the receipt of a copy of the Transactions, presented to the British Museum. 2. From Lieutenant E. F. T. Fergusson, I. N., forwarding a copy of the Magnetical and Meteorological Observations made in the year 1858. 3. Memo. No. 20 of 1860, with a copy of the Selections from the Records of the Bombay Government, No. 53.

The President then called upon Dr. Birdwood, who read the paper advertised for the evening. An unanimous vote of thanks having been passed to Dr. Birdwood, the meeting adjourned.

p 11

SESSION 1860-61.

SEVENTH MEETING.—*March 15th*, 1860, 4½ P.M.

President.—Commodore G. G. Wellesley, C.B , R.N., *President,* in the Chair.

Members.—Captain W. C. Barker, I. N. ; Lieut. E. F. T. Fergusson, I. N. ; Dr. G. C. M. Birdwood ; T. II. Bentley, Esq. ; Sir Cursetjee J. Jejeebhoy, Bart. ; The Rev. W. K. Fletcher, M.A. ; W. F. Hunter, Esq. ; Dr. J. A. Fraser ; Atmaram Pandoorung, Esq. ; Venayekrao Jugonathjee, Esq. ; and Dr. Bhawoo Dajee. The Secretary being unavoidably absent, Dr. Bhawoo Dajee performed his duties.

The minutes of the last meeting were read and approved.

Elections.—J. M. Maclean, Esq., proposed by C. D. Leggatt, Esq., and seconded by Dr. Birdwood ; and Lieut. T. M. Philbrick, I. N., proposed by the Secretary, and seconded by Lieut. W. M. Pengelley, I. N.

Donations.—The following donations were laid on the table, for which the best thanks of the Society were directed to be given to the donors :—

1. Report of the Bombay Chamber of Commerce for the year 1858-1859.   Presented by Government.
2. Correspondence relating to Canal Clearances in the Hydrabad Collectorate in 1855-56 and 1856-57.   By ditto.
3. Catalogue Raisonné of rare, valuable, and curious books. By B. Quaritch, Esq.
4. Transactions of the Medical and Physical Society of Bombay, No. 1., New Series, for the year 1859.   By the Medical and Physical Society.
5. Walker's (W.) Magnetism of Ships and the Mariner's Compass. By Captain Morris, " Balcararis."
6. Becher's (A. B.) Navigation of the Atlantic Ocean.   By ditto.
7. ——————————— Directions for Navigating the Atlantic and Indian Oceans, and the China and Australia Seas.   By ditto.
8. Companion to the Nautical Almanac.   By ditto.

Letters read.—Memo., No. 19 of 1860, from H. Young, Esq., Chief Secretary to Government, forwarding a copy of the Selections from the Records of the Bombay Government.   Letter, No. 4 of 1860, from W. C. Coles, Esq., M. D., forwarding a copy of the Transactions of the Medical and Physical Society of Bombay, No. V., New Series.

The paper read before the Society was a contribution from Lieut. T. M. Philbrick's "Notes on the Andamans."

At the conclusion of which, the best thanks of the Society were voted to that officer; and the meeting adjourned.

SESSION 1859-60.
EIGHTH MEETING.—*April 19th*, 1860.

Present.—Commodore G. G. Wellesley, C.B., R.N., *President*, in the chair. *Vice-President.*—The Honorable W. E. Frere, Esq., C.S.

Members.—Lieut. E. F. T. Fergusson, I. N., F.R.A.S.; Captain W. C. Barker, I. N.; J. E. C. Pryce, Esq.; Sir Cursetjee Jamsetjee Jejeebhoy, Bart.; Dr. Atmaram Pandoorung; Jugonnath Sunkerset, Esq.; and G. C. M. Birdwood, Esq., M.D.

The Secretary to the Society having written to intimate that he was indisposed, Dr. Birdwood officiated for him.

The Minutes of the last meeting were read and approved.

Members proposed.—Dr. H. C. Kingstone, proposed by Dr. Birdwood, and seconded by Mr. Kennelly; and Rev. J. E. Carlile, proposed by the Rev. Dr. M. Mitchell, and seconded by Mr. Kennelly.

Donations.—The following donations were laid on the table, for which the best thanks of the Society were directed to be given to the donors :—

1. Notices of the Proceedings of the Royal Institution of Great Britain, Part IX. Nov. 1858—July 1859. Presented by the Members of the Royal Institution.

2. Numbers of Bottle Logs thrown overboard from H. M. S. *Berenice.* By Lieut. Robinson, I. N., in command.

3. Meteorological Registers kept at Cuddalore and Cocanada during the month of January 1860. By Government.

4. Bulletin de la Société de Geographie. Quatrième Serie. Tome dix-huitième 1859. By the Society.

5. Classified Catalogue of the Raw Produce of the Madras Exhibition of 1859. By the Secretary M. E.

6. Notes and extracts of log during the two Cyclones encountered by the *Wellesley,* April 1857, and *Barham,* October 1857. By Captain Farish.

7.   Fifth Annual Report of the Bombay Benevolent Library and Reading Room for 1859.   By the Sec. B. B. Library.
8.   Catalogue Raisonné of rare, valuable, and curious Books.   By B. Quaritch, Esq.
9.   Notes on Suez, and its Trade with the Ports of the Red Sea. By G. F. Dassy.

Letters read.—1. From John Ritchie, Esq., enclosing notes and extracts of log during two cyclones encountered by the *Wellesley*, April 1857, and *Barham*, October 1857, supplied to Mr. Ritchie by Captain Farish, together with the latter gentleman's suggestions as to the light which the October cyclone throws on the question of the formation of cyclones.   Captain Farish writes—

" A rotatory storm in passing over any place or object appears to have the form of an egg, of which the larger portion precedes the centre or nucleus ; the strength of the winds abating, after the centre has passed, much more rapidly than it increased on the side preceding it.

" May this not be accounted for by the disc of air descending and passing over the surface *diagonally*, the after part being the most raised ? Throughout the part which precedes the centre, rainy, and what may be termed " dirty," weather, accompanied with much lightning, is always experienced. As the centre passes, the most vivid electric discharge takes place sometimes, with sharp hail. After the centre has passed, the weather clears up, and the only lightning seen is that passing onwards with the centre.

" If this is invariably the case, does it not tend to prove that a cyclone is not a surface wind set in motion by any cause, but a disc of air descending from other regions, which, upon meeting the surface currents of a different temperature, disengages thereby rain and lightning, and continues to do so as, progressing onward in its path, it is brought into contact with fresh surface wind ?

" May not this throwing off of electricity and consequent assimilation of temperature afford some clue to the question, How are cyclones terminated ?

" I would invite attention to the regularity and frequency, as shown by a succession of abstract logs, with which cyclonic winds travelling towards the E. S. E., and not necessarily of any great force, prevail beyond Lat. 25° S. in the Indian Ocean, and the important use to navigation, especially in passing between India and the Cape, if this is proved to be as generally the case as my observation leads me to suppose.

" I forward a diagram of a barometric wave in a cyclonic gale off the Azores, which affords a very interesting proof of the close approximation of the tables suggested by Piddington for the measurement of the distance from the centre, not only by the *accelerated fall* of the barometer, but by its *rise* afterwards.

" It was a gale in which I had an opportunity of studying all its phases accurately, and in that instance the deductions were singularly correct."

2nd. The following letter to the Secretary from Capt. Speke was then read :—

"*15th March.*

"DEAR SIR,—I have the greatest pleasure in acknowledging the receipt of your kind letter of the 25th January last.

" Doubtless ere this you have been fully acquainted with the intention of the Government in allowing me to go out again and follow up my last discoveries, to connect, if connection there does exist, the Victoria Nyanza with the White Nile, and to descend by that river to Egypt. Since writing my diaries in *Blackwood*, Mr. Petherick, H. M.'s Consul of Khartum, has shown us that another large river, the Bahr al Ghazal flows, as it were, in a direction coming from my lake, and as there were many other smaller streams flowing from south to north between it and the Bahr el Abiad, it may possibly turn out that the Kevira river is not the Zuboni river which flows past Gondokoro, but was confused for some other one, running in a northerly direction, by the Natives. I shall now start unbiassed in any opinion but the one of supposing the Nyanza is the source of the Nile, whether black, blue, or any other colour. Both Governments, I am happy to say, have been very generous in supporting me. The home one has given me £2,500 for expenses on the way, and the Indian one has given me not only leave to go, but with Indian pay and service to count ; whilst, at my request, they have also added the services of Captain Grant, 6th Bengal Europeans, who is a sterling, good, honest fellow, a zealous officer, and first rate shikari. He was a universal favourite in Bengal, and from having been shooting with him in India, I know him to be well adapted to the work in project. Indeed, nobody could possibly start under more auspicious circumstances than I shall do ; and if it please God to grant me health and strength, the expectation of this country shall not be disappointed by any shortcomings on my part. I have been greatly grieved to find Lord Elphinstone's propositions have not been received with the support which they certainly deserved, of sending some officers from Bombay. It is a matter of purely false economy restricting at this moment any means for the purpose of opening up Africa; and the more expeditions there are on foot at one time, the better chance there is in each one succeeding, as the efforts of one support the other. I earnestly hope before long an expedition will be formed to penetrate Africa from Mombas, and to pass up by Dr. Krapf's route, *viâ* Kituri and Mount Kœnia, to the head of the Nyanza, for it is a land of greater promise than any other for every interest of mankind, whilst the expenses need not be great if the party going there for the first time take advantage of the Arab caravans. Independent travelling is excessively expensive; and for that reason all experimental journeyers should content themselves with travelling only as far as Arab caravans go. This was our mistake last time : we never went beyond the limits of the Arab markets, and therefore could have done for £300 what cost us £3000. I have been trying to induce the Government to advance Mr. Petherick some money to try and meet me somewhere between Gondokoro and Kibuga, but they do not seem inclined. However, Mr. Petherick is a zealous man, and is determined to do something to unveil the mysteries of the Nile. He has promised me every support as soon as I reach his country. He starts in early May : I leave England on the 27th April, and confidently trust to find a Government vessel waiting for me at Aden in May. I have the pleasure to send you a paper entitled " Young England,"* which, though intended for school-boys, contains the only map made, descriptive of the late African discoveries.—I remain, your's faithfully,

J. H. Speke."

Dr. Birdwood observed that Mr. Petherick's statement of the Bahr al Ghazal flowing northwards, as if from the Nyanza, did not deserve any consideration; and that he was surprised that Captain Speke should, on account of that statement, have expressed a doubt of the identity of the Kevira river, and of the connection of the Nyanza with the Nile. Not one, but many rivers must flow between the Nyanza and the White Nile, and as if from the former. There was the Sobat, and another without a name, discovered by the Turks, and cited by

---

* Not yet received.

Lafaraque.   This had its origin in a marsh at the foot of the mountains
of Narea, the drainage of the northern slopes of which must be sufficient
to form several streams.   Other rivers than the Kevira might also pass
direct from the Victoria Nyanza to the White Nile, through gaps in
the range which subtends the Victoria plateau on the north, similar
to the gap by which it has been presumed that the Victoria
Nyanza empties into the White Nile.   This was extremely dubious,
however, both on general considerations, and also on the ground of what
has actually been made known of the country north of the Nyanza, and
between Gondokoro and the Habadia, by the researches of Bruce, Lafaraque, Brun Rollet, and the brothers D'Abbadie, and also the accounts
of Ouare, a native of Limmou, given in the Bulletin of the Geographical
Society of Paris, Nos. 67 and 68 of July 1839.   The Bahr al Ghazal
mentioned by Mr. Petherick, so far as it was known, had nothing to do
with the Nyanza. This river was explored for 40 leagues by Brun Rollet
in 1856, when he found it to be the Misselat of M. d'Arnaud, the
Misselad of our maps.   It is supposed to flow from some marshes in
connection with Lake Tchad, and enters the Nile at Lake Nu, just below the junction of the Sobat or Seboth.   Its course is therefore from
W. to E., and parallel with the Atlas range, which shuts it off from the
basin of the Victoria Nyanza.   It must not be confounded with the Al
Kouan, which also enters the Nile about Lake Nu, being supposed to
be in direct communication with Lake Tchad through the Shary.
Brun Rollet found the Bahr al Ghazal so wide and deep that he believed it to be the true White Nile.   In regard to Captain Speke's remarks, that, after all, the Kevira may not be the same river as that
which flows past Gondokoro, but some other, I would observe that their
identity does not rest on simply Arab evidence, which, however, never
failed Captain Speke, but on the testimony of Brun Rollet and Ulivi,
the former of whom established the station of Bellenia near its banks in
latitude 4° 30' North, according to Antonie d'Abbadie's map of 1852.

Don Knoblecker places a large river to the west of the uttermost
parts of the Nile, and which he supposed to be the White Nile.   The
best authorities agree that this is indeed the White Nile, but that his
astronomical observations are all erroneous, and that is why he has placed
a large river so far west.   The towns and hills he describes along its
banks are identical with those found by others along the White Nile,
and in the same latitudes, but invariably in more eastern longitudes.

Such an error as this is easily understood, and affords Mr. Petherick's assertion and Captain Speke's doubts no argument. Speke's own discoveries now prove, what might have been before quite legitimately inferred, that any large rivers west of the Nyanza and south of the Atlas range must be drainers of the Vallis Garammantica of Ptolemy, and feeders of the Zaire.

In reference to the paper which I had the honour to lay before the Society two months ago, I would wish to state that Antoine d'Abbadie places a portion of a river, which he calls the White Nile, in latitude 3° North, and in about longitude 36° to 37° East. This looks very like the southernmost point of the Habadia; and strange to say, the dotted hypothetical line with which he connects this fragment of a river with the White Nile opposite Bellenia corresponds exactly with the presumed nether bord on the Victoria Nyanza in breadth and in latitude, as indicated by Captain Speke. This, so far as it goes, is very respectable confirmation, I would venture to believe, of my suggestion that the Habahia of Bruce is the ultimate source of the Nile.

On the proposition of the Honorable Mr. Frere, the Society directed that the Secretary should forward to Captain Speke the remarks Dr. Birdwood had just made, as also his paper on the Habahia, in the extended form in which it had been given to the Mechanics' Institute of Bombay subsequent to its reading before the Society.

The paper for the evening was then read.

The best thanks of the Society were then voted to Lieut. Stiffe for his highly interesting communication. It was directed that a copy of it should be forwarded to Government, along with the bottle of mineral water which accompanied it; and that when it appeared in the Society's transactions, a lithography copy of Lieutenant Stiffe's route map should be attached to it.

The meeting then adjourned to Thursday the 17th of May, the Anniversary of the Society.

SESSION 1859-60.

ADJOURNED ANNUAL MEETING.—*May 31st*, 1860.

Present.—The Honorable W. E. Frere, Esq., C. S., *Vice-President*, in the Chair.

Members.—Capt. W. C. Barker, I. N. ; G. C. M. Birdwood, Esq., M.D. ; J. W. Winchester, Esq., LL.D., F.R.G.S. ; J. E. C. Pryce, Esq. ; Lieut. W. M. Pengelley, I. N. ; Rev. W. K. Fletcher, M.A. ; and D. J. Kennelly, Esq., I. N., *Secretary.*

The minutes of the last meeting were read and confirmed.

Elections.—Dr. H. C. Kingstone and the Rev. J. E. Carlile were elected members.

Members proposed.—General Sir William Mansfield, K.C.B., proposed by the Honorable Mr. Frere, *Vice-President*, and seconded by the *President ;* Colonel G. H. Robertson, C.B., proposed by Lieut. W. M. Pengelley, I. N., and seconded by J. E. C. Pryce, Esq.

Donations.—The following donations were laid on the table, for which the best thanks of the Society were directed to be given to the donors :—

1. Catalogué Raisonné of rare valuable and curious Books. Presented by B. Quaritch, Esq.
2. Oriental Budget of Literature for India, Australia, China, and the Colonies. By Saunders, Otley, & Co.
3. Meteorological Registers kept at Cocanada and Cuddalore during the month of February 1860. By Government.
4. Barometrical Observations made at Pahlunpore during the months of October, November, and December 1859. By Government.
5. Barometrical Observations made at Bhooj during the months of January, February, and March 1860. By Government.
6. Journal of the Royal Asiatic Society of Great Britain and Ireland. Part 2nd of Vol. 17th. By the Society.
7. Journal Asiatique Nos. 49, 50, 51, and 52 for January, February, March, and June 1849.
8. Proceedings of the Royal Geographical Society of London. No. 1 of Vol. 14th.
9. L'Expédition Genoise des Frères Vivaldi à la découverte de la Route Maritime des Indes Orientales. Par M. D. Avezac. By the Author.

Letters read.—From Professor Baden Powell, thanking the Society for the honor they have done in electing him as an Honorary Member of their Society.

2. From A. Keith Johnstone, Esq., expressing his best thanks for having elected him an Honorary Member of the Society, and inform-

p 12

ing of his having sent a copy of his new work, "The Royal Atlas," forwarded to the care of Principal Harkness, Elphinstone College.

3. From H. L. Anderson, Esq., Acting Chief Secretary to Government, forwarding, for the purpose of being laid before the Society, copy of a letter from Lieut. Colonel C. P. Rigby, dated 20th March last, enclosing a narrative of 16 years travel in Africa obtained from a Zanzibar Arab.

4. From John Harkness, Esq., LL.D., Principal Elphinstone College, informing the Secretary that the "Royal Atlas" alluded to in Mr. A. K. Johnstone's letter must be expected to reach Bombay two or three months hence.

The business of the monthly meeting having been concluded, the voting lists were examined, and the following gentlemen were named the office bearers for the ensuing year.

Vice-Presidents—The Honorable W. E. Frere, Esq., C. S. ; Capt. W. C. Barker, I. N. ; A. H. Leith, Esq., M.D.

Resident Members.—Dr. Bhawoo Dajee ; John Ritchie, Esq. ; G. C. M. Birdwood, Esq., M.D. ; Lieut. E. F. T. Fergusson, I. N. ; R. Haines, Esq., M.D. ; R. S. Sinclair, Esq., LL.D. ; Narrayen Dinanathjee, Esq. ; Lieut. W. M. Pengelley, I.N. ; Dr. Winchester ; Rev. J. M. Mitchell, LL.D. ; W. F. Hunter, Esq. ; Sir Cursetjee Jamsetjee Jejeebhoy, Bart.

Non-Resident Members—Capt. J. F. Jones, I. N. ; Major A. B. Kemball, C.B. ; George Buist, Esq., LL.D. ; Sir H. Bartle Edward Frere, K.C.B. ; Brigadier General Le Grand Jacob ; Captain G. Jenkins, I.N. ; Commander J. C. Constable ; Dr. F. Broughton, F.R.C.S.

The votes of the members present having been taken, the following Sub-Committees were elected.

Sub-Committee of Correspondence.

Chairman.—John Ritchie, Esq.

Members.—Dr. Birdwood ; Lieutenant W. M. Pengelley, I. N. ; R. Haines, Esq., M. D.; R. S. Sinclair, Esq., LL.D.; W. F. Hunter, Esq.

Sub-Committee of Accounts.

Chairman.—Sir Cursetjee Jamsetjee Jejeebhoy, Bart.

Members.—Rev. J. M. Mitchell, LL.D. ; Lieut. E. F. T. Fergusson, I. N., F.R.A.S. ; Bhawoo Dajee, Esq. ; Dr. Winchester, LL.D., F.R.G.S. ; Narrayen Dinanathjee, Esq.

During the Session now closing, the Bombay Geographical Society has met ten times. Nine meetings being the ordinary monthly of the

Session, and the tenth a special one called to transact urgent business, but upon which occasion were read communications from Captain Pullen on the subject of Red Sea soundings, and from Dr. Carter, the results of a microscopical examination of sea bottom from the southern coast of Arabia.

At each of the nine meetings composing the Session, a paper was read before the Society. These papers were as follows—

September 15th, 1859.—The Hurricanes in the Eastern Seas from 1854 to 1859. By Dr. Buist.

October 20th.—Observations on the Bed and Delta of the Nile. By Dr. Birdwood.

November 17th.—Notes on the Geography of India in the 4th century before Christ, and in the 1st and 7th centuries after Christ, illustrated by maps. By Dr. Bhawoo Dajee.

December 15th.—On the present state and requirements of our Surveys in the Indian Ocean, with reference to the existing Errors of its Physical Geography. By Lieutenant A. D. Taylor, I.N.

January 19th, 1860.—From Captain Speke. On the Commerce of that portion of Africa lately explored by him.

February 16th.—Is the Habaiah of Bruce the source of the Nile? By G. C. M. Birdwood, Esq., M.D.

March 15th.—Notes on the Andaman Islands. By Lieut. T. M. Philbrick, I. N.

April 19th.—Visit to the Hot Springs of Bosher near Muscat, with a Route Map. By Lieut. A. M. Stiffe, I. N.

The 14th volume of the Society's Transactions, completed by Dr. Buist, the late Secretary, brought down to May 1858, was issued in August last.

The 15th volume, now in the press, will be brought down to this date, and it will, it is hoped, be completed and issued before the Society enter upon the new Session of 1860-61.

At the Society's ordinary meeting of February 1859, a letter was read from B. H. Ellis, Esq., Secretary to Government, intimating that the Government had been pleased to place at the Society's disposal the rooms adjoining those of the Asiatic Society; and it was then resolved that the Secretary be directed to take advantage of the opportunity which the forthcoming change of rooms would present for the construction of a catalogue of the Society's books, maps, and papers.

In anticipation of immediate removal, the books of the Library were, without loss of time, removed from the shelves ; but it was not until the following June that the Society was placed in possession of its new rooms, in consequence of the prior occupant being unable to effect removal.

The catalogue was then commenced, and by the end of December the books' portion was completed. The charts' portion was commenced upon, and is now in progress, and the whole, it is hoped, will be completed by the end of this year.

On the last anniversary meeting, the Society had on its list 69 members. On the present one, it numbers 95. Twenty-nine members have been added during the year, while three have withdrawn or resigned.

During this Session, the attention of the Society has been turned to the seriously imperfect charts of the China and Indian seas found in common use on board of the vessels of the English mercantile marine traversing those waters. Old and erroneous charts are renewed from time to time as demand may require, and vended by private sellers, to the imminent hazard of life and property, while the later Admiralty Charts seem to be rarely used.

The existing Indian Hydrographical system was shown to be extremely disadvantageous, wanting not only unity and system, but also that wholesome supervision absolutely necessary to the success of this branch of science, and the Society considered that, to remedy the defective Chartography of the Indian and Eastern Seas in general, it would be necessary to appoint to India an Hydrographer, who would be confined to the supervision of the surveys and charting of those seas alone. The losses of ships, so frequent of occurrence in the Indian and China waters, show the urgent necessity for some such arrangement.

With a view to obtain more perfect data upon which to erect a cyclonological system for the Eastern seas, circular letters have been sent out by the Society for distribution to masters of ships visiting this port, requesting information of the cyclones or hurricanes they may have experienced in passages to and from India. Captain Barker, the Master Attendant of the port, has kindly consented to assist in collecting, and again forwarding to the Society, these circulars as they shall be filled, to be afterwards worked up and compiled by the Society. It must not be omitted to make mention of the indefatigable efforts of Mr. John Ritchie in supplying every information under this head : his contributions to the Cyclonology of the China Seas have been, during the last year, many and valuable.

The dipping circle before the Society was received a short time ago from Mr. Mayes, then in Northern India. The instrument has evidently received severe usage from the effects of bhangy transit, and is so shattered as to be utterly useless. Our proceedings tell us that it was purchased by the Society in 1833, placed at the disposal of Capt. Moresby in 1836, with the view of determining the dip in the Maldive Islands. Subsequently it was, by the sanction of the Society, lent to Mr. Taylor, Astronomer at Madras, and employed by him and Mr. Caldecott in a magnetic survey of Southern India : it was afterwards sent to England for repair, then handed over to Mr. Mayes at Aden, and afterwards taken by him to Northern India, from which place it has been returned at the request of Dr. Buist. It is only to be regretted that some safer mode of forwarding it to the Society was not adopted.

Many of the books of the Library require to be rebound, a measure which should be carried out in full as opportunity and funds at the disposal of the Society might permit.

There are a few volumes wholly destroyed by insects ; the names are annexed.

The Society's Library has so increased as to render necessary an enlarged accommodation for its books. It was contemplated last year to introduce into the present rooms a book press similar to those now in it ; but it is feared that this will be found impracticable on account of the very little space unoccupied ; scarcely indeed sufficient to accommodate members with sitting room on occasions of meetings. Several of the Society's spring maps are unhung, its globes are excluded, and it cannot but be desirable that steps should be taken to obtain larger rooms, suited to the requirements of the Society.

The Report having been adopted, Dr. Winchester moved that a vote of thanks be passed to Commodore Wellesley for the unceasing interest he, as the Society's President, has continued and continues to manifest in all that tends to the Society's well-being and usefulness. Unanimously carried.

A vote of thanks having been passed to the office-bearers of the past year and also to the Secretary,—Mr. Kennelly read a narrative of African travel contributed by the Government, and of which the following letter from Colonel Rigby to Government forms a preface :—

" 1.   As the exploration of Central Africa at present excites great
interest, I have the honor to report for the information of the Right
Honorable the Governor in Council, that a Zanzibar Arab, by name
Said bin Habeeb, has recently returned to this port after an absence of
sixteen years in the interior of Africa, during which time he three
times visited Loanda, on the West coast, and Dr. Livingstone mentions
in his book having met him in the neighbourhood of the river Zambesi.

2.   As I believe that Said bin Habeeb is the first person known to
have crossed the African Continent in so high a latitude, I herewith
annex a short narrative of his travels.   Unfortunately he has kept no
journal or record, and I only obtained the information from him in
reply to questions.

3.   Said bin Habeeb states, that, during the sixteen years he has
been travelling in Central Africa, he has been everywhere treated with
kindness, that the country is generally populous and well cultivated,
the inhabitants being negro races, who make a great deal of cotton
cloth, and have abundance of copper and iron ; he states that one district near Kalanga is inhabited by a race of people with long hair and
resembling Arabs in colour.   On his return towards the East coast, a
few months ago, his followers met with Dr. Livingstone near Lake
Shirwa ; he states that he himself was one journey in advance, and
as his followers were alarmed at hearing white men enquire for their
master in such a spot, they pretended to Dr. Livingstone that they
knew nothing of Said bin Habeeb.

4.   I have frequently heard it stated here that large districts, in the
interior, towards the Lake Nyassa, are becoming depopulated in consequence of the export of so many slaves from the East coast of Africa.
Said bin Habeeb confirms this, and states that he travelled for seventeen days through the Jhahow country without meeting any inhabitants,
although the soil is rich, and there were ruins of towns and villages
over the whole district.

5.   Dr. Albrecht Roscher, an enterprising young German traveller,
who left Zanzibar to explore Central Africa during the month of June
last, has reached the great Lake Nyassa, being the first European who
has ever penetrated so far.   He speaks of the country through which
he travelled in high terms.   The latest information I have received
from him is dated January 1st, 1860, from Nussewa, on the shores of
the lake ; he was then in a deplorable state of weakness from starvation

and sickness, owing to the infamous treatment he had received from a Keelwa slave-dealer, by name Salim bin Abdallah.

6. On leaving Zanzibar, Dr. Roscher told me that all his efforts to procure persons here to accompany him in his journey had proved unsuccessful. He was therefore obliged to trust himself entirely to this slave-dealer at Keelwa, who robbed him on the road of all he possessed, and left him utterly destitute on the shores of the Lake. I trust, however, that supplies which have been sent to him from Keelwa will have reached him in time, and His Highness the Sultan has sent an order to the governor at Keelwa, directing him to arrest the slave-dealer Salim bin Abdallah, and send him here in irons."

The following remarks were made on the subject.

The Honorable Vice-President observed that he feared Said Bin Habeeb was a slave-dealer himself, as he appeared to have chiefly travelled among the chief slave marts of Central Africa. His information regarding Cascrube was valuable as supplementary to that furnished by Livingstone, but in regard to the country about Loanda on the Atlantic coast nothing new was stated.

Dr. Birdwood observed that Livingstone mentioned the people who deprived themselves of their upper incisors. They do it to make themselves look like *cows*, instead of like *zebras*, as they imagine they naturally are. The *Nyassa* had been known for more than 200 years, and as it is the chief feeder of the Zambesi, indicates that the latter cannot be navigable to any great extent.

The Honorable Vice-President asked if Dr. Birdwood remembered where Dr. Livingstone mentioned Said Bin Habeeb?

Dr. Birdwood did not remember. Dr. Livingstone mentioned Zanzibar Arabs in three or four places. [After note Napier's travels, page 902, Zanzibar Arab slave dealers; 924, Zanzibar Arabs, "who disliked the English because they thrash them for selling slaves;" 476, those before referred to.]

The meeting adjourned.

Balance Sheet, for the Year 1859-60.

Date.	Receipts.	Amount.
		Rs. a. p.
1860. May 1	To Balance in the hands of the Treasurers on this date	769 8 3
" "	Ditto in the Secretary's hands	10 11 6
" "	Govt. Subscription for 12 months	588 0 0
" "	Annual Subscription from Members, viz:—	
	On Account of 1858-59	210 0 0
	Ditto of 1859-60	840 0 0
"	Amount realised from the sale of Philosophical Instruments during the year:—	
	On account of Single Lens (Six)...... Rs. 6 0 0	
	" of Double Lens. 1 8 0	
	" of Sympiesometer. 52 0 0	
	" of Wind Gauge. 10 0 0	70 0 0
"	ditto ditto from the sale of Society's Transactions	99 1 3
"	Amount checked	3 7 4
"	Interest	37 12 3
	Total Rupees....	2,628 8 7

Date.	Disbursements.	Amount.
		Rs a. p.
1860. April 30	By Cash paid—	
	To Office Establishment	603 3 1
"	To Extra Clerk Allowance	102 1 0
"	For Contingencies, Postage, &c	414 3 0
"	For Printing Transactions and Advertising	479 12 0
"	For Binding Books, Maps, &c.	29 12 0
"	To Messrs Smith, Taylor, & Co.'s Invoices	142 6 0
"	For transcribing	23 8 0
"	For Commission	7 4 7
"	By Balance in the hands of the Treasurers on this date ....Rs. 809 15 11	
	Ditto in the Secretary's hands. 16 7 0	826 6 11
	Total Rupees....	2,628 8 7

D. J. KENNELLY,
Secretary.

(Audited, and found correct)
W. M. PENGELLEY, Lieutenant I. N.,
Auditor.

TRANSACTIONS

OF THE

BOMBAY GEOGRAPHICAL SOCIETY.

ART. I.—GEOLOGY OF LOWER EGYPT,—*especially of the portion betwixt* ALEXANDRIA *and* CAIRO, *and* CAIRO *and* SUEZ. *By* GEO. BUIST, *LL.D.,* *F.R.S. London and Edinburgh, F.G.S., Corresponding Member of the Geographical Society, Vienna, &c.*

THE only portion of the following paper, which is the result of direct personal observation, is that which relates to the region betwixt Alexandria and Cairo, and Cairo and Suez. Having traversed this seven times, on my way to and from Bombay, when on several occasions I had a tolerable abundance of leisure, I have enjoyed the means of making myself much more familiar with the country around, than the present racing-rate of speed, with which travellers hurry through, permits. As the subject has not hitherto been before the Bombay Geographical Society at all, and as the memoirs written on it have appeared in half-a-dozen of different periodicals—the Reports of the Royal Society, the Transactions of the Royal Asiatic Society and Geographical Society of London, and those of the Asiatic Society of Bombay,—it has appeared to me expedient, with a view to perspicuity, to lay a very brief general outline of the whole before you, embracing the substance of what has been written, claiming nothing as my own, but that which is the result of personal observation, and carefully assigning to each of my fellow-labourers the share which is his due. I have gone little further into these than to make my own observations intelligible.

1 *g*

On approaching the shores of Egypt at the season of low Nile, long before any portion of the land becomes visible, its proximity is indicated by a bright white glare over the southern horizon, occasioned by the reflection of the sun's rays from the dazzling bright salt crust which covers, in the winter and spring seasons, the shallow portions of the lake Mareotis. The Mediterranean now shoals suddenly to a few fathoms, changing its colour at once from indigo-blue to bright green. The vessel has to thread her way through intricate and dangerous channels, so that large men-of-war require to be lightened of their guns before reaching the harbour. The rocks off shore, like those everywhere around, are a soft fine-grained nummulite, easily sawn or dressed by the axe. Amongst the fragments of the remains of old Alexandria, to be found in every quarter of the modern city, are sculptures, sometimes of the intricate carvings of the capital of the Corinthian column, of nummulite nearly pure white, as compact and as highly crystallised as Carrara marble.

The whole Mediterranean shore of Egypt, over a sweep of about 300 miles, is low and marshy, abounding in lagoons, where the sea seems to have thrown up a barrier of shells and shingle, sometimes in fresh-water lakes.

The first of these latter, and that which most strikes the stranger, is the lake Mareotis, to the westward and southward of Alexandria. This, though now occupied by salt-water, is entirely cut off from the sea, and I hold it to have been a true fresh-water lake, for reasons that will presently appear.

LAKE MAREOTIS is about 150 miles in circumference. Strabo describes it as being, at the date the foundations of Alexandria were laid (223 B. C.), a lake filled by several canals from the Nile, and kept full for the purposes of navigation,—more commodities reaching the city through this channel from the interior, than by the sea. In the time of Pliny it was a marsh, and might become a permanent sheet of water,—when, as appears from its present state, the evaporation betwixt one inundation and another is incapable of drying it up,—a swamp, or dry land; the last of these being the condition in which it had, for a long period, existed, till nearly the close of the last century. Its channel is somewhere about ten or twelve feet below the surface of the sea adjoining, from which it is divided by a barrier of sand-hills, about a mile across. It was said to have furnished the sites for

300 villages, and to have formed one of the most fertile portions of the Delta—a circumstance almost necessary, seeing the extent and the regularity with which it might have been inundated, and the facility with which it might be made dry or be kept watered long after the natural flood had subsided. In 1788 the necessities of war compelled us to cut through the barrier, and admit the sea. Since then it has formed a lagoon, diluted by the Nile at the periods of flood.

We find it so difficult to familiarize our minds with the constant upheavals and depressions occurring on almost every spot of the earth's surface, that rather than resort to the supposition of one of these as the most obvious solution for a case such as this, we summon to our aid the most untenable of theories. A lake of no exit, once cut off from the sea, must remain salt in perpetuity, as we see in the case of the bitter lakes in the Isthmus close by, and in numberless other instances in every quarter of the world ;—Mareotis itself furnishing an example, ninety years old. The basin of the lake must originally have formed a portion of the Delta of the Nile ; and after this was raised above the level of the inundation by subterraneous upheaval,—for by no other means could the site of Alexandria and other spots, not reached by the inundation ever have attained their present altitude at all,—the basin of Mareotis must have subsided, and so become the channel of a lake the Nile was at hand to fill. The Mahmodee Canal near by, is cut through rich alluvium. The railway now passes between this and the margin of the lake, close beside the latter, and often traversing its waters. The country for the next 60 miles rises occasionally into dry irregular clayey knolls, on which villages are built, far above the highest flood : where level, it is marshy, covered with a layer of moss and black barren heath ;—both conditions of things which remain to nearly the crossing of the Nile, and being about as wide of the stranger's conceptions of the extreme fertility of the Lower Delta as can well be imagined.

Herodotus informs us, that the priests had assured him that Egypt was " the gift of the Nile ;" and there is every reason to believe the assurance correct. Rennel adds that "the configuration and composition of the low lands leave no reason to doubt that the sea once reached the base of the rocks where Memphis now stands."

According to the learned of those days, when the Egyptian monarchy was founded by Menes, 2200 B.C., or 4,000 from the present time,

" the land of Egypt from the Theban Province northward was a marsh, and that from the Lake Mœris, 150 miles south from the sea-coast at Alexandria, was permanently under water." On the Red Sea shore, and across the Isthmus, from Suez to the Mediterranean, is a raised beach of gravel, shells, and corals, the latter consisting exclusively of varieties now in existence. The bed of the Nile within the past 4,000 years has, in all likelihood, repeatedly sunk and risen again; and Dr. Lepsius mentions a series of monuments at Semneh in Nubia, which record the highest points reached by the inundation, and bear dates of King Amenemba, the third of the twelfth dynasty, whom Lepsius supposes to have reigned 2,200 B.C. Fifteen of these are still available for reference, the height of them proving that the Nile then rose 25 feet higher than in modern times. From the dates of these it appears, that there was, for a series of years, a steady increase in the rise of the flood, and then a gradual decrease, corresponding exactly with the theory of depression and upheaval.

The very important fact of the order of the dates was first adverted to by Mr. Hurley, in the *Athenæum* of June and July 1857. On my pointing out the conclusions just stated as emanating from them, Mr. Hurley replied, that the river would rise and fall with the elevation or depression of its basin. And this would have been true had the debouchure of the Nile been as remote as it now is from the site of the monuments referred to. Four thousand years ago, up to the borders of the Theban provinces, two hundred miles south from the present shores of the Mediterranean, was an estuary or a marsh, where the gradients and speed of the river would be directly affected by the rise or fall of the basin to the northward; the existing delta from Cairo south, becoming ultimately dry land, or marsh, or lake.

A principle that seems to have been too often lost sight of in the formation of deltas, should be constantly kept before us. No delta could ever rise permanently above the surface of the inundation at all, by the agency of silting up exclusively, and unless there was an upheaval of the land or subsidence of the water. At Cairo the deposit of each flood is as thin as a sheet of drawing paper; when this accummulation goes on till it has reached within a few inches of the highest inundation, it must become evanescent altogether. Neither Alexandria, Cairo, Calcutta, Hydrabad in Scinde, New Orleans on the delta of the Mississippi, nor any other deltoid city, could ever have found a site at all, unless by upheaval ; and so with the sites of the villages from Cairo to the Sea, and the bulk of the area of the delta which the Nile, even at its highest floods, now never reaches. Yet these are all composed of river-mud of exactly the same description as that now being deposited.

If this, which is not a hypothesis but a principle, be kept in view, and if it be remembered how much more rapidly mud is precipitated in stagnant than in running water, it will be at once seen, that the rate at which alluvium now accumulates on deltas, merely overlaid by a shallow film from the surface of the stream, affords not the slightest ground for drawing conclusions as to the time taken for the accumulation of the whole mass, laid down, as it must have been, under circumstances utterly unlike those now existing. The mud of the old delta of the Nerbudda, in Goozerat, now forming a bank of 70 feet in thickness, the surface of which, above Broach, 20 miles from the Gulf of Cambay, is 30 feet above the highest flood, divides into flakes of from $\frac{1}{4}$ to $\frac{1}{8}$ of an inch ; and yet we are not certain that each of these may not be the deposit of a single freshet of a few days or hours duration, rather than the accumulation of an entire season.

The layers of sharp desert sand, seen in many places on the banks of the Nile below Cairo to alternate with the mud, may probably have been deposited on the dry surface of the soil, during some of the movements referred to. A descent of the land, after this had occurred, would permit the mud, now lying many feet in thickness over them, to be deposited without disturbing them ; running-water would have removed the sand, and mingled it with the mud. The extreme abruptness of the transition from delta silt to desert sand, from extreme fertility to absolute barrenness, astonishes the stranger : near the Pyramids you may actually, and without figure, have one foot on rich arable soil, the other ankle-deep in desert sand.

Rich as the delta soil is, and moist as it must always be a few feet below the surface, it is curious to observe how speedily it is reduced to barrenness, either by excess or deficiency of water. I have noticed the black moss and barren heath along the line of the railway a little above Lake Mareotis, reminding one of the moors of Rannoch or the desolation of Lochnagar. On the other side of the river, wherever the surface is too high for the inundation to reach it, and artificial irrigation is omitted, the silt is covered with bent and other dry

long-rooted grasses, like the sand-hills along shore forming the
sandy dunes or links on the low-shores of Britain. Conversewise
again, irrigation, with the most moderate amount of manure, makes
the barren sand of the desert, in a few years' time, almost as fertile as
the alluvium of the river.

ROCKS AND GRAVEL.—Having thus far dealt with the solid matter
along the margin of the Nile in process of deposition or induration, I
shall take the formations that immediately follow, in the order in
which I find them along the way, rather than in that of geological
sequence, deferring that which, were chronological order observed,
would follow next, till I have crossed the Desert to the shores of the
Red Sea.

NUMMULITE AROUND CAIRO.—The rocks around Cairo are a soft
fine-grained nummulite, abounding in many sorts of marine with some
land remains. The multilocular shell which gives them their name,
believed by the Egyptians to be the money of the Jews, cursed
and turned into stone, is the most abundant ; and the little
money-stones may often be found loose on the surface in heaps.*
Next in abundance to these are the remains of Crustaceans and
Echinaderms, shark's teeth, and most of the other remains found in
the limestone of Malta and of North-Western India. There seems
abundant evidence to show that this vast formation presents itself in one
continuous and unbroken sheet from the frontiers of Burmah to the
shores of the Atlantic. Just to the south-eastward of the citadel
it rises in a magnificent mass, with fine mural precipices facing the
city. Near the Pyramids it is in thin layers, with caverns of some magnitude in the cliffs. The Pyramids and the Sphynx are constructed
of it : the latter having the appearance of being, to a considerable
extent, cut out of the rock. At both places its external surface is
full of borings of lithodomi. The nummulite which, in the portion
of the desert eastward of Cairo, is covered over by sandstone, and
conglomerate, re-appears within 20 miles of Suez near the last of the
old stations, (as I presume they must, since the opening of the

---

* A tradition similar to this in reference to nummulites, prevails in Cutch.
A holy man, who had been refused charity by a miser, cursed his money, and it
became stone at once, so that it is now found in the rocks. A transverse section of
this little shell certainly very closely resembles a coin.

railway, be called,) and is one mass of fossils. It so continues on to
Suez, where it becomes hard and compact, forming the mass of mountain
called Gibbel Ataka, and probably the bulk of the rocks and hills
around.

The highest point on the old line of road across the Desert, and I
believe also on the railway, is 15 miles from Suez, where the elevation
is about 900 feet above the level of the sea. The hills to the south
now begin to ascend ; the actual increase in altitude, being magnified
by the lower position of the spectator. Gibbel Ataka presents itself
as a majestic wall striking into the sea, 5 miles south of Suez anchorage, ten south of the town, and terminating in the head-land called
Ras Ataka. The mass is 22 miles in length, running W. by S.,
before the range is depressed or intersected, and above 10 across : the
nearest spur is about 9 miles from the town of Suez, the highest peak
is about 2000 feet above the sea. The external appearance and
magnitude of the mass very closely resembles that of Gibbel Abu
Diraj, " the father of steps," which, commencing 10 miles to the south,
just southward of Wadi Musa, presents a face of about 10 miles in
length, running parallel to the Red Sea, with a long ridge stretching
westward, and forming the boundary of the Northern Wadi. The
mountain masses seem as if cut out in steps nearly horizontal and
parallel, and at distances apparently of from 100 to 400 feet from each
other. These are interrupted and cut across by great ravines ; the
result apparently either of rupture or of grooving by cataracts of
water ; probably both have assisted in producing them. Along
nearly all the lines of steps there are, at irregular intervals, semi-cones
of what seem stones and gravel—a sort of tali such as a water-fall
might have thrown over the cliff, until its base found a resting-place
on the platform below. These cones, judging from the aspect presented by them, seen at a distance of from five to six miles off, and
referring to the known altitude of the hill, look about a quarter of a
mile or so across the base, in the line of the hill ; and if so, they must
be half this at right angles to it, indicating a platform of support of at
least 300 yards in breadth.

TRAVERTINE ON THE NUMMULITE.—The Nummulite of Egypt,
like that of Malta, and the tertiary limestone of Gibraltar, is remarkable
for the beauty and the magnitude of the encrustations of variegated
travertine it exhibits.

I have not seen the Egyptian travertine *in situ*, as I have that at Gibraltar and Malta. Captain Newbold describes it as a stalagmite or stalactite, coating crevices or caverns, or depending from their roofs. The surface is mamillary on its lower side, the calcareous solution hardening as about to drop, forming the individual mammæ; each succeeding coating of moisture thickens that first indurated, in somewhat parallel layers, giving additional prominence to the original protuberances, until the whole attains a thickness of sometimes as much as 30 inches of solid rock, beautifully variegated with white, pale, and deep honey or amber-colored layers. The little faults and crevices with which it everywhere abounds, greatly interferes with its beauty as an ornamental stone. The Malta travertine, or alabaster as it is called, formed exactly in the same way, is darker in hue, more transparent, and much more highly crystallised, but is never found in such abundance, or in masses of such size. The older forms of the Gibraltar travertine have been shivered into fragments, commingled with masses of other rocks, and re-cemented by a newer travertine, the same in aspect and structure as the first,—a fate the other travertines just mentioned have escaped.

NEWER SANDSTONE.—PETRIFIED FOREST.—I have not had the means of examining the great sandstone formation under the nummulite limestone, and shall make no attempt at a description which must be a simple transcript. Over the nummulite is a higher sandstone or conglomerate, to be seen a little to the southward of Cairo, and at intervals, all along the route across the Desert. The beds of sandstone vary in thickness from a few inches to 100 or 200 feet. Those just referred to, of which alone I can speak, are composed of rounded or ovidal pebbles, nearly all more or less quartzose; the Egyptian jasper being peculiarly abundant. They are cemented by hard siliceous sand, which, when disintegrated and blown about in the desert, is large-grained, sharp, and semi-transparent. Notwithstanding the abundance of limestone close by, the desert-sand is all sharp-grained and siliceous, and shows no signs of effervescence with acid, the finer and more easily comminuted material being probably drifted away to a distance. The late Dr. Malcomson, I believe, was the first to draw attention, in 1838, to the fact of fossil-wood being embedded in the sandstone. In 1842, Captain Newbold describes it as "in many localities embedding silicified trunks and fragments of trees, particularly near Gebel Ahmar near Cairo, and Wadi Ansan, about eight hours' journey to the eastward." And this circumstance, singular as it appears, is what every Indian geologist ought to have expected. The Trevicary fossil-wood in the Madras Presidency, which has been longest known to us of all the petrified forests, is embedded in a coarse siliceous conglomerate. The conglomerate in Scinde consists chiefly of rolled fragments of the nummulite and other subadjacent rocks. This is conspicuously manifested in the cliff at Minora, near Kurrachee, adjoining beds of oysters and other sea-shells, *in situ* along with fossil-wood like that of Cairo, and bones nearly identical with those of Central India, Burmah, and the Sewallick range. The bones of the celebrated Island of Perim, in the Gulf of Cambay, are embedded in a conglomerate, consisting mostly of rounded portions of trap in a clayey cement, and along with these are numberless fragments of fossil-wood. The wood of Perim is nearly all rounded at the extremities, as if exposed to the action of running-water, or the breakers of the shore : it is, moreover, full of worm-holes, all emanating from its lower, and rising and radiating out towards its upper surface, as if mineralised and hardened subsequently to its being placed in the position in which it is now found : the perforations being effected while it was still soft. The Egyptian wood, so far as I know, bears no signs of being water-worn, nor has it any indication of decay. The fragments, associated as they are exclusively with rounded pebbles, are sharp and angular, and the organisation and structure of the wood as distinct as when it grew.

The sand, the pebbles, the Egyptian jasper, and the wood found strewed along the desert, are obviously the results of the disintegration of the sandstone. Near the old centre station, at an altitude of 700 feet, fragments of sea-shells, especially the operculæ of the lesser univalves, are found amongst the sand. They bear all the appearance of belonging to species now in existence ; and, taken in conjunction with the borings of the litho-domi, seem to indicate a vast emergence from the sea at a date subsequent to the pliocene.

On approaching Suez, a level plain from 1 to 6 miles across is found to extend itself betwixt the base of the hills and the sea. This is formed of fragments of corals, sea-shells, and calcareous sand ; sometimes loose, sometimes cemented into an extremely hard and compact rock. It extends all along the border of the sea to the southward, for a distance of 30 miles at least, and though here broken by the advance of the mountain towards the shore, resumes whenever the level permits. To the northward it extends to the Mediterranean, constituting the entire surface of the isthmus. The shells have all been found identical with those now existing in the sea around, and the whole is a fragment of that vast post-pliocene formation which skirts the shores of almost every existing sea, and seems to have been produced by a subsidence, and subsequent upheaval; giving us curious exhibitions of marine and fresh-water remains, alternating with each other in bays and estuaries, into which streams discharge themselves.

Traversing this bed in all directions, may be observed thin veins of gypsum, from an inch to a foot across, and generally extending about a similar distance into the ground. These have obviously been formed after the waters of the sea finally withdrew. They are indeed forming at the present time; and they are the result of that pasty decomposition where moist soils or mud containing carbonate of lime become saturated with salt-water.

NUMMULITES, BRECCIAS, AND RAISED BEACHES OF GIBBEL ATAKA.—Having thus given a general sketch of ground frequently examined and described by those much more competent than myself to examine it, I now come to attempt an account of the rocky mass called Gibbel Ataka, or the mountain of Deliverance; historically as well as geologically speaking, one of the most interesting localities on the surface of the globe, of which I hope to be able to give a more minute description than any that has hitherto appeared.

I have assumed the existence of platforms, which I consider old sea-beaches, on grounds which will presently appear, from the aspect of the gravel semi-cones. I have on no occasion been able to get such a profile of the rocks as to show their actual shape. Most of " the raised beaches "—such for shortness sake they may be hypothetically called—exhibit an edge of a colour totally different from that of the adjoining rock. In most cases it is whitish; in some, when the air is damp, it is reddish, or just after rain a bright blood-red; the colours in this case being the most intense and unnatural that can well be imagined.

Having described the hills as witnessed from the steamer, at a distance of from 2 to 5 miles, through the intensely transparent atmosphere of Egypt,—if the reader will accompany me from

Suez, and cross with me ten miles of desert, we shall come to have a more clear conception of things than might otherwise be obtained. The total distance is about 9½ miles. The first three is over sand and shingle, abounding with shells,—pieces of selenite scattered everywhere about. In dry weather the surface feels crisp, like that of damp soil slightly hardened by frost, giving way not the less at once to the foot, which sinks over the instep, making walking very slow and tiresome. About 4 miles southward the ground is found beneath the level of very high tides, and it is evident that, when the south-east wind blows, the sea, to the depth of a foot or two, must extend several miles to the westward of its ordinary shore; an occurrence which, from the appearance of the surface, does not seem to happen oftener than once in two or three years. Here the ground is sprinkled all over, with small glittering fragments of selenite, about the size of the little finger; they look at first like tufts of weathered grass till their lustre betrays them. They are obviously due to the same cause as the selenite already described, appearing on a larger scale in veins. Their greater abundance and less size is explained by the recency of their formation. Here, from the effect of refraction, the anchorage and shipping loom high above the level of the land. Crossing this, and now some 7 miles from Suez,—you know the fact, the feeling of fatigue would lead you to suppose yourself twenty,—you come to the verge of a gentle slope,—which it took me one hour to ascend, and which I therefore guess to be, at least, two miles,—rising some 200 or 300 feet to the base of the cliff. This is a great semicircle of gravel 4 or 5 miles in diameter, measured along the base of the hill. I advanced by the radius of two miles, over slightly water-worn stones and gravel, obviously precipitated over the cliffs by torrents, and spread along the plain, which, from the regularity of the heap, I should suppose to have been at this date slightly under water. Formations of this sort appear all along the margin, where the hills meet the plain, their extreme edges being frequently in contact with each other. They are all deeply grooved with dry water-courses from 6 to 10 feet in depth and from 50 to 150 feet across, obviously of modern date. The base of the cliff, as seen on this and on a subsequent visit to Ras Ataka, 5 miles further eastward, is rent into wild caverns and ravines. The central rock is, as already stated, a very compact nummulite, but this is crusted over with breccia, the blocks varying from a few inches to many feet or fathoms; the cementing matter is that on which we, in India, have conferred the name of " Littoral concrete," a sandstone of sea gravel and shells united by carbonate of lime. Masses of this have been grooved through or undermined by cataracts, and other masses have tumbled down, and become piled up over each other in the wildest confusion. Unable from heat and fatigue to proceed quite up to the base of the cliff, I looked about to see whether I could not procure any of the material which gave colour to the upper hills, and accordingly found in abundance the mineral I sought for ;—crystalline or earthy gypsum of all sorts, from pure white to bright blood-red. The colour I assumed due to the *Protococcus Hæmatacoccus*, the prevalence of which, at certain seasons, appears to have given the Red Sea its name.* It always makes its appearance in salt water of unusual density. It indicates to the Bombay salt-maker that the brine has been sufficiently concentrated to be drawn off into the pan, as it has been shown to form the colouring matter of the rock-salt of the Punjaub.

Captain Newbold says, that, on the bank of the waterless river, about 50 miles in a direct line from Alexandria, and 21 from the western branch of the Nile, are six lagoons or large shallow pools, so nearly saturated with salt, that in the hot season, crusts of salt are deposited on the sides or banks of the pool, from whence it is collected for use. It is usually tinged of a red colour, by a substance of a vegeto-animal nature, and has .a highly fœtid ammonical odour, and caustic alkaline taste. As already stated, it is now well ascertained to be the Protococcus Hæmatacoccus, something kindred to both the animal and vegetable kingdoms, and familiar to us in our eastern seas.

CONCLUSIONS.—The deductions which I think the facts stated will bear out are the following :—

1. That, long subsequent to the date of the formation of the nummulite limestone, even to that of the upper sandstone,—in all probability indeed considerably within the newer pliocene period,— the highest of the hills in this neighbourhood were under the sea.

---

* See the various excellent papers of Dr. Carter on the subject, in the Transactions of the Bombay Branch of the Royal Asiatic Society.

2. That their emergence was accomplished at intervals,—through periods of gradual ascent, alternating with those of absolute repose: that the projecting shelves on which the gravel cones are based, are the sea-beaches to which this state of matters gave rise, and that, in all likelihood, the beaches themselves afford material such as would go far to indicate the relative dates of these upheavals.

3. At this period rain must have occasionally fallen with excessive violence. From the extreme steepness of the slope of the gravel-cones, approaching an angle of 50 or 55, it would seem as if they had become indurated almost immediately after deposit, and probably while as yet the sea bathed their bases. Though, seen from 5 or 6 miles off, they seem as if of gravel of the ordinary character, my impression is, from the fragments found below, that they are of the Titanic breccia already described.

4. That the flattened cones, some 10,000 feet in radius, and 200 or 300 in axis, have been laid down since the last great emergence, but have probably been rounded into their present even form by being washed all over by the waves,—the deep, dry channels being the only vestiges of recent torrents ; and we find the types of these all over the desert up to the present time.

5. The raised beaches bordering the Red Sea, the Mediterranean, and probably every ocean-shore over the globe, and in which hitherto the remains of nothing extinct has been found, I am satisfied, have been brought into their present position long within the human, perhaps almost within the historic, period, and are probably connected with those traditions of extensive local deluges prevalent amongst all the oldest of the races of man. A descent and re-ascent of the earth's surface would meet all the circumstances of rising and subsiding waters ; be conformable with operations we know to be at this moment in progress ; and relieve us of all the difficulties of the elevation of the surface of the ocean, the increase of the mean diameter and retardation of the rotation of the earth, with all their attendant perplexities.

THE TRACK OF THE EXODUS.—An examination of the physical features of these localities, naturally suggests an inquiry into the geography of one of the most wonderful events in history—the flight of the Israelites from Egypt.

The Scriptures leave us the most unbounded latitude for tracing the route; fixing the point of departure near Cairo, that of arrival on the margin of the Red Sea, at somewhere on the upper part of the Gulf of Suez. For the rest we are left to interpret for ourselves. It must be remembered, that the host that fled from Egypt amounted to not fewer than a million and a quarter of souls. "The children of Israel journeyed from Rameses to Succoth, about six hundred thousand on foot, besides children : and a mixed multitude went up also with them ; and flocks and herds, and very much cattle" (Exodus xii. 37, 38). We can hardly set down the force with which Pharaoh pursued this vast body at less than 30,000. Some of the very highest authorities have assumed that the route lay from near Cairo through the long burning valley which yet bears the names of " the Wanderings" or " the Valley of Moses ;" and the celebrated divine and traveller, Dr. John Wilson, Bombay, in 1843 traversed the route, with the view of ascertaining the fact. The route seems to have nothing to recommend it but the name ; and when we remember how often the antiquary and historian have been misled by a tradition or a name,—nowhere more so than in this very neighbourhood, where Pompey's Pillar and Cleopatra's Needle could never have had any connection with the parties with whom, for centuries, they have been associated,—we must be cautious in placing this form of presumption against physical probabilities. All the direct routes from the Nile to the Gulf of Suez are waterless ; the casual pools found in the desert being occasioned by violent torrents of rain which fall chiefly in January and February, and dry up almost immediately. Over the 70 or 80 miles intervening betwixt the river and the sea, there is not a single green blade or herb man consumes ; the Camelthorn and poisonous Henbane, on which the camel browses, afford the only portions of vegetation to be met with. Scripture gives us no reason to suppose that the Israelites were miraculously provided for until they crossed the Red Sea : even had it been so, Pharaoh and his host who followed them immediately, whose pursuit was in accordance with the plan of the flight, had no means of furnishing themselves with supplies, no power of moving horses over 70 miles of ground, just before traversed by a million of people. We must assume, therefore, that the desert was *not* the route pursued ; the line of the old canal through the land of Goshen, and the most fertile part of the south-eastern limb of the Delta, nearly doubles the distance, but gives all that is wanted in the way of water and provisions, both for the flyers and pursuers, and brings them within a few miles of Suez. Here the Israelites might, at the top of the Gulf, have crossed at once into the wilderness of Sinai; but they would have been open to be overtaken and cut to pieces by the Egyptians, and the whole scheme of the Exodus been upset. Here it was that Moses was commanded "to speak to the children of Israel that they TURN and encamp before Pi-ha-hiroth between Migdol and the sea, over against Baal Zephon :—before it shall ye encamp by the sea." Assuming Pi-ha-hiroth to be Gibbel Ataka, the only conspicuous mountain in the neighbourhood, a full view of which, some 14 miles to the south, would first be obtained by them immediately on rounding the low hills north-west of Suez,—they were now turning off the desert line of escape, and doubling back on what seemed as dangerous a position as need be. The mass of Gibbel Ataka, as already stated, is some 20 miles in length, and 10 across, and 2,000 feet in height. This was full in front of them, with no choice but to go back to Egypt, or push on for the shores of the sea. Along the base of the range, as it bends southward, is a border of gently slopening sand and gravel about two miles from the shore to the cliff. Marching over this, and looking southward towards Wadi Musa and Gibbel Abu-Diraj—nothing but a vast wilderness,—an interminable expanse of howling desolation presented itself. Now, while the fugitives were thus pent up, the pursuing host appeared in their rear. When the Israelites in utter despair asked "if there were no graves in Egypt," that they should be brought thus far to perish ; suddenly the Red Sea, here only 3½ miles across, with a coral reef forming a shallow barrier, opened for their advance ; the Egyptians followed and were overwhelmed.

To me it seems, on examining the ground, that this route fulfils all the conditions prescribed by sacred Scripture, and desired for the occasion ; and that much more store is to be set on the probabilities suggested by physical considerations and requirements, than traditions drawn from antiquity so remote, and which must needs have frequently been interrupted, or the analogy or meaning of a name or designation, the date or the origin of which cannot be traced back beyond almost the present day.

A FORENOON IN THE DESERT.—The relation of the adventures of a forenoon in the Desert may be a warning to travellers to avoid the risks so unwisely and so needlessly encountered by me in pursuing these inquiries: the inconveniences occasioned by my own indiscretion afford an example of the danger to life that may be incurred from simple exertion over a period of a few hours duration, without any actual malady whatever. Every time. I had visited Suez—in April 1840, June and again in December 1845, July 1853, August 1854, and February 1857,—I had felt the most anxious desire to examine the extraordinary looking ridge to the southward. From the swiftness of the new steamer "Colombo" from Southampton to Alexandria, we were now 24 hours ahead of the Marseilles mails and passengers, for which the Bombay Steamer at Suez had to wait, when there appeared for the first time the opportunity of realising my desires. We had reached Suez at noon on the 5th September, when the cold of the Desert gave me diarrhœa ; and the food at the hotel was so little attractive, that I started on my excursion at daybreak on the 6th, after a 24 hours' fast, and without any supplies for the way, *fons et origo mali*. The morning was bright and cool, the air crisp and clear,—almost bracing. I felt in excellent health and spirits, and overlooked the want of commissariat supplies. The sand was in many places ankle-deep, and walking very fatiguing. I had my sketch book, specimen bag, measuring tape, and hammer,—no living companion. Seven miles from Suez, I came to a sloping patch of gravel nearly semi-circular, and about 2 miles in width. This it took me an hour to ascend. I now began to feel somewhat exhausted, not from anything resembling the actual fatigue of a long walk or severe exercise of any sort, but from want of animal energy. I breathed in deep long respirations, as if going to faint. I neither felt hot, feverish, nor thirsty, and perspired but little, but began to feel an irresistible desire to lie down whenever a bush, block of stone, or bank of gravel afforded the slightest shadow, and then I fell immediately asleep. Having got close to the base of the cliff, I began to appreciate the imprudence I had committed in crossing even nine miles of desert without breakfast or an attendant ; and made for the sea-shore, along which I had occasionally seen a considerable amount of traffic, in hopes of finding help if matters came to extremities. The distance was hardly 3 miles ; in part down the slope, at right angles to the path by which I had advanced, in part along drift, sand, and gravel. I was now getting greatly exhausted ; and seeing a small lime kiln,—now become notable as the point of departure of the electric telegraph for India from the African shore,—got into the fire-place,—there was no fire in it,—and enjoyed for nearly half an hour the most delightful series of dreamy slumbers I had ever experienced. Ras Ataka, close by, looked a mass of mysterious palaces and towers ; over its burning pinnacles, the sky was of the deepest azure. There was no sound or stir anywhere ; and a carrion crow crossing over,—the only example of animal life I observed,—seemed to indicate that if I remained long enough in the desert I should be duly attended to. By the bight of the bay, I had now got nearly 12 miles from Suez. I could barely walk 100 yards without tumbling over. I had no power of retention, scarcely of speech, and my eye-sight was failing me. I made signals to the steamer, at anchor about a couple of miles off, as I passed, but was unnoticed. Every bush, magnified or distorted by the mirage, seemed some one coming to my assistance. I now no longer waited for a shady bank or bush to sleep under, but every now and then lay flat down on the arid sand under the burning sun. At length, after four hours from quitting the kiln, I reached Suez. Though I was not 200 yards from the hotel, I asked water at the first house I came to, and must have swallowed nearly a gallon, falling fast asleep the moment I drank. The people would give me no more ; so, about 2 P.M., I staggered into the hotel, speechless, and nearly blind, but in full possession of my senses. I believed myself in perfect time for the steamer which was set down as sailing at 4 P.M. I whispered into the ear of a fellow traveller,—I could not speak above my breath, —for a tumbler of champagne. I felt I was suffering from simple exhaustion, and that nothing but restoratives was required. Once on board the steamer, I could get round by chicken broth, jellies, and other stuffs at my leisure.

My medical attendants, of whom there were half a dozen,—all most kind and considerate,—took it into their heads I was sunstruck. I had my head drenched and hands chilled with cold water ; and got ammonia and other abominations, which were of no service. At length, a little recovered by sheer absence from exposure, I attempted to join the steamer, and saw her start just as I was half way to the anchorage. A very able and excellent Bengal physician, to whom I am

3 *g*

under infinite obligations, now complied with my wishes, and gave me good rich soup and a glass of sherry, at night followed by a glass of beer; and after a long sound sleep, I arose quite well, perfectly satisfied that all I had suffered·was requited by what I had seen ; equally so, that with ordinary discretion, I might have had the sights without the suffering : and warning all Desert travellers who have passed their fifth decade, that they never on any account neglect the commissariat.

The feeling of exhaustion and desire to sleep, by themselves resembled the same sensations which overcome one in walking through deep drift in a snow storm. The only time I have ever experienced the other symptoms was in 1841, when on the verge of the grave from brain fever. The fever itself had gone, the pulse was going fast, and sinking nature seemed insufficient for the demands being made on her. Medical men deeply experienced in Indian practice, kept me alive by administering large doses of brandy in gruel. I slept off the exhaustion, and after a long period of weakness completely recovered. Hints like these the juvenile traveller, and surgeon familiar only with the experience of a cold climate, may profit by in the East.

Art. II.—HURRICANES in the EASTERN SEAS from 1854 to 1859. *By* George Buist, *LL.D., F.R.S. L. and E., Corresponding Member of the Imperial Geographical Society, Vienna, &c.*

On receiving from Mr. Hugh Crawford, Allipey, a very valuable series of observations on the Hurricane which made its appearance in the lower part of the Bay of Bengal on the 23rd April last, crossed over the southern extremity of the Peninsula, committing violent ravages on the Malabar Coast, and manifesting itself as far west as Aden, I meant to have endeavoured to give a description of the gale, an account of the area it swept, the direction in which it advanced, and rate at which it revolved. This, however, was the only contribution I received; none of the vessels in our port appear to have crossed its track, and the information contained in the newspapers is so singularly meagre, that my purpose was abandoned.

Since the death of Captain Biden at Madras, and that of Mr. Piddington at Calcutta, and the return of Dr. Leibig to England, there seems no one in India who takes any interest in cyclonology. I hope Captain Tennant, on fairly taking up the office of director of the Madras Observatory, may prove an exception, and supply a want that we ought to have no cause to complain of, considering the extreme importance of the subject to be investigated, and the gigantic dimensions to which our shipping interests have recently grown.

On this side of India, Dr. Thom, of H. M's. Service, and Captain Carless, of the Indian Navy, from each of whom we have an admirable account of the *Cleopatra's* hurricane of April 1847, are the only parties who have written on hurricanes. I attempted to give an account of our own very remarkable tempest of November 1854; more, because there seemed no one else disposed to take up the task, and the material for its performance must have perished with the occasion, than from any feeling of aptitude, or any assumed accomplishment in the science.

In the Appendices to each of the two previous numbers of our Journal, are lists of the hurricanes in the Eastern seas for a century back; and which, for a quarter of that period, may be considered tolerably complete. To preserve the information scattered about in reference to subsequent hurricanes, and with the view of continuing the abstract at all events, I subjoin the various instances I have from time to time collected, bequeathing these as a legacy to others who may wish so much of a contribution which further additions may extend.

I have no doubt but that there is abundance of information regarding them fully recorded ; and it in general requires merely the industry or enthusiasm of an individual to draw it forth ; so soon as it is seen that it will be turned to account, it makes its appearance. It would surely be a matter of much regret were Bombay with its University, its Royal Observatory, its Hydrographer,* and its two millions of tons of outward and inward freight, borne in fourteen thousand vessels departing or arriving annually, its forty millions sterling worth of seaborne commerce—were Bombay, by far the largest shipping port between the Tropics, to be the only one where the collection and promulgation of meteorological information, a matter of such moment to the mariner, was neglected.

List of Hurricanes.

1855.   *April 12th.*—Hurryhurr, Madras Presidency, Lat. 13° N., Long. 77° E.   Seems to have been a local squall of unusual violence, but whether or not possessed of the character of a Cyclone does not appear.

1855.   *April 23rd—May 10th.*—Indian Ocean, South of the Line.

1855.   *May 15th—20th.*—Bay of Bengal, betwixt Burmah and Madras.

1855.   *July 21st.*—Off Hongkong.

1855.   *October 29th and 30th.*—Arabian Sea, betwixt Cooria Mooria Bay and the Gulf of Aden.

1856.

1856.   *April 18th.*—Arabian Sea, betwixt Cooria Mooria Bay and the Gulf of Aden.

1856.   *May 14th.*—Bay of Bengal.

1856.   *October 18th.*—Typhoon in the China Seas.

1856.   *November 18th—21st.*—Bay of Bengal, from 5° to 20° N.

---

* It requires to be explained that the officer formerly designated " draughtsman to the Indian Navy," has, of late, been designated " Hydrographer."   The establishment hitherto known as the " Observatory, Colaba," has lately been termed " The Royal Observatory, Bombay,"—on what warrant, I know not.

1857.*

1857.   *September 4th and 6th.*—Off Chusan, and Northern China Seas.

1857.   *September 30th.*—In China Sea.

1857.   *October 28th.*—Off Ceylon, and in the Bay of Bengal.

1857.   *October 29th, November 5th—12th.*—In China Seas.

1857.   *November 20th.*—Ceylon.

1858.

1858.   *April 9th and 10th.*—Bay of Bengal and Andaman Sea.

1858.   *May 15th and 20th.*—Bay of Bengal and Malabar Coast.

1858.   *August 30th—September 20th.*—North China Seas.

1858.   *October 25th.*—Calcutta.

1858.   *November 8th—10th.*—China Seas, betwixt Hongkong and Shanghae.

1859.

1859.   *April 21st—27th.*—Bay of Bengal and Arabian Sea.

1859.   *June 3rd.*—Arabian Sea, betwixt Cooria Mooria Bay and the Gulf of Aden.

1859.   *June 12th—17th.*—Bay of Bengal, off Akyab.

1859.   *June 20th.*—Violent squall off Jacobabad.

1859.   *July 25th—27th.*—Lower Bengal.

I shall next proceed to give a short analysis or abstract of the gales here enumerated, premising that it is by no means certain that all or even the majority of them are entitled to the designation of hurricanes or whirlwinds.   As they were all at least violent storms, their rotatory character may be afterwards investigated.   At the close of the paper I shall enumerate those of whose general character as cyclones there can be no doubt.

HURRYHURR, MADRAS PRESIDENCY, Lat. 13° N. Long. 77° E.— *April 12th,* 1855.—The presumption is, that this was a local squall of unusual violence.   A series of disturbances occurred about the same time betwixt Bombay and Kurrachee, and at Ajmere in Rajpootana. Neither at Bombay nor Calcutta does the barometer seem to have been materially affected.   At both places the weather was cloudy ; and at

---

* I was absent from India from January till October 1857, and feel by no means certain that the list of Hurricanes is, for this period, complete.

Calcutta there were smart breezes, with much thunder and lightning, on the evening of the 10th.

A VIOLENT HURRICANE.—One of the most violent hurricanes ever known in these parts, is said to have visited Hurryhur on the evening of the 12th instant. The winds blew with such fury as to tear away the roofs of houses, prostrate stately trees, and demolish solitary sentry-boxes. Tiles are said to have been flying about in every direction, glass windows smashed to shivers, and the plastering of walls sadly impaired by the hailstorm. The hailstones which fell are described as being as large as good-sized marbles, some of them between two or three inches in circumference. The hospital lost a great deal of its tiling; and other houses, particularly in the Sepoy's lines, are said to have received much damage, but to what extent is not stated. No mention is made of the loss of human life; but the day after the storm, a gentleman is said to have picked up upwards of 270 perroquets in his compound quite dead, and a considerable number besides these maimed and injured. The river also was covered with dead fish, some two feet long; but how these met their fate is not found so easy to explain. The natives confidently assert that, mistaking the hailstones that fell into the water for grubs, the fishes swallowed them, and were killed by the ice not agreeing with them!—*Bangalore Herald, April 17th.*

The steamer *Bombay,* which returned on Sunday evening from Kurrachee, seems to have encountered rough weather on her passage from Bombay, which she left on the 7th instant. A passenger who was on board writes as follows:—"We had a pleasant time of it the first day, though the clouds seemed to threaten a gale. The storm broke upon us the following day; and the day after, when we got into the Gulf of Cutch, it gathered further strength, so as to threaten destruction. The natives on board abandoned the hope of ever again seeing the shore, as they witnessed the fearfully vivid flashes of lightning that played about the vessel as she floundered in the heavy sea that broke over us every now and then. Within fifteen miles of Kurrachee we lost this weather, and we landed early on the 11th, delighted at, and thankful for, the safe termination of our voyage, which more than once threatened the most fatal consequences."—*Bombay Times, April 17th.*

"*Ajmere, 20th April* 1855.—Three inches of rain have fallen here from the 12th to the 20th of April, an unusual quantity for the time of the year, and indeed an unusual occurrence altogether for the rain to have come down at this time. The thermometer in the house before the rain was 88°, but since the rain it has fallen to 75°; near which degree it stands nearly throughout the day."

INDIAN OCEAN, SOUTH OF THE LINE.—*April 23rd—May 10th.*— I am not prepared to say whether the Cyclone experienced by the *Rockall* betwixt 33° and 28° S. and 68° E., betwixt the 28th April and 1st May, was the same as that so minutely described by Lieut. Fyers to the Mauritius Meteorological Society as occurring betwixt 28th April and 6th May, betwixt latitude 6° and 24° S., and longitude 70° to

83° E. If it be so, then the great Mauritius hurricane must have had a larger sweep eastward and southward than that ascribed to it. Captain Fyers does not appear to have seen the *Rockall's* log, though published nearly a twelvemonth before the reading of his paper. Every meteorologist will concur with him in deploring the character of marine barometers in the mercantile navy. Yet we are hardly to wonder at this, when we find H. M.'s ships-of-war of the Indian Navy, under the eye of the Royal Observatory, no better off in 1859 in such things, than colliers, or whalers, or country craft were in 1855.

A CYCLONE.—The American ship *Rockall*, Captain John Martin, which arrived at this port last week, encountered a cyclone on the voyage, of which the following account, written by a passenger, has been placed at our disposal :—

"From latitude 33° south, and longitude 65° east, to latitude 28° south and longitude 68° east, we had light winds and calms, having on the 21st and 22nd April twenty-four hours of dead calm, the weather being very warm. On the 25th April, the south-east trades commenced very abruptly, and blew very strongly, continuing thus to April 30th. The atmosphere in the trades was very close and oppressive. On the evening of the 29th, sharp lightning was observed to the northward and eastward. On the morning of the 30th April, the barometer commenced to fall fast, from 29·60. The weather wore a threatening aspect, being very cloudy and squally. The ship was reduced to a close-reefed main-topsail. At 9 A.M. (civil time), the barometer still falling and the wind increasing, the topsail was furled, leaving the ship under bare poles. The wind was about S.E. by S., and veered to S.S.E. and South ; the ship lying to, as well as she could, nearly broadside on, her head being to the eastward. An attempt was made to tack ship, but such was the force of the gale, that it was impossible to move her a point. The fore-topmast staysail was no sooner hoisted, than it parted, and was blown to shreds. At 10 A.M., the barometer was 28·90. It is vain to attempt a description of the force of the wind. The sea rose very high, and seemed to come from all points of the compass, the ship rolling very heavily. Several attempts were made to get the ship on another tack, but all proved fruitless. At noon the barometer was 28·60. The gale increased ; and blowing from S.S.E. to S.E., shipped a heavy sea forward and aft, which stove in a portion of the bulwarks, partially filling the cabins with water. At 2-30 P.M., the ship rolled heavily, her main yard-arm being often in the water. It was deemed necessary, for the preservation of the ship, to cut away the top-gallant masts, which was at last effected, though not without some personal peril. Such was the force of the wind that the seamen came down from aloft, having had their shirts blown from them. At 4 P.M., the barometer was 28·45, wind blowing fearfully, the ship unmanageable, and shipping considerable water. At 6 P.M., barometer at 28·55, the wind moderated suddenly to nearly a dead calm, when the ship was headed to the westward. It remained calm until 8 P.M., when the wind commenced with terrific violence from N.W. to N.N.W., the barometer 28·60. At about 11 P.M. it began to moderate, and the barometer rose to 29·30 by midnight. It continued moderating until daylight.

1st May.—The breeze from northward and eastward. During the gale, quite a number of poor birds came on board completely exhausted. The whole of this day the sea was very rough, and the weather unpleasant, with a frowning sky overhead. By the 3rd of May, the weather and the sea seemed to have returned to their usual habits."—*Englishman, May 30th.*

HURRICANE OF MAY 1855 IN THE SOUTH INDIAN OCEAN.—At a special meeting of the Meteorological Society held on Thursday last, 15th instant, for the purpose of electing a new President in place of the late Captain West, Mr. C. C. Brownrigg was elected President, and Dr. Behe, Vice-President, *vice* Mr. C. C. Brownrigg.

The following able and interesting paper was read by Lieut. A. B. Fyers at the same meeting :—

Hurricane of May 1855 *in the South Indian Ocean.*—During the month of May last, several vessels received considerable damage in a hurricane to the Eastward of this Island ; and as the bad weather season is usually supposed to terminate in April, most of the Commanders were taken by surprise.

I have no positive data from which to trace the course, &c. of this storm, until the 6th May ; from which date until the 10th, the information received is most satisfactory, and proves in a clear manner its rotatory and progressive character.

From the weather experienced by several vessels bound to Mauritius from India, I am inclined to think that it must have originated during the latter part of April in 5° to 7° South Latitude and 83° to 86° East Longitude ; for instance, on the 27th April, the *Herculanean* experienced heavy gales from N.W. to W. and E. ; sprung a leak, and was obliged to throw a portion of her cargo overboard.

On the 28th April, in 8° South and 84° East, the Dutch Barque *Watel Stroom* experienced a severe hurricane from W. to E. and round the compass ; lost her sails, and damaged her cargo.

The reason that the wind veered with these vessels from the Westward to N. and E., is, that their courses took them gradually round the Eastern side of the Cyclone, which was progressing very slowly, if at all, at the time.

As data fail me between the 28th April and 10th May, I have merely shown the presumed course of the storm by a dotted line on the chart, and proceed to describe that part of its track about which there is no doubt.

On the 6th May the *Futtay Sultan*, bound to Mauritius, was at noon in 13° 10' South Latitude, 70° 52' East Longitude ; Barometer 29·87 inches ; wind from the eastward ; course W.S.W. ; in royals. P.M. Strong winds and heavy easterly sea ; rolling heavily. 4 P.M. Double-reefed the topsails, and down royal yards ; wind East ; course S.W. by W. ; 7 knots. 8 P.M. Very heavy squalls, with rain and lightning ; Bar. 29·70. 10 P.M. In mainsail, reefed foresail, and close-reefed topsail.

7th May.—A.M. Strong gale with much lightning. 5 A.M. In fore-topsail, and lay to under close-reefed main-topsail ; down top-gallant yards ; rolling heavily· Fore-topmast staysail blew to pieces in taking it in. Noon. Lat. account 13° 58' S. ; Long. Chron. 69° 16' East ; wind E. by N. ; Bar. 29·61. On port tack ; tremendous gusts of wind and rain ; main-topsail sheets gave way ; furled the sail, and lay to under bare poles. P.M. Very heavy gale with rain and lightning, the wind blowing with such violence that it was impossible to stand without holding on ; the ship laying with the lee rail completely under water, and making very much water ; all hands at the pumps. At about 4 P.M., the jib guys began to give way ; and before dark the jib boom went, taking with it all the gear, bowsprit cap, &c. ; the starboard boat also went, breaking both davits. 8 P.M. Wind N.E. Midnight. Blowing a complete hurricane, and gradually hauling to the Northward, the ship coming head to sea and pitching heavily ; stove in the cabin dead lights on both sides, and washed everything about the cabins ; the helm lashed hard a lee, and all hands at the pumps.

8th May.—A.M. Wind N.E. by N. ; ditto weather ; water pouring down through the deck and topsides in streams. Noon. Lat. account 14° 14′ S. ; Long. Chron. 68° 53′ E. ; Bar. 29·50 ; ship frequently driving her taffrail under water. P.M. Tremendous gusts of wind N.N.E. 2 P.M. Both topmasts blew away. 4 P.M. Bar. 28·00 ; mainsail and foresail blew adrift and went to pieces, and ship righted, when a sea broke into the port quarter boat and carried it away, breaking both davits. 6 P.M. Wind N.N.W. Midnight. Bar. 27·80 ; gale abating, with heavy cross sea.

9th May.—4 A.M. Bar. 27·50 ; wind N.N.W. ; strong gale and confused sea. Noon. Lat. account 15° 50′ S. ; Long. Chron. 69° 08′ East ; Bar. 27·52 ; wind N.N.W. The wind gradually abated after this.

As the *Futtay Sultan* was going to the W.S.W. and afterwards to the S.W. by W., and the barometer kept falling with an increasing easterly wind, the natural inference would be that the storm was making more south than the vessel ; and that consequently they would meet, if both continued on the same tracks. The commander of the *Futtay Sultan* hove to ; the centre passed very near him ; and his vessel was considerably damaged. In my opinion, had he, on the 7th, scudded to the westward under as much canvas as could be carried, he would have escaped altogether. We have lately had an instance of this kind. On the 4th of the present month (May), Capt. Barron, in the mail brig *Annie*, found himself on the south side of a hurricane. The wind was East, and the barometer falling rapidly ; but instead of heaving to, he very wisely scudded to the westward, and consequently passed across the storm's track. Unfortunately, however, this island was close under his lee, and he had to heave to, to avoid running on to it ; and in consequence felt the force of the storm more than if he had been able to keep on to the westward. Had he hove to when first he perceived that a hurricane was approaching, the centre would have passed over him, and the *Annie* and her mails would in all probability never have been heard of again. Captain Barron deserves the greatest praise for the thorough knowledge of the science of the law of storms that he evinced, and also for the judicious manner in which he acted.

Should the storm of May 1855 have travelled to the Southward, as indicated by the *Futtay Sultan's* log, we should naturally expect to find some vessels experiencing its force to the South of her position on the 9th, and at a later period. Nature is always true to her laws ; and the logs of both the *Parland* and *Empress* prove not only its course, but the rate at which it travelled. A few extracts from their logs will prove instructive.

4 *g*

The *Parland* experienced strong trades and squalls until the 8th May ; when at 8 A.M., the wind increased, from the Eastward ; double reefed topsails, furled jib and mainsail, sent down royal yards : strong gales with heavy squalls ; close reefed fore and main topsail, and furled the mizen.   Noon. Lat. 17° 73′ S. ; Long. 70° 6′ E. P.M. Strong gales with heavy squalls. 4 P.M. Bar. 29·60 ; increasing gales, with heavy squalls and rain ; furled fore-topsail. 6 P.M. Heavy squalls and barometer falling ; furled main-topsail and foresail, and hove to, with ship's head to the Southward, under the wing of the main-trysail.   Midnight. Bar. 29·58 ; wind E. by N. ; heavy squalls and rain : a heavy cross sea ; making much water.   9th May.—A.M. Wind E.N.E. ; ditto weather. Noon. 18° 3′ S. Lat. ; 69° 35′ E. Long. ; Bar. 29·58 ; wind N.E. ; blowing heavily, with squalls and rain ; rudder-head having split and gone, steered for Mauritius ; the wind gradually veered to N.N.E. and N.   At noon on 10th, wind N.N.W. ; Bar. 29·60; strong gales and heavy squalls.

The Schooner *Catherine* passed in front of the storm, and the wind veered with her to the S.E.S. and S.W.   On the 10th May she was in 17° 57′ S. Lat., and 66° 8′ E. Long. ; wind W.S.W.   The Barque *Anne Laing* also passed in front of the storm.

The last extract I shall give is from the log of the *Empress*, which vessel was on the very verge of the centre at noon on the 10th.   On the 8th May, the ship *Empress* was in Lat. 19° 01′ S., and Long. 73° 35′ E. ; wind E. ; course W.S.W. ; fresh breezes and cloudy. 8 P.M. Double reefed topsails.   Midnight. Fresh gales and heavy sea, shipping much water. 9th.—A.M., ditto weather. Noon. Lat. 20° 9′ S. ; and Long. 70° 0′ E. ; wind East ; course W.S.W. ; fresh gales and rain. 4 P.M. Close reefed the topsails. 7 P.M. The gale increasing with a heavy sea, furled the foresail and fore-topsail, and brought ship to on port tack, under close reefed main-topsail, main-trysail, and fore-topmast staysail.   Midnight. Hard gales and heavy rain.

10th May.—6 A.M. Gale increased to a hurricane ; drove the ship on her beam ends ; blew away main-topsail and main-trysail, and foresail from the yard, the foresail being well stowed at the time ; unbent the gaff-topsail to bend it to mainmast to keep ship to,—it was blown to pieces. Noon. Lat. 20° 46′ S. ; and Long. 68° 30′ E. ; Bar. 28·9 ; wind shifted to W.S.W., and blew terrifically, the ship lying in the trough of the sea, the sea making a clean breach over her.   Both pumps constantly going, several of the chain plates gave way.   The gammon hook of the bowsprit gave way ; both top-gallant masts and fore-topmast went over the side ; also the jib-boom.   At the height of the hurricane the Barometer stood at 28·90, and boiled like lead.   The gale blew heavily until 4 P.M., when the Barometer began to rise, and the sea to go down.

Many other vessels suffered in this hurricane ; but I have given extracts from those nearest the centre.   The logs of the others confirm the conclusions I have arrived at, relative to its course and rate.

It appears that the centre of the hurricane on the 6th May was in 10° South Lat. and 73° 40′ East Long.   Its course from 6th to 7th May about South, 38° 47′ W. : from 7th to 8th, about South, 24° 16′ W. : from 8th to 9th, due South.   The average rate of progression from the 6th to 9th, at noon, about 7 miles per hour.   From the 9th to the 10th its course was about South, 4° 21′ East ; its rate of progression about

10·7 miles per hour.   On the 10th, at noon, it must have been in 20° 45′ South Lat. and 69° East Long.

To those who may still have doubts as to the truth of the law of storms, much interesting and useful information may be derived from attentively studying the course and rotatory motion of this hurricane.   The latter is most clearly and beautifully proved by those vessels in the left hand semicircle having had the wind first about E. to E.N.E., and then N.E., N., and N.N.W. ; whilst with those who were in the right hand semicircle it veered from E. to E.S.E., S.E., S., and S.W. : thus proving the law of rotation with the hands of a watch in this hemisphere.   Its progressive motion is also clearly proved by different vessels having been dismasted at different dates according to their position relative to that of the centre.

The diameter of this storm must have been about 500 to 600 miles.   The Barometer on board the *Futtay Sultan* fell to 27·52 close to the centre : and that on board the *Empress* to 29·80.   I imagine that the instrument on board the former must have been set too low.   It is very annoying that most barometers are perfectly valueless in a scientific point of view, their having never been compared with a standard ; rendering it impossible to make any comparisons as to the atmospheric pressure on board of different vessels at the same time and in different positions.   It is to be hoped that the new system of having instruments compared at Kew, and all observations made on a uniform system, will soon admit of a class of valuable data being collected, which will clear up many points of doubt or mere hypothesis, both as to the circulation of the atmosphere, the currents of the ocean, and the causes of hurricanes.

A. B. Fyers, Lieut. Royal Engineers.

Observatory, Port Louis, 15th April 1856.
—*Commercial Gazette, May 27th.*]

Bay of Bengal, betwixt Burmah and Madras.—*May 15th— 20th,* 1856.—There can be no doubt that this gale possessed all the characteristics of a genuine Cyclone ; but the notes of it which I have been able to collect are too meagre to permit any analysis of its features to be attempted.

Burmah.—The following is from a correspondent at Thyat Mew, dated 21st May 1855 :—

"The only occurrence of note since my last is easily described.   On the 15th instant, a strong breeze set in from the North ; it gradually increased to a hurricane ; then veered to the West and West by South, and concluded by totally demolishing the barracks of the 25th Regiment recently erected ; by damaging all, and destroying two, of the barracks of H. M.'s 29th Regiment ; by levelling with the ground the stables just completed for the artillery horses ; and by unroofing and otherwise injuring one or two private houses.   I am afraid to mention the loss sustained actually by Government ; but this I can state, that the repairing of the damages will occupy the executive department for some time to come.   Several lives were lost.

At least two of the 25th died within a day or two of the accident, and I hear that
sixty or seventy are in hospital : about five-and-twenty of the 20th were also injured."

BAD WEATHER IN THE BAY.—Extract from a letter from the Commander of the
Brig *Harbinger* to the Master Attendant at Madras, dated Coringa Bay, 24th of
May 1855.

"Sailed from Coconada on the morning of the 20th instant, with a light southerly
wind and fine weather. Cargo consisting of 1,000 bags of gram, with a few passengers for Madras.

"A.M. on the 21st, weather suspicious and sea getting up fast. At noon, in Lat.
16° 15′ N.; Long. 83° 30′ E.; experienced a severe gale veering from S.W. to South
and S.S.E., with a terrific sea on. Ship under double-reefed topsails, head to the
eastward; found the ship to be making a great deal of water, notwithstanding a
watch being constantly at the pumps. Ship very uneasy, and diving forecastle
under at times. At 5 P.M., puffs still harder, and the weather becoming more
furious; wore ship, and stood to south-westward; wind from S.S.E. Same weather throughout the night; notwithstanding all exertions, two feet water in the
hold. At 1 A.M., in fore-topsail, furled it, and close-reefed the main-topsail;
tremendous hard gusts, with lulls at intervals.

"Daylight. A more favorable appearance of the weather; wind and sea de-
creasing fast; but ship making the same water. Bore away to Coconada, where we
arrived on the night of the 23rd. I purpose discharging the cargo and docking
the ship."

Master Attendant's Office, Madras, 30th May 1855.—*Spectator, May 31st.*

THE WEATHER.—By a report from the Master Attendant's Office, we learn that
a gale was experienced in the Bay on the 21st instant. We should have been thankful of its reaching so far south as Madras. The want of rain begins to be dis-
tressingly felt; and we have complaints to the same effect from Salem in the South,
and Cuddapah in the North. At Bombay they have " put off" their monsoon for
a fortnight; and on the 23rd instant, the usual rains of the season were still holding
off at Ceylon. We had lately to chronicle the novelty of hail-storms in every
direction : now it is drought and heat. In ordinarily cool Colombo, the thermometer stands at 89°; Salem quotes 98°; we have here 96°; and Sind maintains
its pre-eminence by a record of 112°.—*Ibid.*

HONGKONG.—*21st July,* 1856.—I have no means of judging whether
the Hongkong storm was a Cyclone or not; and content myself
with giving the only extract concerning it I have in my note-book,
not doubting that there may be abundance of other information
on record.

THE LATE GALE.—Early in the morning of the 21st, a stiff breeze began to
blow from the eastward. There was nothing, however, in the appearance of the
weather to indicate the approach of such a gale as we have since experienced. The
Unicorn left for Shanghae about noon; and about the same time the *Lancefield*
left for Calcutta; and shortly after two o'clock, the *Lady Mary Wood* also left for
Shanghae. The *Unicorn* had proceeded no great distance, before she got into

trouble. The heavy sea encountered outside, caused her to spring a leak, and this mishap was immediately followed by the bursting of one of her boilers. She remained for some time in a position of great danger, when she slipt from her anchors, and was making her way back to port, when she was fallen in with by the *Lady Mary Wood*, which vessel towed her into harbour, when from her leaky state it was thought advisable to beach her, which was accordingly done on the bank opposite Spring Gardens.

There have been a number of casualties in the harbour among the smaller craft, and the Chinese shipping. Messrs. Bowra & Co's small steam water boat has been thrown ashore, and has sunk opposite the P. & O. Co.'s office. Some thirty to forty Chinese vessels also have been thrown ashore, which has occasioned a considerable loss of life; and on shore several buildings have been thrown down, which has led to the loss of six or more lives.—*Hongkong Register, July 24th.*

ARABIAN SEA BETWIXT COORIA MOORIA BAY AND THE GULF OF ADEN.—*October 29th and 30th*, 1855.—This, as will afterwards be seen, is the pre-eminently stormy region in the Arabian Sea, this being the first of three well-defined Cyclones occurring in four years,— on the 29th October 1855, 18th April 1856, and 3rd June 1859.

We have been favoured by Captain C. J. Grimmer, of the ship *Chevalier*, of Glasgow, 852 tons, with the following extracts from the log of that vessel, which was totally dismasted in a Cyclone, on the voyage from Aden to Bombay, on the evening of the 29th ultimo, whilst in Latitude 14° 24′ North, Longitude 55° 28′ East, betwixt the island of Socotra and Cape Ras-el-Morebat on the Arabian coast. This would seem to be the same hurricane in which the French ship *Bayadere* was so roughly handled :—

"*29th October* 1855.—At 6 P.M., weather looking very threatening, sea making very high from the eastward, reduced ship to three close-reefed topsails; wind at that time about E.N.E. At midnight, blowing a complete hurricane; clewed up the mizen-topsail, and whilst in the act of furling it, Alexander Mitchell, able seaman, was unfortunately lost overboard. The ship at the time lying over on her beam-ends, totally overpowered by the force of the wind and sea, nothing could possibly be done to save him, it being at this time exceedingly dark. At 1 A.M. of the 30th, the fore-masthead was struck by lightning, cutting the mast away at the eyes of the lower rigging, taking with it the fore-topmast, top-gallant and royal masts, with their yards. About 10 minutes afterwards, the mainmast was also struck by the electric fluid, totally destroying all the masts and yards; the mizen-topmast carried away by the main-topmast. At daybreak, compelled to cut everything free from the ship, as the wreck was tearing the ship's side to pieces. During all this time the wind and sea had increased to a fearful height, the ship labouring and straining very heavily, and making a great quantity of water. At noon, the weather the same, and no observation could be taken.

"*Tuesday, 30th October* 1855.—At 2 P.M., the weather a little more moderate, the wind veering from N.E. to S.E.; but at 6 P.M. the gale again increased to fearful violence, with a very cross sea, which struck the ship heavily and increased the damage, destroying much of the ship's stores, carrying away the gig, &c. &c."

The vessel was eventually got safely back to Aden on the 7th instant, under the lower-masts, where she must remain until she can be refitted by materials sent from Bombay. The *Chevalier* first arrived at Aden about the 15th of September, from Liverpool, with coals for the P. and O. Steam Navigation Company, which she there discharged; and afterwards took in part of a cargo of coffee, ivory, and gums for Bombay, and a number of native passengers, some of whom were injured, though none very seriously, by the falling of the masts. Captain Grimmer arrived at Bombay in the steamer *Pottinger* on Monday last.

Amongst our shipping intelligence of the 14th, we find the following notice :—

" *November* 12*th.*—French Ship *Bayadere*, H. Gaignaux, commander, from Aden, 12th October. Intelligence : On the 27th October, in Lat. 16° 30′ North, Long 58° East, experienced a most severe hurricane from the North-west; courses, top-sails, and topgallant-sails blown away from the yards after being furled ; boat blown from the stern, and the cabin filled with water. During the whole time that the hurricane continued, the barometer was quite steady."

The 27th of October is not one of the periods of our regularly recurring storms, unless we suppose that from the early drying up of the rains, all our weather epochs have this season got disturbed. But the *Bayadere's* squall, seems to have been con-comitant with a very extensive series of atmospheric disturbances, though not at a date at which they were looked for. We find the following entry in a Bombay meteorological journal of this date :—

" 27*th.*—Cloudy, fresh, morning ; Barometer at 9-30, 30·035. The sky, cloudy most part of the day, drift north-easterly ; the sea breeze set in late, and from S.W. by S. At 3-40 P.M. thunder in the S.E.; in the N.E. a long singular looking wreath of rain clouds, with heavy showers, from Elephanta to Tanna. Night cool and fresh.

28*th.*—Sunday. Slight showers about 3 A.M., morning very cool; a fine bright rainbow in the west at 7 A.M. Barometer 29·980. Showers all over the N.E. throughout the afternoon. Wind south-easterly during the evening."

This, it will be observed, is a very anomalous state of matters for the fair season, indicating, notwithstanding the height and steadiness of the barometer, trouble to the S.W. of us. On the 28th there was severe weather at Mahableshwur. On the same day there was heavy rain with squalls or storms at Agra, Delhi, Simla, and Lahore. On the 27th and 28th there were heavy falls of snow on the hills north-ward of the Indus, with a hail-storm at Sealkote, during which the barracks were struck by lightning. At this time there were heavy falls of rain all over the Deccan, though we have not been able to make out the precise day on which the heaviest of these ocurred—in all likelihood they were on one of the two already named. The southernmost point, that at which the *Bayadere* felt the storm, was in 16° 30′ N., and 58° E. The hills to the northward of Sealkote may be set down at 32° 30′ N., while Simla, the easternmost point from which intelligence has reached us, is 31° N. and 78° E. The storm therefore was felt for sixteen degrees, that is, 1,120 miles North and South, and twenty degrees or about 1,400 miles from East to West ; and over all this vast space of 156,800 square miles, it may be pretty safely affirmed that there was everywhere a strong and sensible disturbance in the air, manifest to the eye, though not indicated by any of our instruments within the space of thirty-six hours.

The next Cyclone on our list occurred just five months afterwards, in the very same region as the previous one. The logs of the *Haddington* and *Malta* would probably afford all the information wanted to enable us to work out the path and area of the gale.

The continued absence of the *Queen* steamer begins now to occasion uneasiness. She left Aden twenty-six hours before the *Malta*, and this latter vessel took no less than ten days to cross. On the 18th she experienced a very heavy gale such as the Indian Navy steamer, which has now been fourteen days out, was certainly not well prepared to stand. Our hope is that she may have put back and returned to Aden; but we cannot dissemble our apprehensions that some evil thing may have befallen her.—*Bombay Times, April 29th.*

Fears are entertained for the safety of the H. C.'s steamer *Queen*. This vessel left Aden twenty-six hours before the P. and O. Co's Steamer *Malta*, which arrived here last Thursday. The *Malta* made a long passage of ten days, having encountered very bad weather on the way. The *Queen* is,—we trust we may still say *is*, —a notorious old tub, and if she fell in with a heavy gale or sea, it might very likely go hard with her.

The *Punjaub* was sent on Sunday evening in search of the missing steamer, and the *Punjaub* returned yesterday morning under sail, her machinery having broken down again !

The *Feroze* arrived yesterday from Suez and Aden. She left the last-named port two days after the *Malta*. She saw nothing of the *Queen* on the voyage. The *Feroze*, we learn, was coaling yesterday afternoon, and is probably off this morning, for a cruise in search of the missing vessel. We trust she may be successful in picking her up.—*Bombay Gazette, April 29th.*

For the benefit of nautical men, we feel much pleasure in publishing the following extract from the log of the *Malta*, which has been kindly placed at our disposal by the Commander, Captain Purchase :—

Friday, April 18th.

Barometer.	P.M.	
	1	Moderate ; increasing breeze and fine ; wind N.E.E.
29·62	4	Fresh breeze ; wind N.E.
29·56	7	Strong breeze, with threatening appearance to the northward and eastward.
29·54	8	Strong increasing breeze.
29·50	9	Do.
29·50	10	Strong gale.
29·46	11	Do.
29·45		Midnight : Hard gale ; wind N.E.

Saturday, April 19th.

Barometer.	A.M.	
29·28	2	Hard gale ; wind E.N.E.
29·26	4	Do. do.
29·24	5	Do. do.
29·36	6	Do. wind E.S.E.
29·45	8	Strong gale, and high sea; wind S.E.
29·48	10	Gale slightly moderating ; wind S.S.E.
29·50		Noon : Hard gale, with severe gusts.
	P.M.	
29·45	2	Heavy rain squalls, and decreasing sea; wind from S.E. to E.S.E.
29·45	4	Gale decreasing, with thick cloudy weather.
29·58	6	Thick cloudy weather, with very vivid lightning from N.W. to N.E.
29·60	10	Decreasing wind and swell.
29·63		Midnight : Fresh breeze, and cloudy weather.

—Telegraph and Courier, April 30th.

There really somehow seems a fate to hang over the Indian Navy Steamers. The *St. Abbs*, containing the first supply of machinery intended to replace that first referred to, perished at sea, and the *Haddington*, which reached Bombay on the 26th with another cylinder, was very nearly lost in the hurricane, which caused the *Punjaub* to be sent in search of the missing *Queen.—Bombay Times, May 6th.*

The *Punjaub* has, we observe, been sent in quest of the *Queen* Steamer. The arrangement is a judicious and humane one, and the case is one in which no time should be lost so long as there is hope of succour. The apprehension we presume is, that the *Queen* may have been driven out of her course and wrecked, or that she may be still drifting about at sea disabled. If able to turn and run down the wind, she would probably reach Aden in safety, the heaviest of the gale being from N.E., although it seems to have had all the character of a true circling storm. If wrecked, her remains will probably be found on the Arabian Coast, the track at this season from Aden being nearly a direct one. It is quite possible that she may have been disabled in her engines and rigging. The *Punjaub* may gain tidings of her from native craft, and so be able to render her assistance. It is seldom we have a gale of so much violence, the influence of which extends to so short a distance beyond the sphere of its occurrence. The *Malta's* Barometer, which does not seem to be a very good one, stood at 29·62 at 4 P.M. on the 18th, and had risen again to 29·63 by 10 P.M. on the 19th ; the first hour being that of the minimum, the second that of the maximum. At 5 A.M. at the latter of these dates, when the wind was at its wildest, it had sunk to 29·24, or by nearly four-tenths of an inch, a long plunge in twelve hours from one minimum to another. At Bombay betwixt the 17th and 19th, the mercury only fell by seven hundredth parts of an inch, and there was nothing in the sky to indicate that a tempest was passing probably within seven hundred miles of us. There comes to be a possibility, therefore, that the *Queen* may either have escaped it, or experienced it in much less violence than the *Malta.* This is the second time within the past seven months, that we have had distinct and well pronounced cyclones developing themselves in the Arabian Sea betwixt the 54th and 56th meridians, and which scarcely seem to have extended over ten square degrees in all.—*Bombay Times, May 1st.*

[The *Queen* managed to return to Aden in safety. Her log would be valuable.]

BAY OF BENGAL.—14*th May* 1856.—From the vast area over which this gale prevailed—from 10° to 24° N.—I have little doubt of its having been a Cyclone. The information possessed regarding it is so scanty, that it gives us no sufficient grounds for computing its elements. I give the extracts I cut out of the newspapers at the time, as I find them in my note-book:—

THE GALE.—The hurricane we had last night has done considerable damage, though fortunately the loss of life has not been great. Some 70 or 80 country boats have been destroyed, and three men have been reported to have met with a watery grave. A large number of the poor natives have been left without a home, some 900 thatched huts having come down in three divisions of the town. A lady very narrowly escaped being buried under the ruins of a pucka house in Zigzag lane; she left the house just five minutes before it was levelled with the ground. The Police removed a carriage from the Serpentine tank, and have not up to the present time heard anything about the driver or the horse; the harness, which was in tatters, was found lying near the vehicle. Three ships got adrift near the Bankshall, and were seen going down with the stream in company, and they were entangled in such a way that it was with some difficulty they were freed. A vessel off Coolie Bazar reported she was sinking, but somehow or another managed to keep her head above water till she received assistance, and was all right again. Two large up-country boats, laden with coal, belonging to the Coal Company, sank, and the dandies had a very narrow escape of being drowned.

Meteorological Observations taken at the Surveyor General's Office, Calcutta, during a gale which occurred on the evening of the 14th May 1856.

Time.	Barometer unreduced.	Attached Thermr.	Dry Bulb Thermr.	Wet Bulb. Thermr.	Direction of Wind.
P. M.	Inches.	Deg.	Deg.	Deg.	
6 0	29·720	92·0	90·0	82·6	S.E.
7 0	·874	88·0	84·0	74·8	E.
10	·886	85·4	71·0	68·4	N.N.W.
20	·862	81·4	69·2	68·0	N.N.W.
30	·867	77·5	71·4	70·2	N.
40	·845	74·8	73·1	71·9	N.
50	·797	75·0	74·6	72·5	N.E.
8 0	·783	75·2	75·5	73·5	N.E.
10	·778	75·4	76·2	74·2	N.E.
20	·756	75·8	77·1	74·4	N.E.
30	·734	76·0	77·5	74·7	N.E.
40	·752	76·2	77·5	75·3	· N.E.

5 g

The direction of the wind was S.E. till little before 7 P.M., at which hour it suddenly veered to E., which was the commencement of the gale. The gale blew for 25 minutes; during which time, and also for 25 minutes afterwards, there was much rain and lightning, and an incessant fall of hailstones,—the total fall of rain being 2 inches.

This is the most violent gale that has occurred this year, and in general characteristics it very much resembles that which happened on the 14th May 1852.

RADHANATH SIKHDHAR,
In charge of the Observatory.

—*Ibid.*]

MADRAS SQUALLY WEATHER.—Madras was favoured yesterday morning with squally weather, and some heavy showers,—very acceptable relief to her previous dryness. Appearances threatened more than we realized, but we must be thankful for what we got; which is, we think, less than we may anticipate the reception of, during the present month of May. The banking up of clouds to the Eastward, and the frequent play of lightning, led us on Thursday night to anticipate what followed. There is every probability of our hearing of heavy rain inland. We understand that both wind and rain have visited, to a large extent, the Nellore district, and the volume of surcharged clouds that passed over Madras yesterday, without dropping more than a fraction of their contents, give sure promise of a benefit elsewhere.—*Spectator, May 17th.*

CHINA SEAS, 18*th October* 1856.—The Typhoon of the 18th October 1856, in which the *Malta* and *Shanghai* were involved, was a true revolving gale, marked by all the customary characteristics of such storms. The logs of the two steamers, like all those of the P. and O. Company's ships, are beautifully kept; they give us nearly all that is wanted in reference to the centre of the gale. Observations, from a greater number of points, and more extended time and space, are requisite to determine its sweep.

THE CHINA SEA.—A TYPHOON.—The P. & O. Co.'s steam-ships *Malta* and *Shanghai* experienced a typhoon on the 18th October. The former vessel left Hongkong for Singapore at 2 P.M. on the 15th, and the *Shanghai* at 2 P.M. on the 16th.

The Malta.—The first intimation of bad weather on board the *Malta* was at 4 P.M. on the 17th, indicated by the gradual falling of the barometer; the wind blowing from N. to N.N.E., the ship was made snug. At 8 P.M. the barometer had fallen to 29° 25′; the wind from N.E. by N., and the sea rising. The subjoined is an extract of the *Malta's* log on the 18th:—

Hours.	K.	P.	Courses.	Winds.	Bar.	Sun.	Ther.	Remarks, Saturday, October 18th, 1856. C. T.
								A.M.
1	7	4	South	N E b N	29·18	29·20	81	0 30. Hard squalls with rain; and squalls increasing in violence, with lightning at S.W. to North.
2	7	4	....		15	....	..	2 30. From the regular fall of the Barometer, prepared for a Typhoon.
	3			to				2 45. Put the ship's head round to stem the wind and sea, which had greatly increased. Eased the engines; ship labouring heavily.
3	2	..	NNE	N b W	11	....	..	3. Wind hauling round to westward, convinced us the storm was travelling to the northward of our position.
			to					The heavy sea not admitting of our running, kept
4	1	..	North	N W b W	05	29·16	82	the ship's head to the wind and sea as much as possible; ship behaving well.
5	1	..	NNE	N W	05			Strong gale with heavy gusts; ship labouring heavily and taking a great deal of water on board.
6	1	..	N E b N	....	28·98	....	..	6. Sudden shift of wind to the W. Squalls increasing in violence. Barometer very low.
7	1	4	NNW	West	98			
8	1	4	West	W b N	99	29·00	82½	8. Do. W.
9	1	..		WSW	29·05	....	..	9. Gale increasing in violence, heavy cross sea and incessant rain. Barometer rising.
			to					
10	1	..	SW	....	11	....	..	10. Put the ship's head to the S.W.; increased the speed as much as possible; ship labouring, and shipping much water.
11	1	..	S b E	SW	17	....	..	Between 10 and 12 wind very violent; more so after rise of Barometer, and the shift of wind to S.W.
			·to					
12	1	..	S E b S	....	21	29·23	80	Noon. Violent gale, heavy rain and sea.
1	3	..	S ½ E	SW				**P. M.**
2	3	..	....	....	....	....	..	2. Wind decreasing, and sea going down. Barometer rising.
3	3							*(continued)*

Hours.	K.	F.	Courses.	Winds.	Bar.	Sun.	Ther.	Remarks, Saturday, October 18th, 1856. C. T.
								P. M.
4	4	0	....	....	29·26	29·32	82	4. Every appearance of better weather. Set on full speed, the wind having travelled from N. E. to West and round to South during the gale.
5	4	2	....	South	....	....	..	Sunset. Fresh breeze and cloudy ; sea going down.
6	4	2						
7	5	6						
8	3	..	....	....	29·31	29·36	84	8. Moderate breeze with a calm sea.
9	5	4	South	S b W				
10	5	4						
11	5	4						
12	5	4	....	....	29·41	29·38	83	Midnight. Moderate breeze and fine clear weather.

The Shanghai.—At noon on the 17th, the barometer had fallen $\frac{10}{100}$ths since leaving Hongkong, and was gradually falling throughout the night. Captain Roskell did not consider there was much cause for alarm, as there were none of the ordinary phenomena presaging a typhoon, except the gradual sinking of the mercury in the barometer tube. On the 18th all doubt was removed. Captain Roskell says :—

"It was not until the 18th, at 9 A.M., with the barometer at 29° 66′, and the wind beginning to veer more northerly, that a typhoon was apprehended ; the squalls were more frequent, and the ship was made snug. At 10½ A.M., the engines were eased, and the ship's head brought to the westward, in order to ascertain the veering of the wind and the bearing of the centre of the cyclone. At 11½ hrs. the wind was veering N. and N.N.W., and inclining more westerly. I now felt satisfied that the vortex bore north-east, and was passing rapidly to the northward of our position. At the full power of steam I ran to the southward, so as to increase our distance from the centre. At 2 P.M., the barometer stood at 29·20 ; the wind had now veered to the S.W., blowing in terrific gusts, with a very confused sea, and the ship laying E. to E. by S. In running to the southward at full speed, I endeavoured to clear Triton's Bank, bearing E. distant 40 miles, and soon run out of the typhoon circle ; but by 2 P.M. the wind had veered to the S.W., and to avoid Triton's Bank the steam was slackened to dead-slow : hove the ship to on the port tack with her head to the westward, the vortex then bearing N.W. In wearing ship the sea did considerable damage, causing loss of head rails and knees, starboard cutter, and part of the port bulwarks. The masts were uninjured, but the lower rigging was strained considerably, and the tack seams opened by the straining of the ship.

It is a well-established fact, that during the month of October the typhoon tracts are from between N. 12 deg. E., and S. 45 deg. E., to the S. by Westward and N. Westward (Pid. II. B. p. 40). Both the *Malta* and *Shanghai* came down inside the Paracels instead of outside, and were therefore exposed to the dangers of that wide-spread group, where so many vessels have perished; and both vessels were crippled on their endeavours to run from the centre of the cyclone, in consequence of the proximity of Triton's Shoal. Under the circumstances, Captain Roskell did the best thing possible, namely, running at full speed to the southward, and thereby endeavouring to remove his ship as far from the vortex as possible. We cannot say so much for the *Malta*, which vessel literally followed up the cyclone; and if she had steamed some twelve knots per hour, she would, in all probability, have been near the vortex. For example, at 4 A.M. on the 18th, according to the *Malta's* log, the wind was from N.W. by W., which would give the centre bearing N.E. by N., yet the *Malta's* course is N.; at 5 A.M. the wind is stated to be N.W. so that the centre must have been N.E., yet the *Malta's* course is set down at N.N.E.; again at 7 A.M. the wind is stated to be a strong gale with heavy gusts from West, so that the centre bore about North, the *Malta* being kept in a N.N.W. course. *To run to the Southward at full speed was the only safe course;* owing to the proximity of Triton's Shoal and the Paracels, no easting would be safe without an observation. The bearing of the centre of a cyclone can be readily ascertained by a reference to the table given at page 68 of Piddington's Horn-Book of Storms, or by the use of the horn-card itself, which simple contrivance may be placed on the chart, and all the surrounding dangers be seen at a glance.

The *Lightning* and *Fiery Cross*, which vessels left Hongkong on the 18th, experienced a heavy sea, but moderate weather. These vessels came down outside the Paracels.—*Ibid.*

BAY OF BENGAL.—*November 18th to 21st.*—LAT. 5° TO 20° N.— This Cyclone seems, even from the information possessed of it, to have been very well defined. It travelled northwards, and was felt in its strength on the 18th, at Lat. 5°; and at Lat. 14° on the 20th.

EXTRACT FROM THE LOG OF THE BARQUE "FANNY," CAPTAIN J. MIDDLETON, FROM MASULIPATAM TO VIZAGAPATAM, 19th *November*, 1856.— P. M. Strong N.E. breeze, with heavy squalls and rain; every appearance of an approaching gale; close reefed the topsails and courses, and set them. Vessel labouring heavily, straining and making more water than usual; secured everything about decks; and pumps constantly going.

Midnight. N.E., gale increasing; in fore-topsail and courses and spanker; split main-trysail into shreds; with much difficulty secured it; bent a fore-topmast staysail, for a mizen staystail, and brought ship to, under a close-reefed maintopsail, mizen staysail, and foretopmast staysail. Vessel labouring very heavily, and plunging bows under; also shipping much water. Hands up all night securing yards, sails, &c., aloft and about deck. Brought to on the port tack, head to the S.

20th *November*.—A.M. Terrific squalls, and heavy rain, with every appearance of a continuation. Found the lee pump choked with sand, through the water rushing over the stern on to it, and washing it to the pump. On account of the ship having made more water than usual, and the pump constantly going, the chief officer and second with a gang clearing away the bales of tobacco on top, which were found to be thoroughly damaged and saturated by salt-water; also to clear a passage to the pumps. Hands employed in the meantime baling out with buckets. Vessel still labouring heavily, and making much water, owing to the severity of the weather, and the heavy sea. Violent gusts of wind during the frightful squalls and rain, throwing her at times nearly on her beams. Lascars unable to exertion, and have to drive them to perform the necessary duties on deck. Serang and Tindals perfectly useless, having been up the previous night. Deemed it necessary to put her on the other tack, to keep the port-pump going. Wore ship to the N., and set on the pump without intermission till midnight. Found also that a good deal of the cargo forward had shifted, owing to the heavy lurchings, which at times were frightful. Put rolling tackles on the yards, and preventer weather-braces to main-topsail and main-yard.

9. Set the reefed foresail and foot of the mizen, as it appeared to moderate for a short time. Midnight. Compelled to take in the foresail; the mizen spars carried away, and brought the gaff down on deck with the boom. Employed securing them for the night. No appearance of the gale abating, but raging more furiously.

Sun at Noon indifferently obtained, Lat. 14° 3′ N., Long., by account, allowing for a S.W. course, 6 points leeway, 82° E. Course S.W. 50 miles.

21st November.—A.M. Continuation of heavy gales, accompanied with violent squalls. Terrific gusts of wind and a tremendous heavy sea. Vessel at times on her beam ends, and labouring heavily; shipping heavy seas; dismal gloomy appearance all around.

Daylight. Hoisted out one of the pumps to endeavour to clear the well, but without avail; set hands on at both hatches with buckets, to bale out, having tried to put the pump down the main hatchway, but to no purpose, the sand continually choking the pump.

Noon. Compelled to clew up the main-topsail, and fore-topmast staysail through the violence of the incessant squalls.

Lat. indifferently obtained, 15° 9′ N.

Long., by account, 81° 23′ East.

Course N.W. 50 miles.

Ship heading during the last 17 hours N.N.E., allowing 8 points leeway. Winds from E. to S.E. Continuation of the hurricane ; hands employed the whole of the time baling with buckets, as the pumps were rendered useless ; carried away two standing main shrouds, starboard side, and split mizen staysail, sea still raging high, causing the vessel to lurch heavily ; an appearance of the gale moderating, set close-reefed mizen topsail and fore-top mizen staysail.

8. Set reefed courses. Unable to set fore-topsail, as it had been split at the commencement of the gale.

Midnight. Light squall with rain ; hands all night at the pumps.

C. BIDEN.

Master Attendant, Vizagapatam.

Memo. of Vessels in this Roadstead put to Sea.

Nov. 7	Chieftain	at 9.30 P.M.
„ „	Laidmans	„ 9.30 „
„ „	Castle Eden	„ Midnight.
„ 8	Chieftain	„ 2 A.M.
„ „	Minerva	„ 3.15 P.M.
„ „	Canada	„ 4 P.M.
„ „	Stamboul	„ 4. 7 P.M.
„ „	H. C. Steamer Coromandel	„ 4.10 P.M.
„ „	Sir Robert Sale	„ 4.12 P.M.
„ „	Thetis	„ 4.13 P.M.
„ „	Victory	„ 4.15 P.M.
„ „	Bengal	„ 4.30 P.M.
„ „	Nonpareil	„ 4.48 P.M.

The first burst of the Madras monsoon appears to have been attended by a cyclone. On the 19th, 20th, and 21st, more especially on the day last named, it blew with extreme violence, the wind veering round to N.N.W., and then suddenly to N.N.E. We have not as yet been favoured with the state of the Barometer. We mentioned in our last Saturday's issue that the mornings had all at once become cloudy upon us, and the mercury irregular, and this state of matters corresponded, in point of date, with the commencement of the Madras disturbance. From the 1st of the month, when our customary gun-powder plot perturbations occurred, we had a great atmospheric wave rising upon us, the crest of which seemed to have passed over us about the 11th; the mercury, during the day preceding and following, being extraordinarily high. It seemed as if travelling eastward; the crest passing over Poona on the 16th; we have as yet no returns beyond this. The descent due to the present gale commenced here on the 19th, and probably reached its maximum on the 22nd—we have no readings for the 23rd,—but on Sunday morning we had the wind from south-east,—a very unusual direction for this season,— blowing fresh from dawn till long past noon. The weather became settled on Monday; and by this date we have no doubt the Madras gale has blown itself out. The idea that the Coromandel monsoon materially affects the weather here, though generally prevalent, is a delusion, as may be seen by a comparison of the registers of the two Presidencies. Our Elephanta is a purely local gale, experienced over a very limited area—we are ashamed to say—of unknown limits. The first week of November presents us with disturbances of a class peculiar to themselves; and it is the hurricane, not the monsoon portion of the Madras gale, that has made its appearance at Bombay.—*Bombay Times, November.*

NELLORE.—We learn from Nellore that the late gale was experienced in that locality on Thursday last (20th). The glasses began to fall from nearly "fair" early in the morning, and the gale commenced about midday, the wind blowing from N.N.E. The next morning the Aneroid was below "damp." Shortly after daylight the wind veered round to the north-west and then to the west. It blew hardest about midday. The Aneroid by 1 P.M. was below "rain," when it began to rise rapidly. The other barometer was not so greatly affected. Between noon on Thursday and an early hour the next morning, 8 inches of rain fell. A great many of the largest trees were blown down. About 1 P.M. (Friday) the wind began to go round to the south-west and the south. Between 3 and 4 P.M. it had comparatively gone down ; and by 5 P.M. the rain ceased. About 4 inches of rain fell up to that hour from about 6 A.M. There has been a sad destruction of trees, old and young. At the date of our correspondent's letter (22nd) there had been no tappals at Nellore later than the 18th instant.—*Ibid.*

SHIPPING INTELLIGENCE.—The ship *Chieftain*, from London to Madras, experienced severe weather on the 18th instant between Lat. 5° and 6° North, and Long. 87° East. Barometer falling, P.M., wind veering from N.W. to West and S.S.W. with rain, then backing to S.E. by S., and keeping steady at S.E. by E. until the 20th ; at noon, shipped heavy seas. Apprehensive of worse weather near land, kept away S.E., hauling to the Eastward as the wind veered to the Westward for several hours, and then steered due North ; and at noon on the 19th, observed in Lat. 9° 41' N., Long. 87° 49' E.

On the 20th, had some hard squalls, much rain, and lightning ; ship making much water.

On the 21st fresh breeze, A.M., blowing hard with a tremendous sea, ship rolling fearfully and pitching bows under ; wind S.E. to South. Wore ship at 8 A.M., and stood E. by N. ½ N. till noon. Barometer 29·77. At noon, Lat. 12° 55' N. Long. 85° 48' E.

From 21st, moderate winds from the Southwards, and fine weather.

Anchored in the Madras Roads on the 24th. Barometer 29·95.—*Ibid.*

To the Editor of the Spectator.

MR. EDITOR.—In continuation of my hasty communication of yesterday's date, I have now the satisfaction to state that, from the direction of the wind since the fleet shipped and put to sea, they must have escaped the perils of being driven on a lee shore. I have obtained the following information from the Observatory :—

The wind at 11 A.M. yesterday, was nearly due North, and between 1 and 2 P.M. from North to N.N.E., and from 2 till the present time (3-30 P.M.) tending rather westerly, so that the ships will be able to make a good offing. The highest pressure has been about 13 lbs., which was in one gust about 3 o'clock.

From daylight until the shipping slipped cables, they were more or less riding heavily and labouring much ; but the *Stamboul*, the outermost ship, had not drifted, and rode with the greatest ease.

2 P.M. (Friday). I can now relate, from information just received from the Observatory, that from 4 P.M. until 2 A.M. the gale was pretty steady from N.N.E. to nearly N.E. ; after that, it backed to the Northward ; and between 5 and 6 until now, about N.N.W. to N.W. ; force not exceeding 12 lbs., and that only in occasional gusts, until 4 A.M., when it blew a gale until 5-15 ; force nearly reaching 20 lbs. ; since that time gradually moderating.

Barometer began to rise at the usual time before 4 A.M. ; and continues to rise yet, though usually falling at this time of day, and is now 0·29 above the lowest point which was 29·54.

Total fall of rain this month up to 6 A.M. 16·76 inches, of which 6·22 inches fell last night.

From the fearfully high rollers which broke with such force and irregularity to nearly 8 fathoms, any ship in these roads at 3 P.M., when the gale was blowing in heavy gusts, would have been in imminent peril, and still more endangered when the gale veered from N.N.E. to N.E., and reached the great pressure of 20 lbs.

I sincerely hope no ship has suffered any serious accident, and that all are in perfect safety; and that approaching fine weather will soon restore them to their respective anchorages, when every exertion shall be used to recover their anchors and cables.

Hoisting the Red Flag with a swallow's tail as the well known signal to "Cut or slip and run to sea," is a determination involving great responsibility on all sides. But when any reasonable person considers that ships at anchor in these roads may suddenly be placed upon a dead lee shore, and at the mercy of wind and sea, they would never hesitate, when the weather is suspicious, to avail themselves of a favourable opportunity to cut and run into where sea-room will place them, under the blessings of Providence, in perfect safety.

The sea is now remarkably smooth, and surf very moderate.

CHRIS. BIDEN.

Master Attendant's Office, Madras,
    21st Nov. 1856, 4 P.M.

Such a glorious downpour of rain as we have had in the day and night of Wednesday and Thursday, has not been known in Madras for years. It was accompanied by a tremendous gale of wind. On Thursday, from 10 to 11 o'clock, guns at intervals of five minutes proclaimed to the vessels in the Roads, that there was no safety for them unless they stood out to sea. Yesterday morning not a vessel was to be seen, and old ocean twisted his wrinkles into a smile as grim as if he had swallowed them all up. Trees rooted up by the force of the wind are to be seen on all sides. The island yesterday morning had disappeared, and mud houses of the natives are filtered down in all directions. "From the middle of the night until the noon of Thursday," says the *Spectator*, "Captain Biden, and his Assistant Mr. McKennie, were most indefatigable in the fulfilment of their responsible duties; and we trust that neither of them, more especially the former, will suffer from the effects of his continued exertions in the wet, for, we believe, a period altogether of twelve hours."

Since writing the above, we have been favoured with the following memorandum from the Observatory, by which it will be seen that the fall of rain was something very remarkable indeed :—

MEMO.—Fall of rain, as noted at the H.C. Observatory :—

		Night.	Day.
Nov.	19th	In. 2.70	In. 0.00
,,	20th	6.22	2.56
		8.92	2.56

making a total of 11.48 inches.

The gale attained its greatest force between 4 and 5 A.M. on the 21st, at which time the pressure nearly reached 20 lbs. on the square foot.—*Madras Athenæum, November 22nd.*

G *g*

THE GALE.—We have been favoured with the following account of the shipping during the terrific storm of wind and rain which has been bursting over Madras during the last few days :—

Madras, 22nd November, 6½ P.M.—At daylight on the 20th instant, the signal ' surf impassable' was flying at the Master Attendant's flagstaff, quickly followed by ' veer more cable' to the shipping, as the surf was very high, and the weather assuming a threatening aspect. At 6-20, the *Attist Rahman* parted her cable, and soon was ashore abreast the lighthouse, when a hawser was made fast to the vessel by the labour of the authorities on the beach and their establishment; who also used every exertion in their power in landing the crew, which to their credit was safely effected without loss of life; and the energetic boat overseer Veerasawmy Naick was seen knocking about the beach making himself useful. At 9-45, the signal ' let go another anchor,' was made to the barque *Eleanor,* owing to her being anchored so very close in and rolling very much ; which was replied to by that vessel ' my bower has been parted with.' Immediately after this signal a general one to the shipping was hoisted, ' strike top-gallant masts.' Whilst this was flying, the *Defiance* from the roadstead signalized ' I have no anchor left.' At 11-20, the *Gold Digger* dragged her anchor, and drifted along the shipping, coming in contact with the *Dinah Muloch,* carrying off her own jibboom, causing what damage to that vessel is not known, but apparently little or none.

At 1 P.M. the *Defiance* signalized ' sprung a leak,' and the Master Attendant replied ' keep pumps going.' At about 2-45, the *Eleanor* parted her anchor, but almost immediately let go another and rolled very much ; and at 4-20 she signalized ' I have one anchor and 40 fathoms cable :' the Master Attendant replied, ' spring on the cable and put to sea.' It was accordingly obeyed by her at 4-50, when she put to sea quite clear of the shipping ; and at 5 the *Gold Digger* was seen to have put to sea, as she lay very close in, and not in a favourable position.

The authorities on the beach remained and were on the look out the whole night, and even on Sunday attending to what was requisite. During Saturday night, two vessels appeared to have parted their anchors and consequently put to sea, causing what damage to the shipping is not known.

At daylight on Sunday (the 21st), three vessels were found missing in the road-stead, viz., *Aberfoyle, Defiance,* and *Cleveland.* At this time the Master Attendant's flagstaff displayed " surf impassable." At 6-30, the *Gallant Neil* signalized ' I have been run on board by a vessel :' as the Captain was at this time present at the Master Attendant's Office he signalized ' Have you received much damage ?' which was answered ' Have carried away my foreyard.' At 7, the *Britannia's* Captain signalized, ' Is all right ?' which was answered ' Yes.' At 7-40 the Master Attendant signalized to the *Negotiator,* ' What cable out ?' answered, ' I have abundance.' At 8-30, also signalized the same query to the *Beatrice,* which vessel replied ' 90 fathoms cable.' At 9-25, the Captain of the *City of Durham* signalized the following to questions ' What cable out ?'—' Is all right ?' answered ' I have abundance'— ' Yes.' At 10-20, the barque *Madras* drifted, and a few minutes afterwards she sprang on her cable and put to sea. At 11-30, Capt. Farley (Commander of the *Gallant Neil*) signalized ' when damage is repaired put to sea.' She answered ' I have only part of a cask of water left.' At 12, the *Chieftain* (which considerably dragged herself since the night of the 20th) put to sea.—*Athenæum, 24th Nov.*

The air continues moist and heavy, the clouds obviously charged with electricity. We have magnificent exhibitions of thunder-cloud over the ghauts just before sunset, with displays of sheet lightning immediately after dark.   Throughout yesterday the air possessed that extraordinary degree of transparency which usually attends on thorough saturation.   The Mahabuleshwur hills were beautifully distinct and clear, and it was difficult to be believe Matheran much further off than Elephanta usually seems.—*Bombay Standard, November 26th.*

The weather has, for the past four days, assumed an unusual appearance for the end of November; had it been as it is now, in the beginning of the month, it would have been highly orthodox.   Since Saturday we have had a cloudy sky, despite the principle laid down by Sir John Herschell that the full moon is remarkable for the transparency of the atmosphere.   The barometer has been falling, and the thermometer rising.   The minimum yesterday morning was 76°, the minima of the most of the previous week having been 68°.   The air for 18 hours was in a state of almost absolute stagnation, and so damp that the difference betwixt the wet and dry bulb only amounted to 6 instead of 12 to 14, the previous depression.   The sky all yesterday was covered with clouds, with showers flying about in all directions.—*Bombay Standard, November 24th.*

Off Chusan, and Northern China Seas.—*September 4th and 6th,* 1857.

"No sooner had I got on board, than the breeze became a gale, and the misty rain a driving storm.   Then rose the tempest—a tempest such as the China Seas only can show.   It lasted all night, and the next day, and the next.   During a momentary pause we saw through one of the narrow islet channels a large screw-steamer, carrying her funnel abaft her mainmast, struggling down under the mainland.   Some one has since said it was the *Durance,* French transport, and that she grounded at the height of the typhoon.   The " Shanghai Shipping List" afterwards repeated this latter report.   It may be so, but I doubt it.   I believe it was the same steamer I saw two days later in company with the *Capricieuse,* frigate, off Lookong.   She might be the *Durance ;* but we did not make her out to be aground, or any otherwise in "durance vile."   Whatever she was, however, she passed like a spirit on this hurricane.   Outside, the typhoon was sweeping the seas and ravaging the coasts.   It drove the light ship at the mouth of the Yang-tse-Kiang from her moorings, it strewed the junks about in pieces of floating wreck, it broke down walls, it cast away a three-masted English ship, and lifted a schooner over the sand of the south bank, and deposited her in the paddy-fields.   It damned up the waters of Wang-poo and the Yung; and here, in this bay of Chusan, it put junks adrift and bands of wreckers upon the alert.   The *Rosina* had ground-tackle made for such emergencies.   She drifted at first, but her second anchor brought her up.   We were, fortunately, in the best harbour on the coast of China. After this experience I have a right to speak well of the harbour of Chusan.

"On the night of the third day we sailed forth with a moderate wind and a bright moonlight."

*　　　　*　　　　*　　　　*　　　　*　　　　*

"Every day elapsed since the occurrence of the typhoon has brought tidings of some disaster occasioned by it. Sir Frederick Nicholson, of the *Pique* frigate, has occupied himself with the phenomena of this storm. He says,—

"'Commencing with the log of the *Antonita*, a three-masted schooner, under Buenos-Ayrean colours, we find that she rode out the gale at anchor. On the 3rd of September, she was under the island of Chinki; finding, however, that a heavy sea rolled into this anchorage, she weighed, and bore up for Lotsin Bay, where she rode out the remainder of the gale. It is evident that this vessel was in the northern semi-circle of the cyclone, for the wind gradually veered round from N.E. to E.N.E., then to E., and finally to E.S.E., as the gale moderated.

"'If we now turn to the *Lanrick's* log we shall find that she was nearly at the southern limit of the cyclone. On the 4th of September, at noon, she was in lat. 24° 54' N., long 119° 47' E., 67 miles south of the White Dogs, the well-known islands at the entrance of the river Min, and about 220 miles south of the *Antonita* in Lotsin Bay.

"'The *Lanrick's* log on September the 4th notes a strong gale from W.N.W. to W.S.W., veering eventually to S.W. These winds from opposite directions experienced by the two vessels, afford a convincing proof that the centre of the cyclone passed between them,—a fact we are enabled to verify by the log of the *Water Witch*. This vessel had the singular good fortune of escaping with comparatively slight damage, after passing through the vortex of this severe cyclone. Her commander, Captain Baker, places the centre, at midnight, September the 3rd, in lat. 26° 12' N., long. 122° 18' E. It bears N.E. by E. 160 miles from the *Lanrick's* position at noon on September the 4th; a position differing but little from her place at midnight; and from the *Antonita* the centre bears S.E. by S. 130 miles.

"'Most striking are the phenomena noted in the log of the *Water Witch* and in the account of the gale received from the Peninsular and Oriental Company's steamer *Cadiz*, which vessel steered into the centre of the cyclone, while endeavouring to get an offing in the neighbourhood of the White Dogs.

"'The hurricane blowing from the north suddenly ceases, and gives place to a dead calm, lasting for a quarter of an hour. The sky is clear overhead, and the stars are seen shining brightly, while all around is gloom and darkness. Birds, and even fishes, are dropping and tumbling about the decks in great numbers. The tumultuous sea breaks in all directions, sweeping over the ship from end to end. After a brief interval of treacherous calm, the hurricane again bursts forth from the south with redoubled fury. All these are well-known symptoms of being in the vortex of a rotatory storm.

"'On the 3rd of September, while the *Banshee* was at some distance from the southward of the most severe portion of this gale, 'a tremendously heavy swell from the E.S.E.' is noted in her log.   On the 5th of September she fell in with the Siamese ship *Friendship*, which had been dismasted in the gale.   The position of the centre for midnight on the 3rd of September then bore S.S.E. 60 miles.

" ' The log of the *Friendship* will no doubt prove that vessel to have been dismasted not far from the vortex of the cyclone.

" ' The French ship *Mansart* met the cyclone between the north end of Formosa and the island of Kumi in the evening of September the 2nd.   Finding the gale rapidly freshening from N.W., Captain Gravereau bore up for shelter under the Meiaco Islands.   After having in vain attempted to heave to, the *Mansart* continued scudding with the wind right aft, gradually altering course as the gale veered round from N.W. to W., and finally to S.W.   This vessel thus sailed round the southern portion of the cyclone, and passed out to the northward between the Meiaco and Loochoo islands, when the wind had moderated, and was blowing from S.E.   The *Mansart's* log shows the gale to have been at its height on the afternoon of September 3rd; the wind was then S.W., and the centre, as fixed by Captain Baker, of the *Water Witch*, bore N.W. by W. 220 miles.

" ' Captain Gravereau describes both wind and sea as terrific, his crew were constantly at the pumps, and he was obliged to throw overboard a portion of the cargo to save his vessel from foundering.

" ' The intelligence from Tamsui, at the N.E. corner of Formosa, announces the loss of several vessels.   Exposed as that anchorage must have been to the whole fury of the worst portion of the cyclone, the centre of which must have passed within a very moderate distance of Tamsui, it is not surprising to hear that serious disasters have occurred at that place.

" ' At Foochow the gale was felt in all its severity.   A number of the houses were unroofed, but we do not hear of any serious damage having been done to the shipping in the river Min.   On the 4th of September, when the gale was at its height, the wind is stated to have been N.W.; and on the 5th of September, the gale having moderated and the barometer having commenced rising, the wind is reported as S.E.   Hence it is probable that the centre passed very nearly over Foochow.   Three barometers are said to have fallen to 28·85, 28·30, and 28·40 respectively.

" ' The gale was not felt at Amoy.' "

" The most important lesson to be derived from this storm is the relative safety of the harbours of China.   While I was riding it out in Chusan harbour in a little vessel of Chinese rig, square-rigged vessels were being torn from their anchorage in the so-called harbours of Formosa, dashed to pieces, and all their crews drowned."—*G. W. Cooke's " China."*

IN CHINA SEA.—*30th September* 1857.—The following is the only notice on which I can at present lay my hands of the hurricane betwixt Hongkong and Singapore of the 30th September.   I have no doubt the Straits papers of the day contain abundance of information, but I have none of them to refer to.

"This was an action brought by Messrs. Gladstone, Wyllie, and Co., to recover Rs. 17,500 as for a total loss upon a policy of assurance, dated 24th September 1857, granted by the defendants upon the half block of the ship *Albion*, of 535 tons burden. The risk was for six months certain, commencing from the 21st September 1857, and the amount was payable in case of a total loss, but free from particular average.

" From the evidence, it appeared that the vessel sailed, on the 28th September 1857, from Hongkong on a voyage to Singapore; and whilst on her voyage met with a typhoon on the 30th September, which so disabled her, as to prevent a prosecution of that voyage, and compelled her to put into Manilla as the nearest port, where she arrived on the 23rd October."

OFF CEYLON, AND IN THE BAY OF BENGAL.—*28th October* 1857.— The only information I possess in reference to this gale is the following scrap in reference to the H.C.S. *Auckland*, 25th October. I was not aware whether it was a revolving gale or not.

NARROW ESCAPE OF THE STEAMER "AUCKLAND," WITH THE 37TH ON BOARD.—We regret to learn that three days after leaving Trincomalie, the *Auckland*, with the detachment of the 37th on board, was caught in a severe cyclone. But for a knowledge of the laws of storms on the part of the first lieutenant, and the consequent change of course and a run of 60 miles out of the influence of the storm, it is supposed the steamer must have foundered. As it was, great danger and frightful discomfort were undergone. The soldiers were, of course, on deck all the time, exposed to the fury of the elements, rain falling incessantly for three days. One soldier had his leg smashed, and the collar bone of another was broken. Mrs. Dames, and the other ladies on board, were forced to go on deck in the midst of the storm, to escape suffocation. Indeed, the water came pouring in below, through the closed hatches and ports. The damage to property was great; Mrs. Dames alone losing to the extent of £150. Mrs. Dames suffered from fever for some days after her arrival at Calcutta. Colonel Dames, we are glad to learn, was well at Ghazeepore, and by issuing tea to his men when on night duty, kept them in good health. Dr. Fleming had so far recovered, that he had given up his intention of going to England.—*Colombo Observer, Nov.* 19th, 1857.

[The *Auckland* reached Calcutta on the 7th of November. She left Colombo with Detachment of H. M's. 37th on the 25th October, and encountered the Hurricane on the 28th.]

CHINA SEAS.—*29th October, and from 5th September to* 12th *November* 1857. The China Seas seem to have been scourged by a series of violent gales betwixt the 5th September and 30th October. We have not information enough to prove whether or not they were revolving. The ship *Waverley* was about the middle of October (precise date not given) wrecked at the north of Formosa, bound from Shanghai to Swatow. The *Louisa Baillie* experienced heavy gales betwixt the 29th and 31st October in Lat. 12° N., Long. 119° E. :—I have no doubt the same as those which proved fatal to the *Waverley*. Betwixt the 5th and 16th November, the *Trafalgar* was nearly lost, somewhere to the north eastward of Hongkong (exact position not given). A second gale overtook her about a week afterwards near the same place, and drove her back to Hongkong. Betwixt the 12th and 16th November, the ship *Hamilton* experienced a violent hurricane, about Lat. 21° N. and Long. 142° E., and was compelled to bear up for Hongkong. Even from the meagre notice given from the Hongkong Register there can be no doubt that this was a genuine Cyclone ; and I have little doubt that the whole series of facts prevailing in the same, for nearly six weeks on end, were connected with each other,—probably a group of whirlwinds. There must be still abundance of information in existence to make out the fact.

The *Louisa Baillie* had very heavy weather on 29th October, which continued to the 31st, in Long. 119° E., and Lat. 12° 30′ N. Wind from N., varying to South, which obliged the Captain to put into Manilla in distress. Discovered a leak to be above the water line ; he caulked and started again on the 11th, with a strong N.E. wind ; and had to lay the ship to, under close-reefed main-topsail and main-trysail for 36 hours.

The American ship *Intrepid*, Captain Gardner, reports having fallen in with the British ship *Waverley*, off the north end of Formosa, from Shanghai bound to Swatow, water logged. The *Waverley* left that port with about 500 Chinese soldiers— 350 of whom, with the crew, had been taken off by some vessel (unknown) ; the remainder have been brought here by Captain Gardner, who set fire to the *Waverley* before leaving her.—*Hongkong Register, 25th November* 1857.

The *Trafalgar* experienced a series of heavy gales, commencing on the 5th instant, in 16° N., when she carried away the port bulwarks—wind from the N.E. and N., with a terrific sea running, which lasted for several days. On the 13th, shipped a heavy sea which stove in part of the front of the poop, and filled the lee cabins with water, and damaged a great quantity of stores. During the gale, the cargo shifted, which gave the ship a considerable list to port. She was within 40 miles of Hongkong, when she met another gale with head wind, which drove her back 6 degrees. She arrived in Hongkong this morning.

The *Hamilton* encountered a heavy gale of wind on the 12th instant and four following days, in Lat. 21° 27′ N., Long. 142° 11′ E.—The wind increased towards morning. On the 13th it blew a terrific gale from the N.E., with a very high sea, the ship labouring very much, which caused the ship to spring a leak, was obliged to cut away the fore, main, and mizen topmasts and flying jibboom to ease her. The water increased so rapidly on her, that she had 7 feet of water in her hold in a very few hours. The crew were kept at the pumps night and day from that time up to her arrival in Hongkong. The men were completely exhausted when they arrived in harbour, water-logged.—*Hongkong Register, 24th November* 1857.

CEYLON.—*November 20th*, 1857.—Just three weeks after the *Auckland* storm, Ceylon was assailed by a hurricane of unusual violence, which proved most disastrous to the shipping. It does not appear from my extracts, whether it was a true Cyclone or merely a violent gale. No mention is made of the shifting of the wind.

CEYLON.—THE STORM.—A fierce storm of wind has blown since Thursday night (20th November), accompanied by heavy and incessant torrents of rain. Rain, indeed, has fallen with little intermission for the last week.

Three Native square-rigged vessels, the *Fattal Louisa*, the *Antelope*, and the *Dolphin* came on shore last night.

The *Mohidian Box* foundered this morning. In these cases we have not heard of any loss of life.

An Arab vessel is in much danger. Some 30 persons have been got off from her, but 4 are still on board. An offer of £5, last night, failed to induce any boatmen to put off.

To-day the wind freshened and shifted to the west. The result was that the *Sibella*, fully laden and ready to sail, was driven on the Galle Buck*, and in one short hour went to pieces. Every possible effort was made to render aid from the shore; the Governor and his son being conspicuous in directing and assisting. Happily the Master Attendant returned from the inspection of the Pearl Banks two days ago, so that the resources of his department were put in full operation. Every attempt to throw a line to the *Sibella*, by means of a mortar, failed; and when she went to pieces, the second mate and a boy, at least, of her crew perished. The survivors, one of whom, we are told, was rescued from the waves by Mr. Ward, are receiving every possible attention from the Governor and others.

We regret to say that the *Tyburnia* and several other large vessels, amongst them the *Fortitude* and *Clara*, and more especially the *Tartar* and *St. Augustine*, which are said to have fouled each other, are in extreme danger, while there is at present no prospect of human aid reaching them. No boat can live in the sea, while all the anchors and cables available in the Master Attendant's Office have been already sent out.

The only ground of hope is that a kind Providence may abate the fury of the wind and sea; or that if any more vessels are wrecked it may be in situations where life at least may be saved.

---

* About 200 yards north of the Lighthouse.

The scene of mingled wreck of ship, boats, coffee, and oil casks, &c., presented all along the Galle Face, is pitiable in the extreme.

We fear we shall have sad accounts of inundation and destruction of property, and even life, from various parts of the country.

God grant that the steamers and transports, with the brave soldiers of England on board, may escape, or safely weather the storm.

Since the above was written, we have heard that the *St. Augustine* is all right, but that the *Cotte d'Or* is in danger. It is the *Tartar* and the *Fortitude* that have fouled each other: the former vessel is in imminent danger. Three lives were lost in the *Sibella*.

P.S.—2 P.M.—The *Tartar*, after signalling for boats and warps, has just made the fatal signal ' Struck !'

¼ to 3.—An offer of £135 has failed to induce a boat to go to her relief. It is heart-rending to feel that there may be but a step between the brave men on board and death. Every inch of chain is out, but the hapless vessel is drifting shorewards.

The *Cotte d'Or* has not yet begun to drift, but she is in a critical position. The *St. Augustine* is said to be drifting.

The Arab barque is on shore at the Custom House.

Beside the three Europeans, two native coolies were drowned in the wreck of the *Sibella*.

Another small Native craft has gone on shore; and the Schooner *Pearl* is within a dozen fathoms of the shore.

The *Geraldine Roche* is in a dangerous position.

The *Clara* and *Fortitude* are reported as in danger of getting entangled.— *Colombo Observer Extraordinary, November 27th.*

The narrative contained in our Extra of Saturday was necessarily fragmentary, but we believe the only marked errors were the statements of vessels getting fouled. No vessels actually fouled, although the signalman at one time reported that the *Fortitude* and *Clara* were in danger of getting entangled. The officer in charge of the *Tartar* did make the signal ' struck !' as stated by us. It turns out, however, that he mistook a more than usually severe jerk for a bump on the bottom. Had the gale not moderated just when it did, nothing, humanly speaking, could have saved this vessel. Next to the *Tartar*, the *Cotte d'Or* was in most danger. The *Augustine*, although she originally drifted into very unpleasant proximity to the sunken rock called " the drunken sailor," latterly held on well. The *Tyburnia*, we understand, was never in any danger. There were nine persons on board the Arab barque during the storm, all of whom have been safely landed. Of the crew of the unfortunate *Sibella*, we learn that four perished, the 2nd and 3rd officers, the carpenter, and a boy. We learn that the first officer, in whose charge the vessel was, possesses the highest certificates of competency. The captain was on shore, for the object, we are told, of hastening the shipment of the small portion of cargo still to be taken on board. One or two boats next morning would have completed the lading ; and the *Sibella*, if she had lived, would have carried away 900 tons of valuable cargo. The coffee is of course irretrievably lost, but about two-thirds of the oil will be saved. This result is mainly due to the unremit-

7 g

ting exertions of Mr. D. Wilson, of the firm of Wilson, Ritchie, and Co., the agents of the *Sibella*. Mr. Wilson with his establishment was at work while daylight lasted on Saturday, and subsequently by torchlight. Of the ship itself we suspect nothing beyond fragments and a few of the sails will be saved. We have heard the total loss estimated at £40,000, and we believe this is below the mark.

As we came in this morning, a body was observed floating, and a canoe was sent out to rescue it. It turned out to be the body of Zachariah Pinkham, the second mate, over which the coroner and his jury are now sitting.

The barometer sank only a tenth during the storm. It commenced rising on Saturday afternoon—the weather immediately moderated. Yesterday was bitterly cold but fine; and to-day it is sunny and cheerful.

The Arab barque is of the burden of 228 tons, and was originally English. She left Singapore in January last. Unable to make Juddah, she landed and sold her cargo at Cochin and Allepee. She arrived here on the 11th with cargo from Cochin, three-fourths of which she had managed to land, and some of which can still be landed. The master is anxious to show that he was not negligent. He had 4 anchors out—2 ahead and 2 astern. The fact of an English ship having been wrecked will, we should think, be his best excuse.

Ever since the wreck, the natives have been busily engaged picking up the coffee berries, saturated as they are with sea water and the worst of abominations.—*Ibid, November 23rd.*

THE LATE STORM AND ITS EFFECTS.—To the Collector of Customs we are indebted for the following list of the casualties at this Port, and at Barberyn, consequent on the storm of Friday and Saturday last;—

COLOMBO.

Sibella, of Sunderland, 721 tons; laden with coffee, oil, &c., for London.

Louisa, of Singapore, 228 tons; laden with sugar, dry-fish, coir yarn, rattan, &c., from Cochin.

Antelope, of Bombay, 82 tons; laden with empty casks for Cochin.

Dolphin, of Ceylon, 156 tons; ballast.

Mohedin Box, of Ceylon, 31 tons; sundries from Tuticoreen.

BARBERYN.

Mercy, of Ceylon, 71 tons; laden with coir and arrack, from Galle to Colombo and Jaffna; wrecked at Barberyn.

Hydroos Pale Letchiny, of Ceylon; laden with copperah, from Galle to Colombo.

Mohedin Pale, of Ceylon; laden with timber, from Batticaloa.

Cader Box, of Ceylon; laden with salt, from Calpentyn.—*Ibid, November 26th.*

BAY OF BENGAL AND ANDAMAN SEA.—*9th and 10th April* 1858.— Betwixt the Ceylon gale of November 1857 and the Andaman hurricane of April 1858, an interval of tranquil weather of unusual duration occurs. At the latter date, a revolving hurricane of great violence visited the Andaman Sea. From the Arracan Cyclone of October 1854 —on which Mr. Piddington wrote his twenty-third memoir—until 1858 our Cyclones were without a historian. That of the latter date was analyzed and described by Dr. Liebig; the memoir appearing in the Transactions of the Bengal Asiatic Society of April. So I am spared the labour of doing more than including it in my list.

THE H. C's. STEAMER "COROMANDEL."—The H. C's. Steamer *Coromandel*, which returned to Madras on Thursday, encountered a Cyclone in the North Preparis Channel on the 9th ultimo, when she fortunately met with no further damage than the loss of her pinnace, and a gun washed overboard with the gunwale. The sea was as heavy and the wind stronger than the Officer on board had ever experienced. The barometer went down seven-tenths of an inch in three hours, its lowest having been 29·20. The *Coromandel* hove to, when the barometer soon rose, and the weather moderated. She reports, however, we are sorry to observe, the loss of the following vessels on the occasion:—The Portuguese Barque *Labuan*, foundered at her anchors off Negrais; all Europeans lost with the Pilot. The Hamburg Ship *Singapore*, a total wreck; all hands saved. The Hamburg Barque *Juno*, driven ashore at Dalhousie; supposed to be totally wrecked. The American Ship *Albert Franklin*, from Calcutta to China, foundered off the Andamans; all hands picked up. The English Brig *Dido*, from Rangoon to the Straits, foundered; all hands lost but one. And finally a Chinese Junk foundered off the Rangoon river.—*Athenæum*.

A CYCLONE IN THE ANDAMAN SEA.—Dr. G. Von Liebig has forwarded through the Home Department a rather voluminous account of a cyclone in the Andaman Sea, which we shall abbreviate. The cyclone to which he refers occurred on the 9th and 10th of April last. He says that he happened to be on board the steam frigate *Semiramis*, which had left Calcutta on the 4th of March for the Andaman Islands and Moulmein, so that he had an opportunity of collecting some information with regard to the gale of the 9th of April, at which period, it may be in the recollection of our readers, the Brig *Dido*, bound from Rangoon, foundered at sea. The gale was a well-defined cyclone, and a publication of what took place may be of importance to those who navigate the Andaman Sea.

Dr. Von Liebig observes that it will be interesting to mark the limits of the region in which the cyclone raged, and the winds that prevailed in those limits before and after it; and points out that the region in which the effects of the storm were felt may be included between the 11° and 19° N. latitude and between the 92° and 98° E. longitude. He has no doubt that it must have extended to the west of 92° E. longitude on the 8th and 9th, but no observations being available, he is unwilling to go beyond that limit; and remarks that in this region the polar current prevailed before the commencement of the gale, as shown by the observations of the *Semiramis*, *Port Blair*, and *Mullah*, before the 7th, and the *Alma* and *Coromandel* of the 8th. On the 7th and 8th, a south-eastern current from the equator first entered the south-eastern quarter of the region between 93° and 95° E. longitude, at a time when, in the eastern half, the polar current still prevailed. The entrance of this equatorial current seems to have introduced the atmospheric disturbance, but the rotary motion was not observed before the 9th and 10th, when the cyclone had been found travelling from S.W. to N.E. He seems to think, from the *Mutlah's* log, that the cyclone took its origin west of the middle Andaman on the 8th ; and mentions that after the cyclone had passed, the prevailing winds in the region were westerly with calms, and at a late period the polar current prevailed again.

To the south-west of the region (latitude 6° 10′ N. " longitude 88° to 90° E." ship *Edwards*) on the 8th and 9th, south-westerly winds prevailed, giving way on the 1st to the polar current.

To the north of the region (*Dalhousie, Calcutta,* and *Sea* and *Cape of Good Hope*) the S.W. sea breeze common to the coast of Bengal and Arracan prevailed before as well as after the gale (*Dalhousie, Calcutta* to 16° 5′ N. latitude and 92° 16′ E. longitude, from 7th to 11th). The log of the *Edwards* showed that the south-eastern current which ushered in the cyclone was confined between very narrow limits, at reaching west of the Andamans. The scientific investigator of these meteorological phenomena is of opinion, that on the 7th the cyclone was probably confined to the 92° and 95° or 96° East longitude.—*Englishman, April 18th,* 1858.

———————

Bay of Bengal and Malabar Coast, *betwixt the* 15th *and* 20th *May* 1858.—On the 15th May 1858 we had at Bombay so severe a thunder-storm, that, had there been any case on record of the monsoon setting in at this date, we should have supposed it at hand. It lowered the barometer by nearly two-tenths of an inch, the mercury here being rarely affected by a local squall. A squall of still greater violence than that experienced here, occurred at Cochin and along South Malabar, at the same date.

On the 20th, a Cyclone of great violence swept Lower Bengal. It was experienced in its strength from Dacca, Lat. 23° 50′ N., Long. 90° 28′ E., to Lat. 17° N. Long. 91° E. Though called a North-wester, the area over which it extended was much more extensive than is ever traversed by these local squalls. It travelled moreover, from South, Northerly, and veered with the peculiar characteristics of a Cyclone.

Bengal.—We hear from Chittagong, dated 21st May, that they experienced a severe hurricane at that station the preceding day. The wind commenced to rise at 5 o'clock in the afternoon, and by 7 it was blowing a complete hurricane, accompanied with rain. The wind did not abate till 4 in the morning, having done much injury in the way of uprooting trees, throwing down huts, &c., within that time. Our correspondent says, I have not heard what has been the extent of damages on the river, but undoubtedly it is great. The wind was blowing from the S. and S.W.—*Englishman, May 27th.*

The following is from Rungpore, dated 23rd May 1858 :—

"We were visited the day before yesterday, at 11 P.M., by a storm, which for its violence has seldom been equalled in this district. The lightning struck the house in which the magistrate is living, made a hole in the roof, and made its escape by smashing one of the glass doors to pieces. Two European gentlemen who were sitting in the adjoining room were stunned, and the oil lamp on the table was smashed to atoms. The vividness of the lightning and the crashing of the claps of thunder were sufficient to make one think that the world was at an end, and that we must prepare for the day of judgment.

About thirty of the European sailors stationed at Julpeegorie, have volunteered to remain at that station at Rs. 50 per mensem, but the remaining 60 will return to Calcutta on being relieved. Notwithstanding the comparatively good behaviour of the sepoys of the 73rd N. I. stationed at Julpeegoorie, it is useless to conceal the fact that no sepoys are to be trusted ; and after the experience of the last year, it would be madness to leave any sepoy regiment without the control of European troops, either soldiers or sailors."—*Phœnix, May 28th.*

The following is from Dacca, dated the 24th instant :—

"A very painful and disastrous accident occurred on the Pudda on Thursday last, the 20th instant. Mr. Samuel Robinson, the third Master of the Dacca College, with his wife and family, consisting of two young boys and a little girl, were caught in a storm while crossing that river, when the boat was upset."

COCHIN, *22nd May.*—"Our monsoon has now fairly set in ; and we are enjoying all the pleasures that constant damp can bring with it. We had some few squalls with rain previously to the 17th instant, with every indication of the approach of that great potentate himself ; during the night it blew hard, with a heavy sea and rollers from the S.W. ; and on awaking in the morning of the 18th, we found he had fully established his power."

COCHIN, *26th May.*—"The monsoon has now fairly set in. A terrific gale blew here on the 15th instant, at about 6 P.M., attended with much rain, causing the destruction of some property. Another gale occurred on the morning of the 20th, which lasted for half an hour. Several boats were upset, but no life was lost, owing to the ready assistance rendered by those on shore. The accounts, lately received, of the effects of this hurricane at Trevandrum, are, I regret to say, most disastrous. The rivers Karamana and Killiar have been overflowed beyond their wont, whereby several stone and wooden bridges and hundreds of houses were entirely destroyed, and some families are reduced to utter destitution. The Circar will have to lay out more than ten thousand rupees for the repair of the public buildings, bridges, &c. thus demolished. The paddy cultivation there has also suffered heavily from this sad and unexpected catastrophe."

COCHIN.—"The *Sultan* arrived from Aden leaky on the evening of the 18th, but could not get inside until yesterday. We have had our share of rain,—22½ inches having fallen since 1st instant."

The following is reported by Captain Roskell, of the Steamer *Thebes* :—

"Experienced most severe weather.

"A Cyclone on the 19th instant, Lat. 17° 20′ N. Long 91° 10′ E., veering from S.E. and E.N.E. to North and to S.W. Continued for 10 hours.

" 20th.—A heavy gale from S.W.; lying to under a double-reefed boom mizen-sail. 21st.—Moderated; but still blowing a strong gale from S.W., with a high sea. 22nd.—Received Mr. E. H. T. Bull, Master Pilot, on board; but to enable us to do so, was compelled to send the steamer's life-boat.

" Passed a number of vessels off the Heads. All more or less to the eastward, apparently detained there from stress of weather. Passed ten vessels at anchor at Saugor. Ship *Adelaide* and Steamer *Cape of Good Hope* arrived at the entrance of Rangoon River 16th instant. "

THE LATE STORM IN BENGAL.—A correspondent from Noakhally, writing on the 21st instant, says : —

It may be useful to your paper to have particulars of yesterday's terrible gale.

The morning of the 20th May was damp; at 11 A.M. it was very windy and stormy; the wind was easterly and the rain occasionally heavy. The gale gradually increased; at sunset it was excessively heavy. About that time all houses, except those built of brick, suffered much; such as were in any way unprepared for a storm were swept away. The gale lessened a little after sunset, wind veered latterly to the west; again increased towards midnight, when it was at its height. The full tide in the Megna brought up the salt tidal wave which overflowed the country. Morning disclosed the effects of the gale and inundation; all the lower lands were inundated. The salt water had overflowed the compound of the Sudder station, nearly eight miles from the river. Numbers of houses were blown away; ten cutcha buildings in the jail, the whole of the Sudder Ameen's cutcherry, had disappeared; dead cattle and even buffaloes were washed up from the churs to the sides of the raised roads; and where buffaloes die in a sudden inundation, the loss of human life must be expected. Several bodies of children have been found,—particulars are not known fully. I will, if I can, write again.

Although in the immediate vicinity of the river Megna, the joush dhan is not cultivated, and no crop existed at present, much joush dhan was standing within the line to which the salt water has reached, and must have been much damaged. All the tanks within six or seven miles of the river have been filled with salt water. This visitation will cause great distress, especially as rice, instead of being at 3 maunds for the Rupee—the usual price five years ago—is at 2 Rupees the maund. The accounts from Hutteah and the large churs in the centre of the Megna have not been received, but they may be expected to contain the history of much disaster.

No such gale has been known here since 1832. I was travelling in these very parts on the 14th and 15th of May 1852, when the storm was very severe :—it was not to be compared with yesterday's gale. Had this lasted for four-and-twenty hours, the loss of human life in this country would have been incalculable.

I am still unable to use my left leg from my accident out hog-hunting; but I have made careful enquiries, and you may rely on the particulars I have given.

I hear much damage has been done to the boats in the khalls, and that the Roman Catholic Padre's boat has been destroyed; he however is saved. I will write again if I can get any certainty as to the loss of human life, before your next issue.— *Indian Field, May* 29th.

" A thunderstorm of unusual violence, accompanied by heavy rain and some hail, prevailed betwixt Khandalla and Poona, and over a considerable part of the

Deccan, on Saturday afternoon (15th May). The day had been one of unusual heat. By 2 o'clock the wind blew over the burning plain like the breath of a furnace. The first sharp downpour, when the hail appeared, was drunk up in an instant. For some time the rain fell at intervals. It was heaviest about Tullygaum, where, by sunset, every nullah contained a torrent, every precipice furnished a cataract. The level ground looked the marsh of the middle of August, barring the want of vegetation. Thunder and lightning prevailed in all directions, the electric discharges being all vertical from the clouds to the ground until the ghauts were approached. Here it was occasionally seen to descend from the clouds spreading out into many branches. It approached the earth sometimes to ascend from the South.   Occasionally it shot in one grand zig-zag right across the sky, throwing off what seemed like branches on both sides. On many occasions it appeared to shoot out from a mass of cloud, projecting itself in the direction of the spectator, and throwing off shoots in all directions.   This was probably the same form of lightning seen axially and fore-shortened, as that providing the zig-zag stream across.   The whole thing was grand beyond conception; and the contrast betwixt the aspects of the electric fluid in the Deccan and those amongst the hills, singular to a degree.   During the storm the ghauts were lit up with fire-flies, doing their utmost to imitate the lightning, by those sudden flashes which, occupying about a quarter of a second, occur at intervals of from three to four seconds, when the beautiful little insects, by some strange concert amongst themselves, flash out all their lamps simultaneously.   On Sunday morning every hollow contained a little pool or lake.   The great bull-frog had crept out in that brilliant gamboge yellow coat which distinguishes him on his first appearance for the season, and the loud croaking of their love-makings resounded over the land.   The whole aspect of things was that attending the first burst of the monsoon.   There was heavy rain at Khandalla in the course of the afternoon and at night, with a severe gale of wind early in the morning."

" We subjoin a table showing the altitude of the Barometer from the 10th to the 31st May for the past seven years.

" We have taken the day in which more than an inch of rain first fell the first burst; this occurred in 1854 on the 6th and 7th; in 1856 on the 4th; in 1857 not till the 24th of June. We had heavy showers all yesterday morning and forenoon, with an east wind and thunder. The Barometer in the morning slightly rising.

DATE.	YEARS.						
	1852.	1853.	1854.	1855.	1856.	1857.	1858.
May 10th ..	29·788	29·789	29·864	29·836	29·807	Sun.	29·833
,, 11th ..	797	814	857	817	789	29·832	796
,, 12th ..	814	810	859	841	789	859	748
,, 13th ..	815	866	853		811	877	710
,, 14th ..	732	860		921	816	880	684
,, 15th ..	747	Sun.	856	887	811	863	645
,, 16th ..	Sun.	885	860	883	803	846	
,, 17th ..	838	889	866	863	796	Sun.	
,, 18th ..	864	898	914	806		840	

DATE.	YEARS.						
	1852.	1853.	1854.	1855.	1856.	1857.	1858.
May 19th ..	29·811	29·892	29·819	29·778	29·821	29·839	
„ 20th ..	808	890	839		760	907	
„ 21st ..	781	875		852	758	793	
„ 22nd ..	807	Sun.	754	898	761	799	
„ 23rd ..	Sun.	869	668	862	704	785	
„ 24th ..	822	864			739	Sun.	
„ 25th ..	856	870	711	826		765	
„ 26th ..	842	812	700	837	793	732	
„ 27th ..	818	804	682	849	774	659	
„ 28th ..	812	789	692	851	807	631	
„ 29th .	797	782			659	719	
„ 30th ..	768	Sun.	· 741	917	563	739	
„ 31st ..	Sun.	774	723	880	570	747	

NORTH CHINA SEAS.—*30th August to* 20*th September* 1858.— The China Seas seems to have been scourged with an almost constant series of gales betwixt the 30th of August and 20th September. On the first of these dates, the *Askelde* encountered a typhoon off the Saddle Islands near Japan ; 30° N., 105° E.   On the 16th September a violent gale passed over Singapore ; no particulars are given.   On the 21st, Swatow was visited by a hurricane of such fury as to destroy nearly the whole shipping in the port. This had all the character- istics of a true Cyclone.   My information is too scanty to permit of an analysis of its elements.

The *Askelde* encountered a typhoon off the Saddle Islands. She left Japan (? Simoda) on the 25th August, and was 30 miles east of the Saddle Islands, on the 30th ; when, it being too thick to run for the land, she was hove to.   The typhoon commenced at 8 P.M., barometer fell from 29·44 to 29 14, and was at 29·16 at 8 A.M. of the 31st, when the gale was strongest.   Lost jibboom, fore-topmast, and main-topmast; gig washed from the deck when the ship was lying over 38 degrees, and sails all split and blown into knots.   Wheel ropes carried away.   Hammock- rails under water during the strongest part of the gale.   On 1st September, at noon, lat. 29° 29' N., long. 123° 2' E., by observation.—*North China Herald Shipping List.*

A storm passed over Singapore on the 16th September. The following short notice of it appeared in the *Bintag Timor :*—

This morning (the 16th September) at 8½ o'clock, a most terrific gale swept over Singapore. The real damage occasioned thereby has not yet reached us; but we have heard of boats being capsized ; men walking over a bridge being blown over the balustrade and killed; ships in the roads dragging their anchors, some going ashore, others coming into collision with one another; ships carrying away spars, topmasts, etc.; but we have not heard of any loss of life, except the cases referred to above.   In the Island amongst the plantations, trees have been torn up by the roots, fruit-bearing trees have been prostrated, and in truth every obstacle has had to bow to the tremendous violence of the blast.—*China Mail,* *October 7th.*

One of the most terrible Cyclones ever known in the China Seas visited Swatow on the night of the 21st September, destroying almost the entire shipping, both native and foreign, and causing an immense loss of life among the Chinese.   Large vessels were carried a long way inland by the huge waves; and not only were houses unroofed, but some of them had their walls blown down.   Even the hurricane which visited Bombay in November 1854 was inferior to this, before which everything went down that offered any resistance.   The loss of property to foreigners was very considerable.

HURRICANE AT SWATOW.—The *Yang-tsze* returned to harbour from Swatow at 4 o'clock this morning, having left the latter place at noon yesterday.

The vessels *totally wrecked* are,—the *Anonyma*, driven on the rocks six miles from her anchorage, with three anchors down, and full scope of cable.   The *Hong-kong* drifted into a sandy cove four miles, with three anchors ahead, masts cut away (since sold by auction for $35!).   The *Kinaldie* (Aberdeen clipper, 794 tons, 10 months old) driven four miles on to a ledge of rock, and with four feet water round her at high-water mark: hull sold for $1,510, without the copper. *Gazelle* foundered with all hands: Captain Fox happened to be on shore, and four of her crew were picked up alive the following morning.   She had arrived in the afternoon from Amoy, on her way to Hongkong; and H. M. brig-of-war *Acorn* guards the wreck, till means are adopted to save the treasure.   *Laura* (Oldenburg brig) to be sold by auction to-day.   *Hepscott* (British iron-ship, 575 tons) perched upon a pinnacle rock, which has passed through her bottom up the beams. *Louisa,* with foremast gone, in 4½ feet water; may possibly be extricated.

On board the *Anonyma* were from two to three hundred chests of opium—all damaged; but the *Hongkong's,* we believe, were saved.   Divers have been sent up from this place to try and save the *Gazelle's* treasure, which could probably easily be effected now; but should time be wasted in trying to raise the schooner, and by any unfortunate chance the vessel break up, the boxes would sink in the soft mud, from which it would be impossible to extricate them.

For the hulls of vessels totally wrecked and sold by auction, the most ridiculous prices were paid.   The Dutch brig *Aganita Adriana,* of 300 tons, fetched $1; Dent & Co's *Hongkong,* of 240 tons, sold for $35; the Dutch barque *Thusnelda,* 18 months old, of 450 tons, brought $315; the Oldenburg barque *Laura,* of 500 tons, with her copper on, $1,500; and the *Kinaldie,* 10 months old, of 794 tons, $1,510 without her copper.   The *Pantaloon,* perched on the top of a pile of rocks, 15 feet high, and at a distance from the others, fell a prey to the Chinese, who rushed on board, drove the captain and crew on shore, plundered her of 3,000 bags of sugar, and would have completely gutted her, had not the captain with three

8 g

friends returned on board with fire-arms, and driven the wreckers out. This enabled Captain Mooney to save his sails, chronometer, and small stores. The *Aganita Adriana*, which was also taken by the Chinese, was stripped of everything. The *Glendover* and *Alfred the Great* are still ashore.

The following table, handed to us by Captain Chape, will afford a very slight notion of the position of the vessels ; nothing but a lively pencil-sketch would give a true description of the scene, which must be seen to be understood :—

Hongkong (British barque).   On shore ; total wreck ; three masts and bowsprits gone; 2 miles below Swatow.

Anonyma (British brig).   On the rocks ; total wreck ; dismasted ; 1¼ mile below Swatow.

Louisa (British barque).   In the mud ; loss of rudder, foremast, bowsprit, and starboard bulwarks ; 3 miles below Swatow.

Alfred the Great (British ship).   Found on the mud bank, off Double Island, in a sinking state.

Beverly (British barque).   Loss of boat.

Kinaldie (British ship).   Total wreck on the rocks ; 200 yards from the *Louisa*.

Hepscott (British iron barque).   Total wreck on the rocks ; 200 yards from the *Hongkong*.

Harvest Home (British barque).   Loss of rudder.

Wm. Frederick (British ship).

Glendover (British ship).   Total wreck on the mud-bank above Swatow [?]

Moultan (British ship).   On the rocks ; total wreck.

Gazelle (British schooner).   Sunk at her anchors.

Pantaloon (British brig).   On the rocks ; total wreck ½ mile below the *Hongkong*.

Hazard (British brig).

Dennus Hill (British barque).

Louisa Bailey (British barque).   On a mud-bank 8 miles above Swatow.

Aga Adriana (Dutch brig).   Total wreck on a mud-bank 4 miles above Swatow.

Laura (Oldenburg barque).   On the rocks ; total wreck 100 yards from the *Hepscott*.

Ohio (Bremen barque).   In the mud ; 3 feet water alongside at high water.

Giovanina (Sardinian brig).   Dismasted.

Thusnelda (Danish barque).   On the rocks ; total wreck.

The brig *Hazard* is all right—the only vessel that rode out the storm.

The gale commenced about 11 P M. on the 21st, and the barometer was then 29·85.   At 2, the height of the gale (bar. 28·41), a storm-wave, 25 feet perpendicular, came in from seawards, sweeping everything before it, and driving the ships from their anchorages over a long mud-flat, two miles across, with not more than 2 to 3 feet of water on it.   The tide rose from 18 to 20 feet.   It is said that upwards of two hundred junks are wrecked, and that the loss of life amongst them is very great.   The houses on Double Island are in ruins, and the strength of the wind may be gathered from the fact, that godowns on the water front, with walls two feet and a half thick, were actually carried away.   The bungalows have disappeared ! The town of Swatow is much injured, as might have been expected, and the Chinese report much havoc in the interior.

CALCUTTA.—*25th October* 1858.—The only notice I find of this gale in my note-book is that from Calcutta. From the great fall of the Barometer from 29·70 at noon to 29·35 at midnight, I should assume this to have been a whirlwind, but have no other grounds to go upon.

A STORM.—Calcutta was visited by a heavy gale, attended with much rain, during the night of Monday last (the 25th October).

We fear that disastrous news will be received of its effects on the shipping in the river and at the Sand Heads.

One death occurred in Calcutta from the falling of a house; many dinghies were damaged; and nine or ten country boats, loaded with rice, jute, gunny, cloth, &c., were seen to upset; and all the rice and other things are now floating on the river. Casualties, it is feared, of a still more serious kind, remain to be reported. Nor have we yet ascertained what injury the storm has done to our scanty crop of rice. If the rain has been general, no doubt it will be better for the crops: but the gale must have done great injury. We have heard besides, that two or three ships are ashore not much below town.

We must assign this same hurricane as the indirect cause also of another and still more serious disaster,—we mean the fatal collision last night upon the railway. The up passenger train, which ought to have arrived at Howrah at 5 P.M., was unable to travel at a greater speed than that of *ten miles an hour* in the face of the tempest, which,—although in town it had not reached its highest fury till nearly twelve hours later,—was, in the upper part of the province, blowing with terrific violence, even at that time. The consequence was that the passenger train was belated. In addition to this element of risk, the guards had neglected to light the warning lamp in front of the train. Meanwhile a goods train was proceeding down; and as the hour was not that at which the passenger train was expected to be where in fact it was, the goods train, much heavier of course and travelling twenty-five miles an hour, seeing no light to admonish it, ran full into the carriages of the passengers. Two unfortunate persons were killed on the spot; a greater number more or less seriously injured; and much damage and *dégât* occasioned. Four trees were blown down in the compound of the Roman Catholic College in Park Street.

The variations of pressure during the hurricane, as announced by Sims and Troughton's Barometer, were:—

Noon......................................29·70
8 P.M.....................................29·61
Midnight..................................29·35
3-30 A.M..................................29·38
7 A.M.....................................29·66

—Bengal Hurkaru, October 27th.

The gale has not gone off without leaving its usual damages and wrecks behind; the mischief done has been, however, very small. The principal of these is the loss of some few country boats laden with produce, and the usual complement of dinghees; but, considering the proverbial carelessness of native boatmen and dingheewallas, the loss among them is little enough. Some few houses in the native parts of the city have come down by the run, as they usually do in every little storm, and one or two poor niggers are less in the world in consequence. The fantastic tricks played among the bamboo-work preparations for the grand illumination are great; scaffoldings have been shaken and shattered, and in many cases have lost their perpendicular.—*Ibid.* 28*th.*

CHINA SEAS, BETWIXT HONGKONG AND SHANGHAI.—*8th to 10th November.*—A hurricane appears to have prevailed to the northward of Hongkong in the second week of November. The following extracts from the log of the *Arrow* afford all the information I possess regarding it.

THE WRECK OF THE BRIG "ARROW."—The following extracts from his log, in reference to the wreck of the brig *Arrow* on the Pratas, have been placed at our disposal by Captain Ripley, who is anxious that at least $1,000 should be made up for the Chinese junk which conveyed him and his crew to Hongkong.

"On Sunday, November 7th, the brig *Arrow* weighed anchor from Hongkong harbour. On her passage from Hongkong towards Shanghae, at 9 A.M., the island of Tamtoo was abeam, bearing North, distant about ¼ of a mile. After rounding Tamtoo, experienced a heavy sea from Eastward, and the wind being then about N.N.E., and the ship then heading sometimes E. by S. and E.S.E.; rate of sailing from 4 to 5 knots per hour. About 1 P.M., the wind shifted to about E.N.E., and the ship then breaking off to about S.E. by S., tacked ship to the northward, the ship then lying about North, and continued doing so till about 8 P.M. Fokai Point being then about 8 miles distant, tacked ship to the S.E. Throughout the night a strong breeze and a heavy sea; handed the top-gallant sails, and continued that course throughout the night.

Monday, 8th November 1858.—Very strong breeze, with a heavy Easterly sea; ship pitching and labouring heavily; pumps constantly attended to. 6 P.M. Passed to leeward of Pedra Branca, distant about 5 miles, ship then coming up and heading about E.S.E. About 11·20, tacked ship to the Northward. 6 P.M. Tacked ship to the S.S.E., on the East side of Hong Hai Bay, in 9 fathoms water, and continued on that course till about midnight.

Tuesday, 9th November 1858.—2 A.M. Increasing gales with a heavy head sea; double-reefed fore and main topsails, handed fore and main courses, and stowed the main-topsail; experienced strong gales from the N.E. with a heavy N.E. sea running; ship labouring heavily, and taking great quantities of water over all; forward pumps carefully attended to. Lat. and long., by dead reckoning, as far as can be remembered, at noon, was lat. 21° 46′ N., long. 116° 9′ E., ship then heading about E.S.E. to S.E. by E.; rate of sailing, as far as can be remembered at that time was about 1·4 knots per hour, and continued steering the same.

Wednesday, 10th November 1858.—Strong gales from N.E. by N.; ship then heading E.S.E., with a tremendous heavy N.E. sea; ship labouring heavily and taking great quantities of water over all; fore and midship pumps carefully attended to. Lat. at noon, as far as can be remembered, was 21° 8′ N., long. 116° E., ship then heading E.S.E., 2 miles per hour, with 4 points leeway; ship making a true course, by estimation, of S.S.E. 1-30. The S.W. extremity of the Pratas Shoal then bearing about S.E. by E., distant about 48 miles, kept ship away S.E. by S., and made sail as follows to pass the shoal before dark : set reef-foresail, balance-reefed main-topsail, main-staysail, and hauled aft the lee main-sheet, which course ought to have cleared the south-western extremity of the Pratas Shoal about 8 miles to windward. 4 P.M. Passed through some very smooth water, and had every reason to believe we were to leeward of the Shoal, but still continued on the same course to make sure of the distance. At 6 P.M. observed breakers ahead, and on the weather-bow; ordered the helm immediately to be put hard up, and the main-topyard squared, and the peak halliards of the main-topsail lowered; but so rapidly did the ship approach the breaker that, before she could fall off, the ship struck violently on the reef two or three times before she lost her way through the water. The vessel immediately heeled over on her beam-ends, and all possibility of getting her off was at an end. Attempted to lower away the second cutter, but in doing so a heavy sea rolling in made a clear breach over her, and swamped her, so that we lost her altogether. At about 6-40 P.M., cut away main and fore mast to ease the vessel from lurching so heavily, and making her as safe as possible to pass the night out on board. Employed during the night getting light sails up, provisions and water, ready for leaving the ship at daylight.

BAY OF BENGAL AND ARABIAN SEA.—*21st to 27th April* 1859.— This magnificent hurricane, all but the last on the list, is that in regard to which my information is most abundant. I regret not the less that it is not sufficiently so, to enable me to go into particulars. The gale experienced off the Mauritius by the ship *Devon*,—of which I have no doubt the Mauritius Meteorological Society will give us particulars,—is not to be supposed connected with the hurricane on the north side of the line, otherwise than by proximity in point of time of occurrence. The Cyclone under consideration, is first mentioned as having been experienced off Negapatam, lat. N., long. E., on the 24th April, where it proved fearfully disastrous to the shipping. It appeared at the same time at Port Pedro, lat. 9° 40′, N. long. 80° 20′, E. where the American ship *Colarado* was wrecked. It seems here to have crossed the peninsula, and we find it raging at Allipey on the 25th, and at Tellicherry on the 28th. The only minute account of it I have obtained is that for which I am indebted to Mr. Hugh Crawfurd, Allipey :—this I subjoin entire.

The ship *Devon* from Liverpool, which arrived in this port yesterday, fell in with a severe Cyclone on the 21st April, which compelled her to run into the Mauritius, somewhat crippled by the rough usage she had sustained. The ship *Storm Queen*, bound from Calcutta to the Mauritius, must have experienced the same gale, as she fell in with bad weather on the 22nd of the same month, in lat. 6° 18′ S. and long. 84° 3′ E., when she lost topmast, other spars, sails, and the jolly boat.

TELLICHERRY.—A Correspondent, writing from Tellicherry, under date of 29th April, informs us that a severe storm visited that place on the 28th, accompanied by strong showers of rain. It commenced at 11 A.M., and continued till evening, causing considerable destruction. A great number of trees were uprooted, and several houses damaged. After the storm subsided, the beach presented a scene of complete destruction; most of the fishermen's houses being either completely levelled to the ground or unroofed. Several pattamars and mungees, laden with cargoes, went on shore.— *Times.*

NEGAPATAM, 26*th April.*—HURRICANE; COLLISION AND LOSS OF LIFE.— (From our Correspondent.)—A terrific hurricane has just been experienced at this place. On Saturday evening there were, I am certain, not less than 30 vessels of various tonnage, chiefly native, in the roads. Yesterday, about 11 A.M., when it cleared up a little for a few minutes, and we got a faint glimpse at the sea, there was only one vessel, the fine ship *City of Bristol*, in the roads. She was riding it out most gallantly, with her port and starboard anchors out, and a considerable length of cable. She must have had splendid cables, or her fate would inevitably have been that of the other vessels. The whole coast from Karrikal to 8 or 10 miles south of this, is lined with barques, brigs, and schooners, some still entire, others shattered to pieces ; so that one can scarcely believe they were only a few hours ago floating on the bosom of the ocean, with several human beings on board. Others again are lying keel uppermost, furiously lashed by the surging billows; and one, I believe, has sunk. Within a distance of 200 or 300 yards, I counted 12 vessels on shore. Beyond that the coast takes a bend, so that I could not see further. However, I hear that sixteen more have been wrecked farther down, and amongst these is the *Enterprize*, which left Madras only the other day. She was the first to come ashore, they say. It is also reported that four vessels of those that were lying at Karrikal, and all those at Nagore (4 miles from this), are on shore.

Amongst all this tremendous loss of property, I am glad to say that, with one lamentable exception, which I will presently relate, there has not been much loss of life. There is a report that several men were drowned at Nagore, and 2 or 3 here. This, however, is native report, and needs confirmation, for they almost invariably exaggerate. Several have, no doubt, received wounds and bruises, and some have had their limbs broken. I now come to the concluding, and, at the same time, most painful part of my story. Last Saturday morning the English barque *Monarch*, Commander J. Percival, weighed anchor, and left these roads under press of canvas with a fair breeze, bound for Penang. She had a cargo of native cloths, curry stuff, salt, &c., and 180 coolies as deck-passengers. This vessel fell in with the very worst of the storm, and suffered considerable damage, and was, as far as I can learn, drifting in towards shore. Another large vessel just on her way out from Glasgow, with a cargo of beer for Calcutta, and commanded by a Captain Millar, I hear, was in a dismantled state in the vicinity of the *Monarch*. These two vessels did not see each other till quite close upon one another, and, although they both put their helms up, they came in collision, and the *Monarch*, which already had 5 feet of water in her, began to make more. The chief mate and several of the crew, seeing this, jumped on board the other vessel; which was drifting faster in towards the shore, and about thirty coolies followed their example, and all but one sailor (who, in leaping, fell between the two vessels and got jammed) got to shore. The captain, second mate, and 3 or 5 of the crew, with most of the coolies, were left on board. The coolies then began jumping overboard to attempt making the shore. With the majority, it was a vain attempt, and they met with a watery grave. How many of the 180 have been saved I cannot at present ascertain, but by far the greater number have, poor things! perished. There were some women among them. Unfortunately the *Monarch* was wrecked on a part of the coast where there are no boats. These and Catamarans were, however, sent off, I believe, as soon as intelligence of the state of the vessel, and the danger to human life, arrived.

Two of those who were wrecked, one the chief officer of the *Monarch*, and the other an apprentice on board the other ship, got in here some time late last night, and took shelter in the verandah of an old house, occupied by a Major Mitchell. The Major, noticing the insecurity of the greater part of the house, had moved into the safest corner. At 4 A.M. the larger portion of this house fell with a tremendous crash and buried the two unfortunate fellows (who, having just escaped from drowning, had taken shelter there from wind and rain) under its ruins. Major Mitchell was awoke by the falling of the house, and came out to see what extent of damage was done. Hearing some one moan, he immediately hastened to the spot whence the sound emanated, and finding the chief officer still alive, set about releasing him from his painful position. The mate is very severely hurt, but not so much as to leave no hope of recovery. The other poor fellow, who was farther in, must have been killed in an instant, for he was dug out from underneath brick and chunam, several feet thick, and his head was completely smashed. I have just heard that the name of the vessel which came in contact with the *Monarch* is the *Balslangee*, Commander Millar.—*Athenæum, May 3rd.*

SHIPWRECK AT POINT PEDRO. (N.E. extremity of Ceylon, lat. 7° 40' N. long. 80° 20' E.)—The American ship *Colorado*, 2,200 tons burden, was wrecked off Point Palmyra on the 24th instant. It appears that on the evening of the 22nd April, the *Colorado* was anchored off Point Palmyra, and about one mile from the shore. She was in ballast (sand), and about to ship salt at Tonde-Manaar. It was blowing fresh when the vessel anchored, and continued to blow very strongly till 10 A.M. the following day, when it became quite a gale, which appeared to increase in force every hour. The largest anchor was let go with 60 fathoms of cable; the swell anchor was at the port bow with 75 fathoms. As the gale increased, the heavier chain was slacked till fully 90 fathoms were out. The ship continued to ride in safety until the morning of the 24th; when, at about 3 P.M., the gale being at its fiercest, she began to drag her anchors; those on board not being aware this was the case till she came into collision with, and carried away 2 dhonies.

In about twenty minutes after this occurrence, the ship struck on a reef of rocks running parallel with the coast. In a short time she was in pieces, the masts having previously been cut down. She fell with her decks seaward, which caused her to break up more speedily. The crew were unable to fire a gun, or make any signal of distress. About 6 in the morning, the captain's wife was washed overboard, and in his endeavours to save her, the captain was drowned as well as his wife. At the time of his going overboard, the Captain had a bag containing sovereigns tied round his body. The chief mate does not know the number of sovereigns with the Captain, or the quantity of specie on board, but believes it amounted to a considerable sum; the total amount the chief mate thinks is known to the American consul at Galle.

The wreck was discovered by the natives about 7 o'clock on the morning of the 24th, and, with their assistance, which was promptly rendered, the whole of the officers and crew, 24 in number, were saved, with the exception of one lascar, and one English boy ill in his berth at the time. The captain's son, a boy 7 years old, was saved. Every attention was paid by the magistrate to the shipwrecked crew. No property of any kind was saved from the wreck. None of the bodies have been recovered as yet. The storm is described as the most furious ever witnessed at Point Pedro. Out of 8 dhonies that were at anchor, 6 have been wrecked, and the 2 remaining were momentarily expected to part their cables. Mr. Braybrooke, the police magistrate at Point Pedro, has supplied the crew with clothes and food, and has done everything in his power to meet the emergency. The gale was still too fierce, and the sea too high, to attempt to go near the small portion of the wreck that remained.—*Ibid, May 2nd.*

The following very valuable observations were forwarded me by Mr. Hugh Crawfurd, Allipey:—

Alt. of Mercurial Cistern above the Sea level, 28 feet. Diameter of Tube, ⅛th of an inch. Long. 76° 23′ E., Lat. 9° 29·48′ N.

Date.		Observations made at Sunrise.					Maximum pressure at 9.40. a.m.				
			Temper.		Wind.			Temper.		Wind.	
		Barometer.	Of the Mercury.	Of the Air.	Direction.	Remarks.	Barometer.	Of the Mercury.	Of the Air.	At 10 A.M.	Remarks.
April	23rd	29·922	81¾	81¾	NW 5	N., C., Overcast.	29·984	85¾	85¾	NW 6	Nimb., Squally.
,,	24th	890	79½	79½	NW 5	N. & C., Rain.	No Obs.			NW 8	N., and C., Squally.
,,	25th	872	84½	84½	NW 6	Cr., N., & Cum., over.	912	84⅞	84⅞	NW 8	Cr., N., & C., Overcast.
,,	26th	832	77¾	77¾	NW 3	C. and Overcast.	852	81	81	WNW 7	C., N., Rain.
,,	27th	770	77½	77½	SW 3	Heavy Rain.	826	78½	78½	SE 4	C., N., & Overcast.
,,	28th	846	79½	79½	SE 10	Nimb., &c.	934	82	82	SSW 9	N., C., ditto, &c.
,,	29th	30·010	83	83	SW 4	Haze and Cir.	30·074	86½	86½	SW 4	Cir., & Haze.
,,	30th	002	81½	81½	SE 3	Cir. C., and N., Clear.	088	84½	84¾	SW 3	Cir., Zen. clear.
May	1st	054	80½	81	E 3	Cr., &C., Zenith Clear.	110	83½	83¼	W 3	C., Z. Cirri.

Date.		Minimum pressure Obs. at 4.40. p.m.					Observations at 9.40. p.m.					Rain guage.
			Temper.		Wind.			Temper.		Wind.		
		Barometer.	Of the Mercury.	Of the Air.	Direction at 5 P.M.	Remarks.	Barometer.	Of the Mercury.	Of the Air.	Direction at 10 P.M.	Remarks.	
April	23rd	29·930	$85\frac{3}{4}$	$84\frac{3}{4}$	ESE	Squally to Eastwd.	29·076	$85\frac{1}{2}$	$85\frac{1}{2}$	NW 6	Cum. and Cir	$1\frac{1}{16}$
,,	*24th	838	$85\frac{1}{4}$	$85\frac{1}{4}$	NW 8	N., & Overcast.	930	85	85	NW 7	N. and Overcast	$\frac{8}{16}$
,,	25th	820	77	77	NW	N. &c., Rain & Thunder, heavy rain, thunder, and lightning; lightning bright orange and green, and most vivid. One patimar struck, and 1 man killed.	878	$78\frac{3}{4}$	$78\frac{3}{4}$	ESE 5	L., Thun., & Rain	
,,	26th	744	$79\frac{1}{2}$	$79\frac{1}{2}$	WNW 7	Rain.	826	$79\frac{1}{2}$	$79\frac{1}{2}$	NW 7	Rain.	$1\frac{8}{16}$
,,	27th	730	79	$79\frac{1}{4}$	SSW 11	C., N., &c., O., Fair.	850	80	80	SW 12	Heavy Rain.	$1\frac{5}{16}$
,,	28th	904	84	84	SSW 6	N. and C., Overcast.	30·010	84	84	SW 4	C., Cir., Cir. Cum.	$2\frac{5}{16}$
,,	29th	972	$85\frac{1}{4}$	$85\frac{1}{4}$	WSW 4	Cir. and Haze.	032	$83\frac{1}{2}$	$83\frac{1}{2}$	Calm.	Cir., driz.	$\frac{2}{16}$
,,	30th	30·000	$86\frac{1}{4}$	$86\frac{1}{2}$	W by N 3	Cir. & C., Z. Clear.	082	$83\frac{1}{4}$	$83\frac{1}{4}$	WSW 3	Cir., Zen. clear.	
May	1st	006	$87\frac{1}{2}$	$87\frac{1}{2}$	WNW 4	Cir. Cum., and Cir.	058	$83\frac{3}{4}$	$83\frac{1}{4}$	WNW 3	Cir. C. and Cir.	Dew fell

* ☾ Last Quarter 21h.; Apogee 13h.

Barometer readings, &c.

Date.	Barometer.	Temper.		Direction of Wind, and Remarks.
		Of the Mercury.	Of the Air.	
On 25th May.				
At 6. A.M.	29·872	$84\frac{1}{2}$	$84\frac{1}{2}$	NW. Strong breeze. Cum., Cir., and Nimb. all round, and overcast. High surf; one patimar went down at her anchors.
9.40	912	$84\frac{3}{4}$	$84\frac{3}{4}$	NW. Weather as above; fresh gale; steady at NW.
Noon.	..	..	..	NW. Heavy rain, *vivid* lightning, and loud thunder; lightning bright orange and *greenish blue* colour, very intense.
4. P.M.	796	77	77	NW. Strong gale. Weather as above, with thunder and lightning, &c., &c., and rain.
4.40	820	$77\frac{1}{2}$	$77\frac{3}{4}$	NW. As above.
9.40	878	$78\frac{3}{4}$	$78\frac{3}{4}$	ESE 3. Thunder and lightning taking off; much rain and light wind.
On the 26th.				
At 6. A.M.	29·832	$77\frac{3}{4}$	$77\frac{3}{4}$	NW 3. Light Wind; Nimb., Cum., overcast.
9.40	852	81	81	WNW 7. Moderate Gale. Cum., Nimb., &c., overcast.
Noon.	..	..	..	Rain; Wind veering between WNW. and West; still blowing strong gale.
4. P.M.	728	80	80	W 7. Strong gale and rain.
4.40	744	$79\frac{1}{2}$	$79\frac{1}{2}$	WNW 7. do. do.
9.40	820	$79\frac{1}{2}$	$79\frac{1}{2}$	NW 7. do. do.

(*continued*)

Date.	Barometer.	Temper.		Direction of Wind, and Remarks.
		Of the Mercury.	Of the Air.	
On the 27th.				
At 6. A.M.	29·770	77¼	77¼	SW 3. Light wind; rain and surf gone down.
9.40	828	78¼	78¼	SE 4. Moderate breeze; Cum., Nimb., &c., &c.
1. P.M.	762	78	78	SW 11. Blowing a hard gale, and veering to Southward; overcast, &c., &c., and rain.
2.30	732	78¼	78¼	South 11. More moderate, with heavy rain.
3.	728	78	78	SW 10. Strong gale, constant rain.
3.30	724	78¼	78¼	SSW 11.
4.	do.	79	79½	SSW 11.
4.40	730	79½	79½	SSW 11.
9.40	850	80	80	SW 12. A very hard gale, and heavy rain.
Midnight.	828	79½	79¾	SSW 12. As above.
On the 28th.				
At 6. A.M.	29·846	79½	79½	SE 10. Strong gale; Nimb., Cum., &c., overcast: barometer rising.
9.40	934	82	82	SSW 9. Strong gale as above
Noon.	831	80¾	79½	SW 12. A very hard gale, veering to WSW., stripping the trees of leaves and branches, and blowing numbers down.
1. P.M.	822	76¾	76¾	WSW 12. As above; mercury in the tube jumping; caused I fancy from the vibration of the house.
2.	880	82	82	SSW 9. Gale moderating.
3.	890	83½	83½	SSW 6. do. do.
4.40	904	84	84	SW 6. do. do.
9.40	30·010	84	84	SW 4. Moderate breeze.

N. B.—The numbers after the direction of the wind are intended to indicate its force; as 12, a Hurricane 10, Gale; 5, fresh breeze, &c., &c. I have *not* applied any correction whatever for height or temperature, which are the only two corrections needed (I think) in this barometer, the diameter of the tube making any correction for capillary action unnecessary, and the instrument being a fiducial point.

HUGH CRAWFURD.

Allipey, May 13th, 1859.

The cyclone that passed across the southern part of India about the 26th of last month seems to have flung its tail over Aden in the shape of a terrific rain-storm, accompanied by thunder and lightning. We have the following from a correspondent :—

Aden, 3rd May 1859.—On the night of the 30th of April we had a rain-storm in Aden, such as the oldest Arab inhabitant of the place had never witnessed. The preceding night there had been a copious fall, sufficient to fill nearly the whole of our splendid tanks, but at about 10 P.M. of Saturday it began again, and one might have thought that the dreadful pudder over our heads was determined to swamp us. The rain fell in flakes, and lasted without intermission for nearly three hours. About midnight, screams and cries resounded through the town and camp, but it was not till the following morning that the extent of the mischief done was fully known. Long before daybreak several hundreds of the people were collected on the sea-beach, some looking for their lost property, and others busily engaged in searching after their lost friends and relatives. Nine bodies were picked up during the day, but twenty more are still missing. So sudden was the rush of water from the hills, that these unfortunate creatures were either taken by surprise and carried away whilst sleeping, or in trying to escape from their houses they were met by the torrent and hurried onward by its impetuous velocity. A great number of the *cajan* dwellings were swept away bodily, and upwards of two hundred stone houses have suffered considerable damage. The tanks, which had been filled the night before, stood the renewed strain tolerably well ; but different parts of the new masonry were carried away, and immense quantities of *debris* from the hills have found a lodgment in the capacious basins. It is my opinion, indeed, that the tanks, by breaking the rush of water from the hills, served in a great measure to shield the houses in the plain immediately below ; for had it not been for the interruption which they afforded, the torrent would have been much stronger and much more destructive. The storm was accompanied with heavy thunder and lightning, the latter so vivid and so continuous that one might have thought that the moon was shining. The Arabs maintain that a bolt struck the range of houses in the bazaar occupied by the butchers, and several persons were conscious of several slight shocks as of an earthquake.

The roads in every direction have been cut up fearfully. In some parts, all vestiges of a road have been obliterated, and in others immense masses of stones and earth have been deposited in hillocks across them. The Main Pass was quite blocked up with one of these masses from the over-hanging hills, and it was only with the greatest difficulty that the *cafila* could enter. The road was in the same state all the way to Steamer Point, and rendered quite impracticable for vehicles of any kind. However, very early next morning, our energetic Brigadier was on the spot, and no time was lost in commencing the work of reparation. Every available man was put on the roads, and already free communication has been restored. It will be some time before all the damage is repaired, and the cost will be very large, I fear. But the poor people will be the greatest sufferers. Many have lost their little all, whilst others in losing their houses are left homeless. The soldiers of the 57th turned out boldly at midnight, and did all that brave men could do under the circumstances. The nullah runs parallel with their barracks, and many of them rushed into the rapid torrent, and succeeded in saving a number of horses and camels from being carried into the sea. There has been heavy rain in the interior, and the whole population are now busily engaged in sowing their lands.

(From another Correspondent.)

I suppose you have heard of the great storm we had at Aden the other day,—the like has not occurred in the memory of the oldest inhabitant. I have collected a few particulars respecting it, which I now send, thinking that they might be of some interest to you.

During the morning of Saturday the 30th April, some moderate showers of rain fell, sufficient to fill all the cisterns in the place ; but that night a most terrific storm came on, the heavens appeared to open, and from 10-30 P.M. to 1-30 A.M. of Sunday, the rain came down in sheets, accompanied by a perpetual crash of thunder ; and the lightning was so vivid and continuous that it resembled moon-light. It was altogether most grand, and beyond anything I ever saw in India.

The coolies in the employ of the P. and O. Company were washed out of their huts, and the boats of that Company were only kept afloat by constant baling.

The damage to property, public and private, in the camp, is estimated at between two and three lacs; every cistern but one is destroyed, their walls having burst from the great pressure caused by the force with which quantities of rocks, &c. were washed into them from the rushing hills.

The corporal on duty at the Main Pass had a narrow escape. Hearing the noise he opened the gates, when a perfect torrent rushed through, carrying with it everything that came in its way. I am told the sight was most appalling. The road up the Pass is quite destroyed, the side of the hill having slipped down and carried it completely away.

A resident at the camp states that 187 stone houses are more or less ruined, and between twenty and thirty persons killed :—twelve bodies have been recovered. The water in the nullah, thrown over the bridge and the valley, looked like a sea, and at one time the shrieks of human beings and drowning animals were most dreadful to hear.

The rush of water from the hills into Back Bay, the anchorage of the steamers, was very great; the roads about them are ploughed up. A Parsee had collected 150 sheep in a stone pen,—in the morning not a vestige of either the animals or the building was to be seen, all had been swept into the sea; this will give you some idea of the strength of the torrent. Large quantities of provisions and grain have been destroyed.

I am informed that the stench in the camp is something awful, caused by the filth washed into it from the surrounding high lands. Hundreds of men are now employed restoring the carriage communication between the Point and the camp.— *Bombay Gazette.*

ARABIAN SEA, BETWIXT COORIA MOORIA BAY AND THE GULF OF ADEN.—*3rd June.*

THE LATE CYCLONE IN THE INDIAN SEAS.—(Extract from a Journal kept by Charles William O'Kelly, 3rd Officer of the Ship "Typhoon," on her passage from Aden to Bombay, Lat. 15° 30′ N., Long. 66° E.)—On the morning of the 3rd June, from various indications best known to experienced men, the Captain adjudged that it was going to blow "great guns," as he graphically expressed it; and, accordingly, orders were issued to make everything well secure. Previous to this, royal yards, studding-sail booms, and flying-jib boom, were all sent down, and the ship was hove to under a close-reefed maintopsail. In compliance with the above order, all the other sails were well lashed round their respective yards with preventive gaskets; spars, boats, and all things likely to move, well secured; hatches battened down, &c. About 7 A.M., the wind increased to a terrific gale, and in the same proportion did the squalls and rain increase in frequency and fierceness. A little after 8 A.M., the wind, which, previous to this, seemed to be travelling all round the compass, suddenly shifted to the S.W., and a cyclone, in all its fury, struck the ship, which lay over with her lee bulwarks in the water. The main-topsail held on about ten or fifteen minutes, when the truss-bolt of the yard snapt like a carrot, though of wrought-iron, and about four inches in diameter. The sail flew into ribbons, and great pieces of canvas went flying to leeward. The weather topsail sheet drew the eyebolt out of the deck, carrying with it one half of the belaying rail, and unshipping the crank wheels that work the main pumps. This was the "unkindest cut of all;" for, had she sprung a leak—as all things warranted the supposition that such a misfortune would take place—we should have been half full of water ere the pumps could have been made available for active service. However, on the carpenter sounding, there was no water, or so little that it was of no consequence. 9¼ A.M. All things were now in a critical state, some of the beams in the cabin were broken, the ship working and groaning in a frightful state. About 10 A.M. the cyclone struck her again, laying her over till two or three feet of her main deck were in the water. Consternation was now depicted on every countenance. Main-topsail yard adrift, sail in ribbons, fore-topsail and cross jack blown out of the gaskets, the mainmast bending like a whipsaw, with some of the weather rigging carried away, rendering it utterly impossible for the men just then to go aloft. The rain beating on every exposed part like hailstones, causing acute pain; the roaring of the mountainous seas breaking round us, the gushing of the wind and rain, the loud peals of thunder, the vivid flashes of lightning, the flapping of the torn canvas, the shouting of the officers, and the screams of the Hindoo passengers, all blending together in one bewildering chaos, rendered it a scene awfully sublime in its nature, but most painfully startling in its effects. By this time, the carpenters had made a temporary fixture for the pump, and were standing by, axe in hand, to cut away the masts; and some of the crew had lashed themselves to the weather bulwarks. 12 o'clock. Captain Faulkner encouraged the crew, by telling them that he thought we had got the worst, and giving them a glass of grog; they then got some dinner. After dinner, the men went aloft, cutting away the torn canvas to ease her a bit, and endeavouring to secure the topsail yard. Found that the trap band had sawed into the topmast, rendering it completely useless for future service, and that the topmast rigging was all chafed and cut. However, the yard was secured as well as it was possible to do under the circumstances, and a tackle got on the mainmast, &c. By this time, the wind had visibly decreased, though it was still blowing hard, with a tremendous sea. Lay to all night; and in the morning squared away, and run under a reefed foresail—all our other sails having been blown to ribbons. The carpenter reports foreyard gone, copper started; and no doubt other damages will appear when the weather will permit a thorough examination.

In the monotony of seafaring life, a trivial occurrence often takes the attention of even a casual observer, and what would seem commonplace and unworthy of notice to a landsman, is often fraught with imminent forebodings to the experienced sailor. Thus, previous to this cyclone coming on, there seemed something inexplicably strange in the appearance of nature. Heavy, dark masses of clouds stumbled and rolled about in dire confusion; a calm fell suddenly, and the air became thick and heavy, causing a difficulty in respiration. The sea, imitating the clouds, rose in crested masses. The ship became inundated with numbers of beautiful butterflies, and many species of sea birds crowded the deck, and lay with drooping wing, completely exhausted, some even entering the cabin.

The observant student can see the evidences of a Deity in a blade of grass, or the pebble by the seashore. But in my mind, the man who could witness those scenes " *Cujus sui pars*," without acknowledging the manifest workings of a Supreme Being, that there is a God who " rides on the wings of the wind," and bowing before his Omnipotence, must, indeed, be no better than the brute devoid of soul and reason. Truly hath the Psalmist said, " those whose business is on the great waters, see the wondrous works of the Lord."—*Telegraph and Courier.*

" We lament to find, in the *Levant Herald*, an account of a fearful catastrophe at Erzeroum. On the morning of the 2nd June, the town was visited by an earthquake, consisting principally of one terrible shock, which lasted fifteen seconds, and occasioned immense loss of life and property. It is roughly calculated that 1,500 persons perished; and nearly all the large buildings are destroyed. Slight shocks continued to occur till the evening of the 3rd. Of all calamities, perhaps, none is so terrific as this. Fifteen seconds, and fifteen hundred souls launched into eternity—more than a hundred with every pulse !"

BAY OF BENGAL.—12*th to* 17*th June* 1859.

We learn that the Barque *General Godwin*, Captain Christopher Marshall, which left Calcutta for Rangoon this time last month, immediately after she put to sea, was caught in the very thick of the late gale. For three days and nights, she had to withstand the pitiless pelting of the storm ; but the good ship appears to have weathered it out right gallantly, under the management of her skilful and experienced Commander, who, we believe, a year or two ago, achieved a remarkable passage through Torres' Straits. Subjoined is an extract from the letter of a passenger on the *General Godwin*, giving some particulars of his experiences during the time the hurricane lasted :—

" *Rangoon*, 23*rd June.*—We have been in harbour for the last five days, but the *Baltic* has been here twelve hours only. You will say that we made a very quick passage indeed, and so we have, thank God! but what we have gone through is little known to you. Our troubles, however, are at an end, I hope, and I am now as comfortable and in as good health as I ever was. When the pilot left us, which was on Sunday the 12th, we had beautiful weather; in fact too good almost, for it was nearly a dead calm. We were obliged, therefore, to anchor, lest the tide should drift us away to the westward. We weighed anchor, however, on the setting in of the ebb, and made sail about 5 P.M. About an hour after dark it began to freshen, and continued increasing till about midnight, when it blew very hard; so much so that we were obliged to sail under close-reefed topsails. Towards the morning the top-gallant yards were brought on deck, and every preparation made for a heavy gale.   At daylight it blew still more strongly; the fore-topsail was furled, and a fourth reef put to the main-topsail.   This latter, being a new sail, held on; but so strongly was it blowing that the reef holes split an inch or two.   All this time the sea was running mountains high, and we were shipping water fore and aft.   The pumps were obliged to be kept agoing every hour; everything was afloat on board, and you won't be surprised to hear that my chest of drawers was lying a foot deep in water, so that all my clothes were quite wet; in fact, so were the clothes of everybody else.   All hands had no rest, no dinner could be cooked.   The crew lived on half-cooked rice, and we on a kind of stew made of fowls, ducks, potatoes, onions, &c., boiled down together.   But the worst of all was that salt water got into the tanks, and there was no fresh water to drink.   It was discovered, however, that one of the tanks had escaped the salt; but though this water was not brackish, the rolling of the ship had stirred up the rust of the iron tank, and the water was of a dark copper colour, so that it could not be drunk.   This was the worst calamity of all—the tea was salt, and in fact everything was salt.   All the glass-ware and crockery on board was smashed. The gale continued for three whole days and nights without the least signs of abating ; but on the fourth day there was a lull and signs of breaking up ; but the sea still ran high.   At one moment we were on the summit of a huge hill of water; at another in a hollow with two such hills on each side of us.   On the fifth day, however, the sea settled down, and it blew steadily from S.W., and with this wind we reached Rangoon on the eighth day after we left the pilot.   I have said, we had only stew to eat, and I may mention how I ate it.   Sitting at table or anywhere else was out of the question; so standing up, I jammed myself between the locker and my chest of drawers to steady myself; but just as I was in the act of putting a spoonful into my mouth, the ship gave such a lurch, that spoon, soup-plate, stew and all went flying from my hands, and I should have lost my dinner, but that fortunately some stew was left."—*Bengal Hurkaru, July 8th.*

The Ship *Stree Lutchmy Pursad*, 600 tons burden, J. Shaw, Commander, which sailed from Madras on the 28th May last, bound to Moulmein (in ballast, with 13 passengers), was totally wrecked off Cape Negrais.   The *Rangoon Times* states, that three days after the departure of this vessel from Madras, she experienced strong south-westerly gales, in which she lost her foremast.   She also experienced heavy and terrific squalls across the Bay, which induced the Captain, upon sighting Cape Negrais on the 10th of June, to anchor in 11 fathoms of water with 70 fathoms of chain cable paid out.   This was done with a view to enable some requisite repairs being made to the vessel before proceeding further on the voyage. Misfortunes, however, never come singly, for while at anchor off Cape Negrais, a terrific squall struck the ship on the 14th day of June, which, after carrying away her chain cable, caused her to be blown on shore among the rocks, where she went to pieces.   The ship's boats were lost, and the disaster was so sudden that it was an utter impossibility to save any property.   The Captain, with 20 of the crew, saved themselves by swimming ashore.   The Captain's wife and daughter, with eight female passengers and seven of the crew, met with a watery grave.   These poor shipwrecked men then travelled, partly by land and partly by water, till they reached Bassein, where the Captain entered a protest anent the loss of the ship before Major D. Brown, Deputy Commissioner. The carpenter of the vessel also sustained an irreparable loss by the death of his wife, and some three or four children.—*Ibid.*

OFF JACOBABAD.—*20th June.*

The following is from our Jacobabad correspondent :—

Jacobabad, 21*st June.*—Some of the boisterous winds that are blowing about Bombay at this time of the year, visited us last night. The day had been unusually hot, oppressive, and sultry ; but a slight breeze set in about 9 o'clock P.M., dying away at 10, and freshening again at 11, and finally settling into a furious gale. At 12, its force was something awful. The heavens opened, and large drops of rain descended in smart showers ; loud and prolonged claps of thunder rolled overhead, as if the whole artillery of heaven was being discharged ; and broad vivid sheets of lightning played on the whole expanse of country around, scorching the eyes :—ton loads of dust as usual. The gale lasted about two hours. On awaking at 5 in the morning, I found I had undergone a transformation. I turned in at 9 o'clock after a cold water bath as clean as a new pin, but in the morning the dust was on me half an inch thick. I shook off buckets full. The delicious fragrance of the atmosphere in the morning tempted me to indulge in a walk, notwithstanding that I had scarcely any sleep during the night. I hadn't taken fifty paces when the ravages of the night's furious gale met my eye in all directions ; huge Sind cedars entirely rooted up, large branches of the strong babool severed from the trunk and ready to drop off. Chimney-tops were blown the dickens knows where. The unfortunate telegraph inspector's tent was blown away, and he along with it. I met him just as he was returning on horseback from visiting the telegraph posts along the line, to see if any were knocked down ; not a single one had received any injury ; and it highly amused me to witness the horrid contortions of his phiz, as he related last night's disaster, how he was jammed between the leg of a table and his charpoy, with a large heavy wet tent over him. I have also been given to understand that a gentleman of the engineer department who has his camp pitched about two or three miles away, suffered a similar mishap, but did not come off so cheaply ; in his attempt to rush out when the tent was coming down he ran foul of a trunk, smashed the bridge of his nasal protuberance, and had four of his front teeth knocked out.—The weather to-day is delightful, quite like a summer's day at home, and everything outside looks beautifully fresh and green.—*Sindian, June 25th.*

[We do not know that this storm had anything to do with those in the Bay of Bengal of the same date, but the simultaneousness of their occurrence makes it worth while to mention them together.]

IN THE UPPER PORTION OF THE BAY OF BENGAL, AND LOWER DELTA OF THE GANGES.—*Betwixt the 25th and 28th July* 1859.

THE LATE GALE.—As apprehensions exist for the safety of the shipping at the head of the Bay, H.M.S. *Punjaub* proceeds immediately to cruize about the

Sandheads in search of distressed vessels, carrying down a number of Pilots in the event of falling in with inward bound vessels or others in distress, and the Pilot Brigs not being at their stations. The Steamer *Despatch* has been sent down through Channel Creek to visit the Houses of Refuge.—*Englishman, July 30th.*

We have been favoured with the following letter from Diamond Harbour, dated 28th July 1859 :—

" We left the ghaut at 9 A.M. of the 26th, and had fine weather till we got to Hooghly Point, some 10 miles from Diamond Harbour, when the wind blew strongly from the northward, and by great exertion we managed to get into a creek. At dawn of day of the 27th, it blew a perfect hurricane from the north-west. After undergoing great fatigue, being completely drenched to the skin, and all our baggage and stores damaged by salt water, we got safely on *terra firma* at 8 P.M. After quitting the creek, several of us never expected to get safely to land; it blew so fearfully strong. The seas making over the boat, it became disabled ; her rudder having been unshipped, made things look very gloomy. The steam tug *Canning* is lost off Culpee, with Captain Ludlam and eleven of her crew. The steamer *Forbes* is ashore abreast the station also ; the anchor boat *Hercules* a little below ; and a French ship aground off Canterbury Point. One lascar was lost from the *Forbes*. The ship *Wilhelmsburgh* proceeding down was dismasted at Saugor. The Bund in several places has been washed away, and several trees uprooted ; so you see, we have had some hard and trying times of it. We have Harwood, of the Police Office, here, also the Reverend Mr. Babanau. They were passengers on board the steamer *Forbes*. They have been very hospitably treated, and will leave for town by the first opportunity availing. The crew of the *Forbes* are here ; also those saved out of the *Canning*. The weather continues unsettled yet."—*Ibid.*

The following is from a correspondent at Diamond Harbour, dated the 28th instant :—

" Between the hours of 2 and 3 P.M., on the 26th instant, the wind blew strongly from the N.E., with heavy squalls of rain, and cloudy threatening weather. This continued throughout the night, till dawn of day, when it blew a perfect " hurricane." The tug steamer *Canning* went down at her anchors off Culpee, in four fathoms of water ; and I regret to say, that Captain Ludlam and eleven of her crew were drowned. The chief officer and the remainder of the crew managed to get on shore, and walked up to the Magistrate's cutchery, and ultimately to the Customs' station, where they are at present located. The tug steamer *Forbes*, belonging to the same Company as the *Canning*, parted from her cables, and was driven on shore abreast the Customs' station, where she lies a " wreck." Captain Arrowsmith has written up to town for assistance, as he is sanguine of getting her off. A lascar, belonging to the *Forbes*, met with a watery grave. The crew of the last named tug are also located at the Customs' station. The anchor boat *Purchase* was driven on shore ; also the French ship *Periguy*. The bund facing the Customs' station has been washed away, and several trees uprooted. A brig from the coast, laden with cocoanuts, capsized in Hooghly Bight. Two passengers by the

10 *g*

Forbes,—Mr. Harwood of the Police, and the Reverend Mr. Babanau, also putting up at the Customs' station,—being desirous of getting up to town, signalled to the Government steamer *Despatch*, proceeding up, to give them a passage. " Bear a hand" was signalled in reply, but no attempt was made to stop the vessel. I conclude that the party in charge of the steamer could not have been a " British," tar otherwise he would not have left his distressed brethren in the shameful manner he did. The electric telegraph is out of order. The ship *Sultana*, with emigrants on board, is lying off Canterbury Point. This is the vessel the *Canning* was towing down. The *Forbes* was bound up. I have been given to understand that Messrs. Payne & Co., of the Belatee Bungalow, intend to open a branch of their establishment at this place. To make it " pay," they will have to sell " Marine" stores. The weather still continues threatening.—*Hurkaru, July 30th.*

By the mail steamer *Burmah*, we regret to learn the total loss of the barque *Neptune* off the Megoo River, near Akyab. This vessel left this port on the 23rd ultimo for Bombay, having on board a detachment of about 80 men and officers of H.M's. 31st Regiment. She encountered very heavy weather after her departure; and when in the latitude of the Andamans, a severe gale carried away her spars, which obliged her to make to a port for safety. Jury yards, &c. were rigged, and the vessel headed towards Akyab. The weather continued boisterous and cloudy; no observations could be taken to ascertain the position of the barque; everything depended on the accuracy of the dead reckoning, and it was so far good, that the vessel fetched a little to the northward of the Bolongo Island. At this time the weather became worse; the jury yards, &c. carried away, and the vessel left to the mercy of the elements. She drove between the rocks and the shore, and came to anchor, with the intention of repairing the injury and resuming her voyage, but the sea was too heavy. Her cable snapped, she drove on the reef, and immediately lost her foremast. This occurred on Monday morning, the 1st instant; and guns of distress were fired, calling on the officials at Akyab for speedy assistance.— *Hurkaru.*

LOWER BENGAL.—*25th to 27th July,* 1859.

The following extract from the log of the American ship *Ashburton,* now lying at Alleppie, is published by the *Cochin Courier* of the 2nd instant. From the latitude and longitude given, it will be seen that the English ship was only 12 miles from the nearest land, viz. Anjengo; and it is to be hoped she has been able to clear Cape Comorin:—

" *Friday,* 22nd *July.*—First part of this twenty-four hours, calm. During the night, heavy squalls and rain; hauled up the courses, and clewed down topsail yards during the night. At daylight, saw a large English ship on our weather beam, bearing east, distant five miles, Lat. 8° 35′ N., Long. 76° 25′ E., with fore and main topmasts, mizen topgallant mast, jibboom, and heads of fore and main masts carried away. As she was in sight for eight hours, and showed no signals, or bore down for us, we kept on our course. Could see the hands clearing away the wreck.

" P.S. As she had two topsail yards to the mizen, supposed her to be a six topsail yard ship."

The following is an authentic report of the loss of the *Chinsurah*, a barque of 461 tons, Captain Eastaway, from London to this port, with a very valuable cargo, which was lost on the Gaspar on the 1st instant. On the 24th ultimo, the pilot took charge of the ship, and found the captain in a dying state. Owing to a violent gale coming on, he was obliged to put to sea. The gale continued from the 24th to the 27th, when it moderated. On the 26th the ship seriously damaged her rudder. On the 30th anchored in the Gaspar channel. On the 1st the wind came round to the south-west, and as there was too heavy a sea to ride in the Gaspar channel, weighed and endeavoured to get into Saugor roads, engaging the *Sestos* tug steamer to take the ship in tow. On approaching the centre buoy of the Gaspar, the vessel became unmanageable. Signalized the *Sestos* for immediate assistance, as the rudder was damaged. The steamer took no further notice except hoisting the signal, 'steer N.N.W.' At 2-30, struck heavily in 19 feet 6 inches, Steamer *Sestos* still keeping a long distance off. At 3-30, ship had 7 feet water in her hold, her white paint being then half under water. To the astonishment of those on board, the steamer left them, making the best of her way for Saugor roads, although they must have seen that there were no boats at the quarters.

METEOROLOGICAL OBSERVATIONS *taken at the Surveyor General's Office, Calcutta, during the Week ending Saturday, July* 30th, 1859.

Date.	Reduced Reading of Barometer at 10 A.M.	THERMOMETER.		Daily Range of the Temperature.	Mean Temperature for the day.	Mean Wet Bulb.	Computed Mean Dew-point.	Mean degree of humidity for the day.	Prevailing Direction of Wind during the day.	Rain.
		Highest Reading.	Lowest Reading.							
	Inches.	°	°	°	°	°	°	°		Inches.
July 24	Sunday.	—	—	—	—	81.1	—	--	Sunday.	
25	29.312	91.6	81.0	10.6	85.0	81.1	79.1	0.83	N. & S.E.	0.79
26	.213	85.8	77.8	8.0	81.1	78.2	76.7	.87	N. & N.E.	} 4.04
27	.140	83.8	78.0	5.8	80.4	78.2	77.1	.90	N.E. & S. & E.	
28	.533	87.8	80.1	7.7	83.7	80.9	79.5	.88	S. & E.	0.21
29	.578	92.0	81.4	10.6	85.7	82.3	80.6	.85	S. & S.E.	.
30	.576	90.9	82.6	8.3	85.9	81.8	79.7	.82	W. & Calm.	

The mean temperature and the mean wet bulb are derived from the twenty-four hourly observations made during the day. The dew-point is computed with the Greenwich constants. The figures in column nine, represent the humidity of the air, the complete saturation of which being taken at unity.

The extreme variation of temperature during the past week............   14.2
The maximum temperature during the past week....................   92.0
The max. temperature during the corresponding period of the past year.   92.0
The mean humidity during the past week ....   0·86
The mean humidity during the corresponding period of the past year....   0·85

                                                                    Inches.
The total fall of rain during the past week......................   5·04
The total fall of rain between the 1st January and the 30th ultimo .....   30·93
The total fall of rain during the corresponding period of the past year ..   29·86

On the 26th July, a high northerly wind sprung up about 10 A.M., and continued to blow till 5 P.M., after which a north-easterly wind set in and blew for about 3 hours.   About 8 P.M., the wind veered and became easterly, which rose to a gale; the directions of which, during several hours of its continuance, were as follows :—

From 8 P.M. till midnight, Easterly.
Midnight till 1 A.M. on the 27th July, Northerly.
1 A.M. till 8 A.M., North-Easterly.
At 8 A.M. the gale ceased.

During the prevalence of the gale there was incessant rain, but no thunder and lightning. The ten minutes' observations taken during the gale, show that at 8 P.M., which was the commencement of the gale, the Barometer stood at 29·069 inches; it then continuously descended till it became 28·719 inches at 3-40 A.M.; after which the barometer began to ascend, attaining to the height of 28·870 inches at 7 A.M. The ten minutes' observations were given up at this hour; but the barometer was observed to rise continuously (without indicating the usual tides), till the midnight of the 28th, at which time the height it stood at was 29·458 inches.

IN THE CHINA SEAS.—*July 25th and 26th.*—Simultaneous with the hurricane in the Bay of Bengal, a typhoon occurred betwixt Hongkong and Singapore, a little north of the line. We can hardly suppose that this had any connection with the gale at the same date blowing betwixt the 18th and 24th parallels; but the fact of the perfect coincidence of their dates is curious.

THE " PEKIN."—The Peninsular and Oriental Company's steam-ship *Pekin,* Captain Burne, arrived here on Monday, having left on the 22nd ultimo. She encountered a very heavy typhoon on the morning of the following day, which lasted without any abatement until the 26th.   On the 25th, observed a large junk working heavily in the typhoon; shortly afterwards she sunk, and only 6 lives out of 100 men were saved, being hauled on board the *Pekin* by ropes.   On the 27th, spoke the Dutch brig *Wilhelmina,* in the China Sea; also passed the P. & O. Co.'s S. S. *Granada.—Straits' Times, August 6th.*

The following is from Bhaugulpore, dated 4th August :—

" We had a very severe gale on the 27th ultimo. It began at 7 A.M., and lasted, with little intermission, for upwards of forty-eight hours. The mischief among the native craft on the river must have been proportionately great, if we are to judge of it from the gangs of shipwrecked boatmen passing daily through the station, on their way to their homes up country. Our commissioner, Mr. Yule, who happened to be on the river, near Rajmahal, about the same time, had a very narrow escape from a watery grave : his budgerow was overtaken by the storm, when under sail, and ere she could be put to, was capsized. The presence of mind, and self-possession displayed by the commissioner, on this most trying occasion, are worthy of all praise. No sooner did he perceive the danger of his situation than he prepared himself to meet it ; viz. by making up a small bundle of necessaries and fastening it under his arm, and by shifting his quarters from the cabin to the chopper of the boat. The crisis came—the boat rolled and tossed about, and was swamped at last ; but her passenger had luckily left her a few seconds before, and was already some distance from her, swimming, when she sank. The rest is soon told. Finding himself on *terra firma*, Mr. Yule made the best of his way to the next village, some distance inland, where he passed the next 20 hours, or until he obtained the loan of an elephant from some one, when he pushed on to Colgong, some 40 miles. At that place, he found a horse waiting (for which he had telegraphed from some station down below), on which he rode into Bhaugulpore, another 20 miles."— *Phœnix, August 9th,* 1859.

In the Bay of Bengal, betwixt nearly the same parallels, the number of hurricanes being the same, the proportions for each month differ most importantly from those in the China Seas. In the former region, April and May give us five ; and for three years out of five they occur on nearly the same day of the latter month ;—in the latter we have none. In the China Seas, September is the stormiest month in the year. In the Bay of Bengal it has, since 1854, furnished us no storms at all.

Turning next to the Arabian Sea betwixt the parallels of 6° and 22° N.,—over peaceful so far as cyclones are concerned,—we find that we have only had four within the period under discussion. One of these (26th April 1859) was in reality a Coromandel storm, crossing over to Malabar. The other three all occurred betwixt Cooria Mooria Bay and the Gulf of Aden : though of great violence, as they were singularly circumscribed in their field of action, it is needless to classify them. The following extract from the Appendix to the previous number (XIV) gives an abstract of the hurricanes in the Arabian Seas so far as our records extend. It is not a little singular that, out of nine, three should have occurred in the first week of November.

1648. *May* 27.—"A hellish hurricane," as it is termed by the Portuguese historians, accompanied by an earthquake, shook Western India; and similar things occurred on 27th May 1848, but on this occasion the gale was not revolving.

1783. *November* 3-7.—Violent hurricane from Tellicherry north to Bombay; great loss of shipping and lives; proving fatal to almost every ship within its reach.

1790. *November* 3-7.—Frightful hurricane from Calicut north. H.M. Ship *Resolution*, with about 1,000 small craft and 400 lives lost in Bombay harbour.

1807. *June* 24.—Furious hurricane off Mangalore.—*As. An. Register*, p. 171.

1819. *September* 25.—At Kutch and Kattiawar, lasted a day and two nights.— *As. Jl.* 1820, vol. ix., p. 307 (?)

1827. *December* 20.—Bombay (?)

1837. *June* 15.—A tremendous hurricane swept over Bombay: an immense destruction of property and loss of shipping in the harbour, estimated at nine and a half lakhs (£90,000); upwards of 400 native houses destroyed.

1847. *April* 19.—Terrific hurricane from the Line north to Scinde, in which the H.C.S. *Cleopatra* was lost, with 150 souls on board. The Maldive Islands submerged, and severe want and general famine ensued.

1854. *November* 2-3.—Hurricane at Bombay; a thousand human beings and half a million worth of property supposed to have perished in four hours' time.

In the Appendix to the 12th number of our Transactions (p. 2) the following classification of the hurricanes of the East and West Indies occurs :—

PROPORTIONS OF HURRICANES OCCURRING IN EACH MONTH.

	West Indies.	*East Indies.*
January	5	0
February	7	0
March	11	1
April	6	5
May	5	9
June	10	2
July	42	4
August	96	5
September	80	8
October	69	12
November	17	9
December	7	5

The West India list extends over three hundred years, commencing with 1493, giving a table of four hundred hurricanes; of three hundred and sixty-five of which

only are the dates made known.   The Bombay list extends over a century ; but as
it could only be made anything like correct for the space of twenty-five years, the
abstract is deduced from those occurring betwixt 1830 and 1854, to the north of
the line and betwixt the meridians of Canton and Kurrachee.   We find that in the
West Indies, a hundred and eighty-eight hurricanes have occurred within the present
century, or at the rate of 3·5 annually.   In our seas, sixty-one have been recorded
during the past twenty-four years, or on an average of 2·5 annually.   The space
over which our review extends, includes the singularly tranquil waters of the
Arabian Sea, and excludes the great hurricane track of the Mauritius.

The list I have already given furnishes the means of materially extending this classification ; and I shall subdivide them not only according to the months in which they occur generally, but arrange them
under the heads of the places of their occurrence.

CHINA SEAS, LAT. 8° to 22° N.

Hurricanes.	Date.	Hurricanes.	Date.
None.	January.	1	August 30th, 1858.
None.	February.	4	September 6th, 1857 ; 5th,
None.	March.		20th, and 30th, 1858.
None.	April.	2	October 18th, 1856 ; and
None.	May.		29th, 1857.
None.	June.	None.	November.
2	July 21st, 1856 ; and 25th,	None.	December.
	1858.		

It will from this be seen that for the past five years, nine hurricanes
in the China Seas have been confined to the months of July, August,
September, and October,—September showing the most.   The cyclone
month of November, betwixt the Burmese and African shores, is
barren east of the Straits.

BAY OF BENGAL.

Hurricanes.	Date.	Hurricanes.	Date.
None.	January.	1	July 26th, 1859.
None.	February.	None.	August.
None.	March.	None.	September.
2	April 10th, 1858 ; and 21st,	2	October 28th, 1857 ; and 20th,
	1859.		1858.
3	May 15th, 1855 ; 15th, 1856;	1	November 18th, 1856.
	and 15th, 1858.	None.	December.
None.	June.		

The other gales enumerated in the list do not require to be classified ; and I am not sure besides that they were revolving or true hurricanes.

The talent and labour,—or rather the labour, for no talent is required,—in producing this form of classification is insignificant to the pains and experience requisite for analysing the elements of a hurricane. Yet were the system carried out—for which a little industry suffices—there need not be a degree over the surface of the ocean where the mariner was not provided with the means of guessing his chances of encountering a gale at any given date.

Art. III.—OBSERVATIONS ON THE BED AND DELTA OF THE NILE.—*By Assistant Surgeon* George Birdwood, *M.D.*

Read before the Society, October 20th, 1859.

These "Observations on the Bed and Delta of the Nile" are but a critique on the hypotheses broached by the learned Doctor Buist, in his "Notes on the Geology of Lower Egypt," (a) that the bed of the Nile has repeatedly risen and sunk, and (β) its delta lengthened within the last 4,000 years.

At page 4 of his *brochure*, the learned Dr. Buist writes, "The bed of the Nile, within the last 4,000 years, has, in all likelihood, repeatedly sunk and risen again ; and Dr. Lepsius mentions a series of monuments at Senneh, in Nubia, which record the highest points reached by the inundation, and bear dates of King Amenemba, the third of the 12th dynasty, whom Lepsius supposes to have reigned 2,200 B. C. Fifteen of these are still available for reference, the height of them proving that the Nile then rose 25 feet higher than in modern times. From the dates of these, it appears that there was, for a series of years, a steady increase in the rise of the flood, and then a gradual decrease, corresponding exactly with the theory of depression and upheaval."

The substratum on which Egypt—"the gift of the Nile"—rests, may, certainly, at one time, have been under water ; all North Africa, except the Atlas and Arabian mountains, being an aqueous formation of the secondary and tertiary ages, and then, as it is believed, covered by the Mediterranean, or a corresponding midland sea. During those ages, the rocky foundation on which Egypt has since been laid, was, in all likelihood, repeatedly submerged and emerged ; but all the evidence we possess is against the conclusion of such subsidences and elevations having occurred within the historic period ; while the presumption is of the strongest, that it was completely evolved, in the main as it is to day, before the creation of man, according to its accepted time, and from the first, on a platform permanently above the level of the sea.

11 *g*

Indeed, within historic times, Egypt, " from the Plinthinetic Gulf to
Lake Serbonis," and from " Pharos Isle" to "the Tower of Syene,"
or even "utmost Axume," would appear to have been free from all
geologic change, the effect of subterranean agency. We cannot deny
the marks of such agency about Egypt, but it never appears
to have involved Egypt. We know that, since ancient times,
the Nile has been smitten in all its seven streams,—that its Pelusiac
branch has failed, that its Canopic branch has been supplanted by the
Bolbitine,—that its bed is higher and more westward, and the apex of
its delta further north than when Herodotus was at Heliopolis ; but
these are changes incidental to all strong and muddy waters, flowing
through unresisting soils, such as the " black and crumbly" earth of
Egypt, the tschernozoieme of Pontine Russia, and the " regur" of the
Deccan cotton fields, and have no connection whatever with the perpendicular oscillations of the Nile bed, assumed by Dr. Buist.   The Bolbitine and Bucolic Nile were, indeed, artificial works ; and Menes is
said to have diverted the Nile even above its delta, from Lybia to
Memphis.   The cyclical rise and fall of the Nile inundations assumed
by Dr. Buist, lend no aid to his hypothesis of the alternate upheavals
and depressions of its bed, for the assumption is altogether gratuitous.
There is not a mark, not a record, not a tradition in Egypt of the
Nile flood ever having either " steadily increased" or " gradually decreased ;" the marks, the record, and the tradition of a change in the
Nile level at Senneh, being of a *sudden cataclysm, peculiar both in its
cause and in its effects to that especial locality, and even as such an
isolated phenomenon, far more fairly attributable to the operations of
water and quarrying, than to volcanic action.

Sir Gardner Wilkinson,—"the Nestor of Egyptology," as the Chevalier Bunsen has called him,—in commenting on the statements of Herodotus,—" that the Egypt, to which the Greeks go in their ships, is an
acquired country—the gift of the Nile," and that " the shells found in
the *desert* sufficiently prove that the sea formerly extended farther into
the country,"—observes that, " as marine productions have not been
met with in boring to the depth of 40 feet in the *Delta*, it is evident
that *its soil* was deposited from the very first on a space already above
the level of the Mediterranean."   That the general level of Egypt is
continually rising, is manifest everywhere throughout Egypt ; and is,

* *Sudden,* as compared with a cyclical change.

indeed, implied in the fact of Egypt being simply the deposit of the Nile, simply an apron of alluvium, precipitated from the river, on a secondary and tertiary basis, and gradually elevating the river, to which it owes itself, above that basis. Similarly the Yang-tse-kiang, flowing over a more level foundation than the Nile, has, it is said, in many places, become so earthed up, that it seems to run along the top of a wall, rather than through an ordinary channel. This perpendicular elevation of Egypt, by the ceaseless defecation of the Nile, combined, especially on the immediate banks of the river, with the slow accumulation of vegetable mould, and everywhere of desert sand, is proved by the way in which such monuments as the obelisk of Oristasen, and the vocal Memnon, at Thebes, have become buried; by the fact of Heliopolis, which, in the times of Herodotus, was on the edge of the desert, being now surrounded by Nile détritus; by the gradual increase in the breadth of Egypt, its cultivable area yearly advancing on the desert; and by the necessity which has always existed, for the Egyptians banking up their villages and towns, from time to time, to save them from being overflowed, a labour to which, in his days, Herodotus states, all criminals deserving of death, and war captives, were condemned. The land increases East and West, because the Nile, always rising in proportion to its bed, must, as the latter continually silts up, overflow, and cover with its rich alluvium an ever-widening space of ground. Some, as M. de Luc, have thought that Egypt is being reduced in breadth; but the reduction is only seeming, a result of diminished cultivation. Sand-downs are indeed blown about the whole country; and, on the sub-sidence of the inundations, the desert in turn, overwhelms the river deposit, but only partially, and for a time, the river always steadily, despite all counteraction, encroaching on the desert. It is to this ceaseless wrestling between the Nile and the Lybian sands, for the mastery of Egypt, that the sharp intercallation of desert sand and river mud observed in the Delta by Dr. Buist is owing, and not, as he sup-poses, to volcanic upheavals and depressions. The rise of the land in Egypt is, at any point along the Nile, exactly proportionate to the amount of the flood there. The more northwards the river runs, the lower is its inundation; and we find consequently that, while in seventeen hundred years, its deposit has been 9 feet at Elephantine, and 7 at Thebes, in the Delta it is scarcely appreciable, although there the immediate banks of the river are, in some spots, from the accumulation of humus, as high as anywhere else.   In all these facts, we have no indications of volcanic upheaval ; nor have we on the other hand, any indication whatever of volcanic depression; while the facts *opposed* to the hypothesis of such depression are many and positive.   Sir Gardner Wilkinson observes that, " the grove of Acanthus (Acacia nilotica ; *Sont.*) alluded to by Strabo still exists above Memphis at the base of the low Lybian hills ;" and that " in going from the Nile to Abydus, you ride through the grove of acacia once sacred to Apollo, and see the rising Nile traversing it by a canal similar to that which conveyed the water thither when the geographer visited that city, even then reduced to the condition of a small village ;" that in the Fyoom we have the evidence of its having been tilled by the ancient inhabitants, in some parts of it " the vestiges of beds and channels for irrigation as well as the roots of vines " being found in their old sites " far above the level of the rest of the country ;" and that " in the vicinity of Lake Mœris, are several watercourses and canals with the roots of vines and other trees which are distant more than 12 miles from the nearest irrigated land." " I do not," he continues, " mean to affirm that these are actually of the early time of the Pharoahs, but they undoubtedly owe their origin to the system of cultivating the *hóger* adopted by the ancient Egyptians, and this extensive culture of the vine is, at least, prior to the Arab invasion." Indeed, by the universal confession of the inhabitants themselves, no canals or cultivation have been maintained in this spot within the period of Moslem records ; and tradition asserts, that the province of Fyoom, which now contains about 80 villages, had more than four times that number, in the flourishing periods of the Pharonic kings. Now, if the Nile bed had always been undergoing depression, these primæval groves, canals, and roots should have either been submerged or inhumed ; inhumed, if the depression had always been accompanied by corresponding deposition ; submerged, if not. As neither catastrophe has overtaken them, the fair conclusion is, that the land has not been depressed. We can conclude the same from every monument and town throughout the valley of Egypt, and in the ruins of Bubastis we have a witness far more striking, though not a whit more strong, than those above cited, of the soundness of this argument. But I must delay enlarging on them until it again becomes necessary to speak of depression in connection with the Delta. Dr. Buist asserts that the dates at Senneh prove that there was, for a series of years, a steady increase in the rise of the Nile flood, and then a gradual decrease, corresponding exactly with his hypothesis of depression and upheaval. The facts concerning the inundation bearing on this hypothesis are as follows. In the time of Herodotus 16 feet was necessary to inundate the Delta ; a like rise there is recorded to have been required under the Cæsars and the Caliphs. These are the measurements about Cairo. The inundation, of course, varies along the whole course of the Nile, but at every point where its measure has been preserved, it is found now to be the same as it always has been through the past, except at Semneh. One passage in Herodotus appears to militate strongly against this fact. He says "when Mœris was king, the Nile inundated all Egypt below Memphis as soon as it rose so little as 8 cubits." Mœris was king 500 years before the sack of Troy. From, however, the overwhelming testimony, that the inundation has always reached the same height at the same place, throughout Egypt, " it is clear," says Sir Gardner Wilkinson, in Rawlinson's Herodotus, "that the change from the time of Mœris to Herodotus could not have been what he supposes. The 8 cubits at Mœris were either calculated at a different level, or at some place in the Delta far below Memphis." For examples, the inundation at Elephantine was once measured from a far lower level than that from which it is now computed, owing to the Nilometer there having become silted up ; and about Rosetta and Damietta it is about a fourth of what it is at Cairo. Volney also has suggested that, subsequent to Mœris, " an alteration took place in the measures of the country, and one cubit was made into two * * *. In the time of Mœris, Egypt was not united into one kingdom ; there were at least three between Asouan and the sea. Sesostris * * * conquered and united them. But, after this prince, they were again divided, and this division subsisted until the reign of Psammeticus. Such a change in the measures of Egypt accords perfectly with the character of Sesostris, who effected a general revolution in the government, established new laws and a new administration, raised mounds and causeways, on which to build villages and towns, and dug so great a number of canals, according to Herodotus, that the Egyptians laid aside using wheel-carriages, which they had till then employed." This is a mere conjecture, but deserves remembrance in the present connection. But, again in Book II., Chap. 177, Herodotus writes, when Amasis was king "the river was more liberal to the land." Taken literally, it would

be sufficient to explain this passage by unusual rains among the high
valleys of Abyssinia, and the mocking Mountains of the Moon.   But
the truth is, that Egypt suffers as much from over as under inundation, and the above passage has always been understood to signify
the overflowing prosperity the country enjoyed under that monarch,
an explanation fully justified by the context.*

The monuments at Senneh—or rather Semneh—to which Dr. Buist
appeals as a test of his hypothesis, prove that the river at Semneh does
not now rise within 26 feet of the height it attained during the reign of
Amen-m-he III., a Sovereign of the 3rd dynasty of Manetho.   Nothing,
at first sight, could be more to Dr. Buist's purpose than this fact.
A less superficial scrutiny, however, shows it to be at direct variance
with his deductions from it.   Semneh is in Nubia.   Between
Nubia and Egypt at Silsilis the Nile was formerly interrupted by a
natural plutonic barrier.   At some period or other this bund burst.
While it remained, the waters of the inundation had to accumulate behind it, before falling over into Egypt, and of course rose proportionately higher above than below Silsilis.   When it burst, however, this
disproportionate rise of the river throughout Ethiopia, fell to a point at
which it approximated to the general average of Egypt.   The monuments prove that the fall above the bund—at Semneh—was 26 feet.
Without any monuments, however, such a fall at Semneh is calculable
from the ancient watermarks on the rocks at Silsilis, much more than
26 feet above the highest of the modern inundations.   We find too

* Sir G. Wilkinson observes, that this prosperity can only relate to the internal
state of Egypt, to the wonderful extension of its manufactures and commerce, and the
remarkable wealth of the middle classes of its population, and not to the influence of
the country on the neighbouring nations; for abroad, the Egyptians, at this same
time, were utterly despised, as a people which had purchased peace and plenty
from Babylon at the price of independence.   " Let us buy and sell at our ease," was
their language, "and perish Judah and Tyre! perish all who obstruct the will of
Great Babylon!"   Well, in language referring to this period, did Ezekiel prophesy
of Egypt " it is a base kingdom," it shall raise itself no more to " rule over the
nations," " there shall be no more *a prince of the land ;*"—for, a brief while, and
Cambyses has entrapped the huge camp of Pelusium, " the strength of Egypt,"
and the Empire of the Pharoahs has passed away like a dream ! Media, Lydia,
Tyre, and Babylon itself, are then supplicated in vain, for these natural allies
have been allowed to perish that Egypt might buy and sell at ease!   Such was the
fruit of the system of non-intervention pursued by the cotton supply interest of ancient Egypt.   Has it no lesson for us, already so familiar with the honeyed lie
" cotton knows no politics ?"   It warns us, as does the history of every dead
empire, that if a people once " forget the art of war," once cease to vindicate the right
against every evil doer, however great may be the material prosperity they enjoy,
their decline has begun, and their downfall is at hand.

See note on Herodotus, Book II. Chap. 177, and Essay VII. appended to Book I.

that a like proportion of land in the long gorge of Nubia has become barren. Far up in its valleys from the first cataract to the confluence of the Nile with the Tacazzee, lie Nile deposits which the modern floods never reach. Immediately north of Silsilis, however, the alluvium is at once found coincident with the annual flood, and not a line beyond it. The monuments at Senneh then, if they do not sufficiently demon‑strate that the bed of the Nile has remained stable during historic times, will not admit the directly opposite conclusion Dr. Buist has drawn from them.

The water of the Nile, formerly bunded behind the Jebel Silsilis, must, it has been inferred from the appearance of the country to its south, have then formed a vast lake, and this *à posteriori* inference is corroborated by all the *à priori* arguments that can be derived from the phenomena presented by many other great rivers, in the progress of their development. In its *upper course*, a river is but a mountain brook, boiling along zig zag declivities, and leaping down precipices. In its *middle course*, it descends the steadier incline of a sub‑Alpine region of low hill and wide dale; it winds; its channel is broad, but as yet at the best merely a gorge; and when this narrows greatly or runs into a bar or natural weir, the river must gather volume before it can force its onward way, and form at once a waterfall and lake; the latter of greater or less extent, according as the obstruction causing it occurs in an open or a close country. Such lakes and cataracts nearly always mark the *middle course* of a river, generally marking the tran‑sition from the middle to the *lower course* in which it, so noisy at its source, flows slowly through uninterrupted plains to its termination. The Bahr‑el‑Abiad at present frequently expands into such lakes in its descent from the highlands of Central Africa to the Nile; and just one such undoubtedly was the great lake of Ethiopia, which, in primæval times, stretched between the hills of Silsilis and the island of Meræ. Osburn has represented it in a map in the 2nd volume of his " Monumental History of Egypt," and at page 134 observes, " we apprehend the existence of this vast lake or sea to be *very distinctly* shadowed forth by the Egyptian myths, which have been preserved in the Greek tradition. The Nile, the priests told Herodotus, came from the *ocean** and flowed into the ocean again. *The historian was greatly*

* The " *ocean*" here referred to, was, probably, the Victoria Nyanza or Lake, not the lake behind Silsilis. This does not, however, affect the bearing of my argument. —*G. B. April* 1860.

perplexed therewith.   As he afterwards tells us, he knew no river with such a source.   The fact that, when first known to the Egyptians, the Nile flowed from a great lake, perfectly solves the difficulty.   The same *fact* accounts, *just as fully*, for the myth preserved in the Book of the Dead regarding the nocturnal course of the sun.   It sank together with the Nile and again rose together with the Nile, from a huge abyss containing infinitely more water than the river itself. *This was denoted by the hieroglyphic name " meh-num," " full of water," " overflowing with water."*   Such was *literally* the case at the time the *fable* was *invented ;* and in the infancy of knowledge it was no unnatural conclusion, that the Lake of Ethiopia, whence the river flowed, and the Mediterranean, into which it emptied itself, were the two shores of one and the same abyss."   At page 133, Osburn, referring to the Jebel Silsileh, writes that, north of that point, "the Nile, through the rest of its course to the sea, has undergone no perceptible change of level, through the many ages during which its valley has been inhabited."   These quotations are highly interesting, although all must agree that many of the conclusions they embody are so unwarranted, as seriously to damage Mr. Osburn's authority as an Egyptologist.   In justice, however, to Dr. Buist, and the more so as Mr. Osburn's book is much read, it must be mentioned that the latter, in considering the mode in which the catastrophe at Silsilis, must have occurred, observes "it is evident that it was not by a sudden fissure of the rock of Djebel Silsileh, or any other result of an earthquake, which would have allowed the whole of this huge volume of water (the Great Ethiopic Lake) to burst forth at once, and utterly sweep from the valley all traces of man and his work.   No such event occurred, as it is perfectly useless for us to explain, *and therefore no such disruption took place."*   Mr. Osburn substitutes no intelligible theory for the one to which he objects, although a sudden disruption at Silsilis is supported by every analogy, by the marks of rupture on the escarps of Jebel Silsileh, and by the Ethiopian name of Silsilis, " Gol-gol" signifying "the rent rocks."   Mr. Osburn's objection to the theory of a " sudden disruption," does not, however, arise from its clashing with any facts, but solely from his fancying that it is opposed to certain peculiar ideas of his own on Egyptian history.

The purpose of his book is to reconcile the Bible with the hiero-glyphic chronicles of Egypt.   In due course, he approaches the account in the Pentateuch of the seven years' plenty and following seven years' famine in Egypt ; and the question is,—how to explain it ? "The great lake of Ethiopia" answers,—or rather is made to answer,—in every way. His "readers *are aware,*" he writes, that its "*overflow really did take place,*" "*during the administration of Joseph ;*" and, that settled, of course, the seven years of plenty naturally arose from the lake draining into Egypt in that time, the Nile inundation having then "very far exceeded all that had ever before been known in Egypt ; so that an extent of surface was brought under cultivation in the Delta unparalled in any former or subsequent period." The seven subsequent years of famine, as naturally, were owing to the absorption of the feeders of the Nile by the bed of the emptied lake, and to "at least seven years" having been "required for the river so to work its own defined course over the plain of Ethiopia before the phenomena of the yearly overflow should re-appear in Egypt in their wonted order." The expression "there was neither earing nor harvest" "leave us surely to infer that, in the course of them, the phenomenon of the overflow never appeared at all." Mr. Osburn's argument, stated nakedly, is—a plenty of seven years and a succeeding famine of seven years having occurred in Egypt in the days of Joseph, the Great Lake of Ethiopia must have burst then, and not suddenly, for the above plenty and famine prove that it must have taken seven years to run off, and again seven years to partially refill and resume the broken current of the Nile. Thus would he torture Egypt to witness to THE TRUTH ! He forgets that seven years was a short period for such a huge volume of water as the Ethiopic Lake, to have passed through the channel at Silsilis, a channel which is still being yearly cleared. He forgets that there is nothing in the *theory* of a sudden formation of a sluice at Silsilis necessarily inconsistent with his own hypothesis. And he forgets that the famine in the days of Joseph, having been "in all lands," cannot be attributable to a cause peculiar to the land of Egypt. Of course, we are not concerned to deny the resolution of the lake of Ethiopia during the days of Joseph ; to deny that resolution as the cause of the plenty and the famine which then prevailed in Egypt ; my sole purpose in reviewing Mr. Osburn's arguments against the theory of a sudden disruption at Silsilis being to show that they, when duly and impartially examined, in no way support Dr. Buist's deductions from the records of the Nilometer at

12 *g*

Semneh. Mr. Osburn, it is clear, in undertaking the work of har-
monising the monumental history of Egypt with the Bible, was bent,
as he himself informs us (page 634) "*to regard the issue of nothing
beyond the matter in hand.*"

Growth of Delta.—It would appear that when Mr. Hurley of Tor-
quay opposed Dr. Buist's notion of upheavals and depressions to áccount
for the assumed increase and decrease in the level of the Nile at Semneh, by suggesting that if the whole basin of the Nile underwent a
subsidence and then a subsequent elevation, * * * the waters of the
river must have participated in the event, and have preserved their
relative level with the banks, whereas the registers at Semneh required
for their solution some phenomenon which would apply to the water
alone, not to the banks, the learned Dr. Buist admitted that Mr. Hurley's
view would indeed be true, had the débouchure of the Nile been so
remote then, as it is now, from Semneh. It is predicated that the bed
of the Nile has, within the last 4,000 years, been several times upheaved
and depressed ; and to prove this, it is gratuitously affirmed, in the teeth
of the contrary verdict of history, that the Delta has lengthened during
the last 4,000 years.

This is indeed reasoning like a parson—*incertum per incertius*—with
a vengeance ! Its logic is that of Des Cartes' famous syllogism, or rather
enthymeme, "*cogito, ergo sum !*" I will take nothing for granted, said
the philosopher, will even deny my own existence until I can verify it ;
" eureka, I think, *therefore* I am." So Dr. Buist, not, however,
doubting everything but believing all things, would demonstrate
an assumed second position by an unproved—nay, a disproved—first !
" Four thousand years ago," writes Dr. Buist, at page 4 of the
brochure under comment "up to the borders of the Theban province, 200 miles south from the present shores of the Mediterranean, was an estuary or marsh, where the gradients and speed
of the river would be directly affected by the rise or fall of the
basin to the northward." There is not a tittle of evidence that the
Delta has lengthened during the last 3,000 years ; and there is every
probability that, as it now is, it has been from the very dawn of Egyptian
civilization. Pelusium, Canopis, Busiris, and Taphoris stand now exactly
where they are said to have stood in the earliest records of them.
" Zoan" is yet "in the field," as in the days of Abraham ; the same great
cities now stand on the Delta as when Rameses was king B. C. 1341 ;

and Heliopolis is now as far from the sea, as when Herodotus was in Egypt, B. C. 455. Now, if, since the days of Abraham, Rameses, and Herodotus, the length of the Delta has not visibly increased, the inference surely is that it was what it then was, and now is, immeasurably before the call of Abraham, before even the creation of man according to its accepted time. Indeed, if the Delta was not formed long before the first gleanings of Egyptian civilization we should be forced, as Sir Gardner Wilkinson states, to throw back the origin of the cities of the Delta "beyond the deluge, or even the Mosaic (*Rabbinical?*—G.B.) era of the creation!" Dr. Buist's assertion may be traced to Herod. Book II. Chap. 13;* " One fact I learnt of the priests is to me a strong argument of the origin of the country. They said that, when Mœris was king, the Nile overflowed all Egypt, below Memphis, as soon as it rose so little as 8 cubits."

Now, forgetting awhile the explanation already given of this passage, and bearing in mind that Mœris "had not been dead 900 years, when" Herodotus "heard this of the priests,"† and that Egypt still answers the description given of it by Herodotus 2,300 years ago, are we not entitled to infer that, if it were true that such overwhelming changes had taken place in the evolution of Egypt in 900 years, that some great changes should have occured in the succeeding 2,315 years, the period from Herodotus to ourselves? What does Herodotus himself say?‡ " It seems to me, therefore, that, if the land goes on rising and growing at this rate, the Egyptians who dwell below Lake Mœris in the Delta (as it is called), and elsewhere, will one day, by the stoppage of the inundations, suffer permanently the fate which they told me they expected would some time or other befall the Greeks." In speaking of the geographical evolution of Egypt, Herodotus states that it "was an acquired country, the gift of the river;" that it "appeared evidently to have formed at one time a gulf of the sea;" that "it resembles (to compare small things with great) the parts about Illium and Teuthrania, Ephesus and the plain of the Mæander," and " the sea opposite the islands called Echinades," which had " already joined one-half of them to the continent" by the deposit of the river Achelous. Again, "my opinion is that Egypt was very much such a gulf as * * * the sea called Erythrean." "Now

* Discussed at page 85.   † Herodotus, Book II. Chap. 13.   See also *Smythe.*
‡ Book II. Chap. 13.

if the Nile should choose to divert his waters from their present bed into the Arabian Gulf, what is there to hinder it from being filled up by the stream within, at the utmost, 20,000 years? For my part, I think it would be filled in half the time. How then should not a gulf of much greater size have been filled up in the ages that passed before I was born, by a river that is at once so large and so given to working changes?" This reasoning is correct in principle, anticipating indeed, as regards the general phenomena of deltas, that of the first of modern geologists, but is incorrect in its facts; and, in so far as it concerns the delta of the Nile, can apply alone, as Sir Gardner Wilkinson has observed, to "the original formation of the land, the soil since the time that Egypt was first inhabited being only deeper and more extended East and West towards the Arabian and Lybian mountains; and whatever form the valley may have had in the early ages of the world, it could not have been a gulf of the sea since Egypt was inhabited."

The statements of Diodorus,—that the Ethiopians "describe the Egyptians as one of their colonies led into Egypt by Osiris," and that it was from the Ethiopians that the Egyptians learned to honour their kings as gods, to bury their dead with so much pomp; and that their writings had their origin in Ethiopia,"—have been regarded as so many proofs presumptive of the growth of Egypt from Ethiopia to the sea. Such reasoning is of the loosest. Diodorus indeed, in connection with the above, adds, " they pretend also that Egypt, at the commencement of the world, was nothing but a morass; and that the inundations of the Nile, carrying down a great quantity of the alluvial soil of Ethiopia, had at length filled it up, and made it a part of the continent; and we see at the mouth of the Nile a peculiarity which seems to prove that the formation of Egypt is the work of the river. After the inundation, we remark that the sea has repelled on the shore large masses of alluvial soil, and that the land is increased." So then the Ethiopians would have it that Egypt,—land and intellect and civilization,—was only a crib from Ethiopia. Hoskin, in 1835, his imagination "ardently excited," as he owns, by his discoveries in Meroe, strongly advocates this view, but more recent research has destroyed every argument in its favour as totally at variance with fact. Pliny has stated that the people from Syene to Meroe were not Ethiopians, but Arabs, and modern ethnologists and philologists have demonstrated that the Nile, through its course in Egypt, is peopled by a primeval immigration of the Caucasian race.* When the immigration took place, history does not teach. On this point, Sir G. Wilkinson,—starting with the fact "that Tanais was already built in the age of Rameses the Great," on the evidence of its monuments, "in addition to the positive authority of Scripture,"—remarks, "it is then evident that neither was the period elapsed between the deluge and the building of Tanais sufficient to form the Delta, nor the constant accumulation of the alluvial deposit of the Nile capable of making so perceptible a change in the extent of that district as to authorize us to suppose the upper parts of the country peopled and civilized while the Delta was a marsh; how much less then can we suppose Ethiopia to have been already inhabited by the ancestors of the future colonizers of Egypt, while that part of the valley lying below the cataracts of Syene was undergoing its formation?" Everything indeed goes to prove that the whole of Egypt was completely evolved before the genesis of man, and certainly not that it was a swamp while yet Ethiopia was inhabited and civilized. The remark with which the last passage quoted from Diodorus concludes, affording positive evidence that Egypt has not been increased by that means since his day, is itself strong presumption that it was not so increased from its first peopling. The annual N. W. wind blows from the Mediterranean up the river during the inundation, and the dislocation of alluvium which is thus caused, together with the dispersing action of the currents which sweep along the Northern bord of Africa from Gibraltar up into the Gulf of Skanderoon, must, in the absence of all proof of the Delta *undergoing* depression,—indeed, in the presence of the strong presumption that it never has been and is not being depressed,—explain the fact of its never lengthening. The Etesian winds striking against the Nile flood more or less obliquely, the direction taken by the latter must necessarily be in the diagonal of these two forces. The disgorging Nile thus helps to propagate through the Levant the prevailing whirl of the Mediterranean, and sweeps far away from Egypt the silt it is charged with, saving such proportion of it as may settle down in the calm water between the Delta and El Arish. Admiral Smyth states that this Mediterranean current drifts the Nile sediment Eastward, and deposits it "along the Syrian shores, thereby leaving Tyre and Sidon inland." So strong is this

* *See* Herod. (*Rawlinson*) B. II. Ch. 16. Note by Sir G. Wilkinson; also Appendix to B. II. Essay I.; also Appendix to B. I. Essay XI.; and Bruce's Travels.

circular Mediterranean current that, in 1801, Captain Culverhouse of H.M.S. "Romulus," while on her passage from Acre to Aboukir Bay, thought he had stranded her several leagues off the Nile, so palpably like a mud bank did a stratum of Nile alluvium, on its way to the Syrian coast, appear. Herodotus, it will be remembered, notices (Book II. Chap. 5) the distance you see the Mediterranean discoloured by the Nile, and would appear to have been influenced by it to his opinion that the Nile was lengthening. Says he " when you are still a day's sail (60 miles) from the land, if you let down a sounding line, you will bring up mud and find yourself in 11 fathoms water, which shows that the soil washed down by the stream extends to that distance." Now, as we have all but completely proved, and presently will completely prove, that the Delta has not grown an inch since Herodotus, and that, at present, it is a very unusual and alarming accident to find yourself in 11 fathoms 60 —aye 30—miles off the Nile, is not the above passage strong evidence that the Nile mud is not even accumulating under the sea off the Lybian coast? The projection of the Delta has been adduced as a proof of its having, at some time at least, pushed itself through the sea. But if the Mediterranean currents are sufficient to drift the Nile mud, actually in fields, to the Syrian coast, the shore of the Delta must project solely because it is fixed immoveably on a . rock,—a projection of the Neptunian foundation on which Egypt is throughout erected; and so is it represented to be in the last published geological map of Africa, although the fact has not yet been stated in any book. The whole coast of Asia Minor and Africa is waved, not straight.* The great

* Sir Roderick Murchison, in his address at the anniversary meeting of the Royal Geographical Society, May 23rd 1859, in reviewing the observations of Captain Spratt on the effect of the prevailing wave influence on the deposits of the Nile, observes that Captain Spratt distinctly proves " that the wave stroke from the west, influenced by the prevailing north-westerly winds, has, for ages, been impeding the transport of any Nile deposits either to the West, or into the depths of the Mediterranean on the north, but has constantly driven them to the east. Through this unvarying natural process, Alexandria, which is on the west of the Nile mouth, has been kept free from silt, whilst the deltoid accumulations of the river have, in the historic era, successively choked up and ruined the harbours of Rosetta and Damietta, and have formed a broader zone in the Bay of Pelusium than on any part of the coast." Referring to what I have written at pages 82 and 90, I would here observe that the choking of the harbours of Rosetta and Damietta is not the effect of any volcanic agency and does not indicate any growth of the Delta by Nile deposit. These harbours have been ruined as much by the lateral oscillations of the strong volume of the Nile in the incoherent soil of the Delta, and the engulfment of drifted desert sands, as by partial silting up. The spits in front of Rosetta and Damietta do not *grow*. Formed within shelter of some projection of the coast, no sooner do they attempt to push into the open sea than they are overwhelmed and

argument, however, for the growth of the Delta, is, or rather was—for the controversy has long become obsolete—the passage in Homer, in which he states " that the isle of Pharos from Αἴγυπτος was as far as a vessel with a fair wind could sail in one day." Now, the proper authorities on Homer, innocent of all geology, have proved, that, by Αἴγυπτος, Homer, in the above passage, means the Nile itself, which, before King Nileus changed its name, was called Ægyptus. Thus, Homer himself elsewhere states that " Menelaus anchored his fleet at the mouth of the Αἴγυπτος." Alexandria is now a day's sail to native craft, from where the Canopic branch of the Nile was ; and the rock of Pharos, an advanced post of the Lybian desert, is now no nearer the coast-line of Egypt than when Helen fled there. We know that it has not been gained on since the days of Alexander ; and how should it have been gained on by the continent and by eleven leagues in the far shorter period betwen Menelaus and Alexander, as it must have been, did not Homer refer to the Nile under the term Αἴγυπτος ? Pharos is still naturally an island, although, from modern Alexandria being chiefly built on the Heptastadium by which Alexandria was artificially connected with the mainland, it appears to have become part and parcel of it, from the assumed growth of the Delta. The very word *Heptastadium* is a sufficient argument against both the learned Dr. Buist's hypotheses ; it brings down, as with one shot, both his winged fancies.

M. Savary, in his " Letters on Egypt," states, on the alleged authority of Strabo, that, in the reign of Psammeticus, the Milesians, with thirty ships, landed at the Bolbitine Nile and built Metelis. Metelis, he further states, to be the modern Foua, which, in the Coptic vocabularies, is still called Messil ; and he argues that, as Metelis was a seaport, and Foua is nine leagues from the sea, therefore the Delta must have lengthened nine leagues from Psammeticus to the present day. Now, it is not certain that Foua represents the ancient Metelis, and, moreover, Strabo nowhere mentions Metelis, as Volney long ago showed. The assumption of the growth of the Delta is finally reduced to an absurdity, when we find that, to meet one set of its advocates, Egypt should have lengthened 200 miles from Mœris to Herodotus ; another, eleven leagues from Helen to Alexander ; and another, nine leagues from Psammeticus to Savary. It

---

dispersed. The port of Pelusium is, indeed, being continuously filled, but why ? Because there is no longer a Pelusiac branch of the Nile to continuously clear it. The *port* of Pelusium was simply the *mouth* of the Pelusiac Nile.

has been advanced that, if the Delta is not growing, it must be undergoing slow depression along its sea-bord. The conclusion is justified *à priori*, by the phenomena presented by other deltas, but the *facts* of the Nile Delta altogether forbid it.

The Acanthus groves of Memphis and Abydus, and the deserted vineyards of Mœris and the Fyoom, have already been cited as facts opposed to the hypothesis of the depression of Egypt. In the ruins of the city of Bubastis, we have another, and far more striking, argument against it, applying not only to Egypt generally, but to the Delta in particular. Herodotus has left us a complete description of Bubastis, with the measurements of its temple and ramparts. That the level of the ground on which the temple stands coincides with that of the surrounding country, and that the ramparts have not been silted up, and the deserted city turned into a fresh-water lake, are proofs, among others, of the imperceptibleness of the Nile deposits in the Delta; and that the whole city and its neighbourhood are not under the waves of the salt sea is evidence unimpeachable that the Delta has not been depressed; for its least depression, if not counteracted by alluvial deposition, would lead to its submergence.

How different, in this respect, the Delta of the Nile is from those of other rivers is well illustrated by a recent discovery in the Delta of the Mississippi. Messrs. Dickeson and Brown have found, in Louisiana, a section of 16 fossil cypress groves, arranged vertically one above the other,—above the whole, flourishing a primeval forest of evergreen oaks. Here we have clear proof of the Delta of the Mississippi having undergone 16 successive subsidences. The first grove sank, earth accumulated over it, another grove sprang up and that too sank, and so on to the last. The same thing is yet happening all over the Mississippi Delta. We see nothing of this sort, however, going on in Egypt; we find no traces of anything of this sort ever having occurred there, although it has been bored all over to the depths of forty and fifty feet. You will remember that Horner, in one of his borings in Egypt, found a piece of pottery some 30 feet below the surface, and that he had stated the discovery to be a proof of the existence of man on the globe for at least 17,000 years. Messrs. Dickeson and Brown, however, in the course of their borings in Louisiana, have been enabled, with the wonted good fortune of Americans, to out-Horner Horner himself. As usual, the Britisher whips creation, but the Yankee whips the Britisher. At New Orleans, 16 feet below the soil, in the fourth of the cypress groves above-mentioned, they found a well-preserved human skull; and judging the Mississippi deposit by that of the Nile, and calculating the ages of the cypress and oak groves from the so-called annual layers of their stems, have concluded that this skull is evidence of the world having been inhabited by man for at least 57,000 years. What has been said of the Nile deposit is sufficient to show that it cannot be used as a test for that of the Mississippi, while it is a familiar fact to the botanist that the so-called annual and annular layers of trees are often, and especially in tropical America, the formation not of years, but of months. Messrs. Dickeson and Brown, like Mr. Horner, have calculated from an undetermined basis. Mr. Horner's potsherd, indeed, turned out to be *Christian*, and it will be very good fun, should Messrs. Dickeson's and Brown's skull prove *Caucasian*. But to speak seriously, the question of the age of man is one of the most interesting which at present engages science, and we must be prepared to find, perhaps, that we are of a more ancient race than the *rabbinical* chronology would make us. But certainly, without more exact information on all the conditions under which this skull of the Mississippi was found, we cannot allow it to disturb our accepted conclusions,—or misconceptions if you will,—on the time of the creation of man. None of the recent discoveries, said to have a significance similar to that of this skull, have ever yet been satisfactorily described,—none are therefore convincing. As for this skull itself, for all we as yet know to the contrary, it may be that of some poor shipwrecked sailor, who only escaped from a watery grave to find one in the cypress quagmire lured by the crowning oaks of evergreen. Had he sunk on through the bog to the 16th grove, his skull would have equally well proved the age of man 300,000 years!

I have entered into the examination of Dr. Buist's hypothesis at great length; for, although the controversy which he has inadvertently reopened has long been settled, and so thoroughly argued out on both sides that, throughout this paper, I have not been able to advance a single original argument, indeed scarcely able to express myself in my own words, I yet feel that it is necessary that it should be on record, in the books of this Society, that our late Secretary's notes on the "Geology of Lower Egypt" did not pass unchallenged. This is the more imperative from the circumstance of all the facts of the lands of the Bible having important bearings on certain momentous matters of opinion and belief. That Dr. Buist, in penning his notes, was forgetful of his responsibilities in connection with this circumstance is so clear,

13 *g*

from his treatment of the vexed question of "the track of the exodus" from Egypt, that I cannot bring this paper to a close without referring to it, ill-qualified although I am to espouse any side in that dispute. In opposition to the *consensus* of the weightiest authorities, he assumes that the retreat of Israel must have been by the canal of Sesostris. He rejects the desert, because he supposes it incapable of supplying the fugitives with supplies and water. "Much more stress," writes Dr. Buist, "is to be set on the probabilities suggested by physical considerations and requirements, than on traditions drawn from antiquity so remote." In this controversy, physical requirements must, of course, be considered, the Bible having left us wide latitude to do so, but history must be held of paramount importance. At the word solely of Dr. Buist, who has never visited the desert route and is no antiquarian, we cannot refuse our consent to the opposite verdict of learned men, who, to antiquarian research, have added personal acquaintance with the whole ground under debate. Dr. Buist's assumption, founded solely on physical considerations, is weakened, too, by his own hypothesis that, within the last 4,000 years, Egypt has several times been depressed and upheaved. The exodus occurred, according to Bunsen, under the 19th dynasty of Manetho, in the reign of Menephthah, more than 3,000 years ago, and, by Dr. Buist's hypothesis, its accredited track may, three or four times since then, have been alternately a pool of standing water, and a parched wilderness. If physical considerations are to be all-in-all in such controversies, some physicist hereafter may, in the teeth of all history, refuse the desert as the Haj route, on the identical ground on which Dr. Buist has refused it as the exodus route. If Dr. Buist be in the right, it is tradition alone that will prove him so. His guess owes all the little importance that attaches to it, to the fact that it is indirectly supported by Bunsen's reading of certain of those remote traditions which Dr. Buist so much despises. Bunsen, starting with the conviction that the books of Moses have, only incidentally, an historic character, believes that we must look to Manetho and Eratosthenes for all that is reliable of the history of Israel *in Egypt*. Assuming that a class of lepers, mentioned by Manetho, were the Israelites, it would appear to the learned chevalier, that, after the evacuation of Egypt by the Hyksos, or Shepherd Kings, (*B. C.* 1548 ?) the Israelites were persecuted by the native dynasties ; much because they had been befriended by the Hyksos ; much also because the Egyptians were jealous of the prosperity of the Jews ; but

chiefly because Joseph had aroused against his race, the hatred of the Egyptians, by the conversion of their freeholds into crown lands, during the terrible seven years of famine. Under the fanatical Menephthah, the severest tasks and cruelties were imposed on them, for their opposition to the worship of his people. They were gathered out of every province, and settled on the edge of the Arabian desert, Avaris being assigned them as their chief town. In Avaris the lepers (the said Israelites) seem to have fortified themselves, and summoned the shepherds from Palestine to their aid. United, they drove Menephthah from Memphis to Ethiopia, and ravaged Egypt for 13 years. Menephthah returned eventually with an army, and drove the allies beyond his borders. From this time, we read no more of the lepers in Egyptian records. Israelites, however, appear in the chronicles of their campaigns, immediately succeeding the rebellion of the lepers, although it is worthy of remark that no such race is mentioned in the chronicle of an Egyptian campaign in Palestine, undertaken just *before* the above event. This Egyptian story then of the exodus is complete only up to the suppression of the rebellion. After that, we are left to the Bible and our own speculations. The shepherds retreated by Typhonian Avaris, and their old stronghold by the river of Egypt, afterwards called Rhinocolura. The Israelites, we know, took the way of the peninsula of Sinai. How they got there, Bunsen will not determine ; but he evidently leans to the conviction of Lepsius, that their route was by the canal, *and by its left bank too.* No deductions, however, as to the route can be made from strategic data. At the outbreak of the rebellion, the Jews, we may suppose, were in Avaris. At its suppression, Memphis had been 13 years in their possession. Had they removed their families to the royal city ? If so, would they thence strike direct into the desert for Suez ; or seek it by the canal through fertile Goshen ? Supposing that Avaris was Zoan, and remembering that in Sinai were the copper-mines of the Pharaohs, and that that copper was taken to Memphis by the Sesostris canal, Bunsen would infer that a route so thoroughly familiar and handy to the Israelites, was the one of their exodus. Sinai was garrisoned by the Egyptians ; but, during the rebellion, the Sinaites asserted their freedom, and the Kenite of Midian was prepared to receive Moses with open arms. Bunsen's speculations all rest on the history of Manetho. Manetho derives his information from those priests who told Herodotus one thing, and Diodorus another ; and himself is only preserved in the pages of other writers. Bunsen, a wild reasoner, especially for a diplomatist, will not himself say which way the Israelites took, although he shuts us out of every other but that advocated by Lepsius. Yet such historical speculations alone give Dr. Buist's assumption any importance. Taken alone, as based solely on physical considerations, it is worthless. It was a good enough guess, perhaps, although not new ; but it was unusually hardy to think of upsetting, with a guess, the judgment of men who have devoted to this controversy a lifetime of persevering research, keen criticism, and profound thought. In thus writing, I do not mean to assert that the hypothesis volunteered by Dr. Buist is wrong, and that the views to which he is opposed are right ; I am not entitled to judge between them. All my object is, simply to show on what frivolous grounds he has raised his hypothesis ; on what frivolous grounds *he* has dared to differ from standard authorities on a subject which, of all others embraced in his *brochure*, it was least excusable to handle carelessly. I say this deliberately. *Bear and forbear* should ever be the rule for the regulation of private intercourse ; but in public impersonal discussions, especially on questions of science, the only true chivalry is neither to give nor take quarter.

Art. IV.—PAPER ON THE PRESENT STATE AND REQUIREMENTS OF OUR SURVEYS IN THE INDIAN OCEAN, WITH REFERENCE TO THE EXISTING ERRORS OF ITS PHYSICAL GEOGRAPHY.—*By Lieutenant* A. D. Taylor, *II. M. I. N.*

Read before the Society, December 15th 1859.

Shortly after my return to Bombay, in July last, having been asked by our Secretary to lay before the Society an account of the extent of ground which has yet to be traversed, before we can boast of possessing perfect Charts of every locality, I have been induced to draw up this Paper.

When the news of the Indian Mutiny reached England (more than two years ago), there was evinced such a desire, as was never formerly displayed there, for information about the civil, military, and naval forces of the East India Company, and of the way they were all employed. A work, emanating from one of their servants on the Home Establishment, and entitled "India in 1858," professed to supply the necessary authenticated information.

In this book we read that "the duties of the Bombay Marine consists of surveys on the coast of Arabia, the Red Sea, and coast of Sind ; the force is also used for the prevention of piracy in the Persian Gulf." Such a statement is calculated to mislead the public, and to persuade them, that the principal portion of our time is occupied in surveying, whereas that duty of the Navy is but an inconsiderable fraction of our work.

Too much credit cannot be given to the earlier navigators of the Indian Ocean; and when we read of the wonderful voyages they made, without any of the appliances of modern invention, we are almost led to believe that the boldness of our ancestors has not descended to us. Without charts, little acquainted with the practice, and still less with the science of navigation, the pioneers of commercial enterprise in the East had a difficult task. A quaint old historian thus recorded an opinion of the original maritime service of the East India Company :—" The skill of their Officers, though moderate, was sufficient for those Seas, and for the seasons in which they sailed." The allusion is, of course, to the long prevailing custom of making but one outward and one homeward voyage within the year,—a practice which still obtains with most of the Native traders, particularly to the Red Sea and Persian Gulf.

But soon the value of time came to be better appreciated, and it was seen that without charts, little progress could be expected ; then was encouragement given to industrious mariners to contribute their mite to the general fund of information, and amongst them, Horsburgh, the self-taught cabin boy, shone pre-eminently ; so bright, indeed, was his light, that succeeding navigators seem to have had diffidence in attempting to improve upon his Indian Directory, which still remains the guide and standard work for the Indian and Chinese Seas.

In course of time, the perfection of the Hydrography of the Indian Ocean was deemed of sufficient importance to warrant the appointment of a Marine Surveyor General, whose duty was the supervision and direction of all maritime surveys. This honourable appointment was held for many years by the late Captain Daniel Ross, of the Indian Navy, once President of our Society, whose name and fame we hold in grateful remembrance.

Our knowledge of the coasts of the Indian Seas was then confessedly very limited, and the importance of adding to it was admitted by the rulers of this vast country.

We read in our own Journal, that "the earliest records of the India House bear abundant testimony to the fact of the constant and lively interest taken by the Court of Directors in the improvement of the charts and navigation of the Indian seas." Repeated instructions were sent out, year after year, to the local Government, to cause individual talent to be put into requisition by every species of encouragement : Log-books, astronomical and written observations, to be procured and sent home ; and, where the originals could not be obtained, tracings of charts were directed to be accurately made and forwarded for compilation and publication. The patronage so wisely extended by our then most gracious and excellent Sovereign, George the Third, to the improvement of geographical knowledge, was thus, in spirit and letter, transferred to his people in every quarter of the globe ; and the steady support which other navigators and travellers experienced at the hand of Royalty, was equally evinced by those who watched over the destinies of India.

Under the retrenchment system, India passed a period of six years of hydrographical inaction, in spite of the expressed astonishment and regret of the Royal Geographical Society of London, that after all the expenditure of life and treasure in the surveys of the Persian Gulf, of the Red Sea, Maldive Islands, Chagos Archipelago, and half of the southern coast of Arabia, so much should remain unsurveyed ; —nor was our own Society backward in advocating, from time to time, the claims of Hydrography.

It is impossible that every shoal (invisible, and, therefore, more dangerous to the mariner and more difficult to be found), can be hunted out ; time does not permit of every inch of ground being traversed ; and the omission of dangerous patches may be frequently expected in charts of such coasts as are uninhabited, or whose inhabitants are either hostile or unwilling to point out the neighbouring reefs and unseen dangers.

Many such shoals and reefs have been discovered in the Red Sea, and doubtless many more may be found when that Sea is more frequented by sailing vessels and coasting steamers. Such omissions have yet to be rectified, and that task will need much skill.

Since the resumption of Surveys, in the year 1844, more than one vessel yearly, with a small tender attached to each, have been employed on the coast of Arabia, North Africa, Sind, Kattywar, Kutch, Guzerat, and the west coast of India below Bombay (commonly, though erroneously, bearing the distinctive appellation of " Malabar Coast "). Officers of the Indian Navy have been also employed in the Bay of Bengal.

It is not my intention, however, to narrate what Officers or what Vessels have been employed during the last fifteen years, or how each vessel was fitted out ; suffice it to say, that in no one instance were they supplied with means of carrying on simultaneously all the enquiries which one naturally expects from a scientific survey, viz.—topographical, statistical, geological, meteorological, tidal, botanical, &c., when, at a trifling additional expense, such inquiries should have been pursued. But we have the satisfaction of knowing that, notwithstanding the little encouragement they met with, the labours of our Officers have produced excellent Charts, on a large scale, of the shores of India, Arabia, and Africa. Now our grand desideratum is, accurately compiled navigating sheets on a much smaller scale ; and I think our Society might press the urgency of this want upon Government. We must not be contented with mere track Charts, which, in too many instances, have only tended to mislead navigators, and may yet tend to painful results, if not suppressed.

A description of the work which remains for our naval surveyors, I would preface with the report of the Hydrographer of the Admiralty, which relates to the East. This is taken from the Admiralty Manual :—

" The Charts of the whole of the Cape Colony are exceedingly defective ; and from thence, to the Portuguese settlements of Delagoa, we know scarcely any thing.

" From Delagoa to the Red Sea, and the whole contour of Madagascar, are sufficiently represented on our Charts for the general purposes of navigation, though many further researches along the former coast might still be profitably made.

" In the Cape Colony, the coast from Table Bay to Cape Agulhas, with Algoa Bay, and Port Natal, have been surveyed. The rest of the coast, as far as Delagoa Bay, remains as before. The islets and dangers off the north-west, north, and north-east of Madagascar, from the Comoro Isles to Diego Garcia, require to be examined.

" In the Gulf of Persia, the longitudes are very vague. The east and south coasts of Ceylon require examination, as well as the Andaman and Nicobar Islands, and from St. Mathew's Isle, in 10° North Latitude, to Prince of Wales' Island. The coasts of Malabar and Coromandel are all but completed by the Officers of the Indian Navy. The Straits of Malacca and Singapore have also been surveyed, as well as those of Rhio and Durian. The east coast of Summatra, from Malacca Straits to Sunda and Banca Straits, require examination.

" With the China Sea we are becoming daily better acquainted ; but much is to be done there, for probably not one of the multitudes of rocks and shoals with which it is almost covered is put exactly in its right position, and, while some are repeated two or three times, others have been omitted.

" On the coast of China, the charts are excellent from Canton round to the mouth of the great river Yang-tse-Kiang ; but of the Yellow Sea we know very little, and still less of the Corea, Japan, and the coast of Tartary up to the confines of the Russian Empire.

" Java and all the Islands eastward, including Timour, with the Java Sea, Flores Sea, with the south coast of Borneo, Celebes, &c., and islets and rocks in that region, have been partially examined by the Dutch, but no regular survey has been made. The west coast of Borneo, from

Tangang Api southwards to Sambhar Point, has not been surveyed, nor have the islands and passages from the Straits of Gaspar to the Natunas. The west coast of Borneo, from Tangang Api northwards, and Palwan Islands, have been surveyed, as well the east coast of the Malay Peninsula, and the Gulf of Siam. Cochin China, with some other trifling exceptions, a part of the coast of Hainan, and the whole of the Gulf of Tonking, may be considered as unknown.

" Some detached portions of the coast of Corea and Tartary, and of Japan, and some few of their harbours, have recently been examined ; but of the coast of China northwards of the Yang-tse-Kiang, the Gulfs of Pechele and Leatong, we still know very little.

" The southern passes into the China Sea have never been examined with the care they deserve ; and all that is known of what are called the eastern passages through the great Malay Archipelago, are only the results of the casual observations and sketches made years ago by industrious seamen.

" The Spaniards have surveyed a portion of the Philippine Islands, and the Dutch have made some partial surveys ; otherwise the eastern passages remain as before.

" The islands and surrounding shores of the Arafura Sea, if better known, would offer many ports of refuge, and probably an increased opening to commercial enterprise.

" The Straits of Torres have been satisfactorily surveyed ; but before it becomes the highway for steam-vessels to and from Sydney, its approaches, and also its contiguous coasts of New Guinea, should be more intimately known.

" The outer dangers off the east coast of Australia, in what is termed the Coral Sea, require careful examination.

" The whole circuit of the great island of Australia has been well explored, and the *general* characteristics of its several shores are suffi- ciently known for all *general* purposes ; but far more minute surveys of its immediate waters and maritime resources must precede their being inhabited, beginning with the eastern coast, along which the tide of colonisation seems to be already creeping.

" The survey of New Zealand has been completed ; and the chart of the coast, and plans of all the ports, with ample sailing directions, are published."

Here we have a good general description of late surveys and of what remains to be done ; but we need a more detailed exposition of the
14 *g*

finished and unfinished work close to our three Presidencies, which I shall here endeavour to give, beginning at Point de Galle, the southern port of Ceylon, which island some people are facetiously pleased to term the key of India.

From Point de Galle to Kurrachee we now have good charts, except for the 90 miles south of Bombay Light-house, which portion of coast is to be done this season. From Kurrachee to the westward, along the Mekran coast, through the Gulf of Persia, and down to Muscat, we have charts; but so many errors have been detected in them, that the entire set are looked upon as doubtful; that portion, indeed, of the Persian coast, from Ras Farsah, in 61° 30′ E., to Bunder Abbas, is no survey at all, but a flying sketch, acknowledged by all navigators to be very erroneous. From Muscat, round the south-east coast of Arabia, to Bab-el-Mandeb, and for the Red Sea, our charts are good; but, as noticed above, many new rocks may be found along the shores, as the surveys, especially that of the Red Sea, are done to a very small scale. And here I may remark, that the originals are not to be found in our record office—where are they to be found?

On the African coast, south of the Straits of Bab-el-Mandeb, there is a short unsurveyed piece of less than twenty miles to Ras Bir; but from that cape to Ras Hafoon, the coast has been well surveyed and mapped. The whole of Socotra, and its adjacent islands and banks, are well delineated. From Hafoon southwards to the Cape of Good Hope is but imperfectly surveyed; and this is acknowledged to be the case by the Hydrographer of the British Navy, in the new edition of the Admiralty Manual, from which we took the foregoing notice. His statement, however, that the coast of East Africa (including, of course, all the small islands), as well as Madagascar, are sufficiently represented on our charts for the general purposes of navigation, is not borne out by facts, for Lieutenant Sedly, who was there very lately, in the sloop *Clive*, assures me that every year one, if not more, vessels are lost in the vicinity of Zanzibar; and I hope to show presently that the popular idea regarding the currents in those parts, as gained from the people who profess to cater knowledge for the public, is very erroneous.

But though it is easy to find fault with the statements of others, I find it a difficult job to produce a correct account of the extent of our knowledge of that vast expanse of ocean, between the southern point of Africa (or Cape of Good Hope), the eastern point of that Continent (or Cape Guardufui), and the Islands of Ceylon, Summatra, and Australia. Most of the dangers attendant upon the long sea voyage from Europe to India, are comprised within that oceanic space—whether they be terrene, as low islands and sunken rocks ; marine, as conflicting currents ; or atmospheric, as hurricanes and other storms. The dearth of *positive* information is lamentable, but of *speculative* we have more than enough ; and from the chaos of published dangers, each chart-publisher seems to take or reject what he likes.

A chart, by Imray, has a dozen questionable shoals between the Cape and the Mauritius, but Walker's copy chart has only eight : the former has some doubtful dangers in the Bay of Bengal, which the latter omits, perhaps on authority, but the question should finally be settled as to the existence of all doubtful dangers. The Cargadas Garagos group should be properly examined, and, in short, the numerous islets and dangers (as the Hydrographer says) off the north-west, north, and north-east of Madagascar, from the Comoro Isles to Diego Garcia. A new shoal is noticed on our observatory charts, as discovered in 1858; it lies 165 miles to E. by N. of Cape Ambre, the north point of Madagascar.

In our Transactions, we find that Captain Robert Moresby, I. N., a distinguished surveyor, on his return to Bombay with the *Benares*, in September 1837, recorded the following suggestions as to what should be explored in that coral region :—

" Of the Chagos Archipelago, ' Owen's Bank ' still remains to be examined to complete that survey. Of the unexplored portion of the Saya de Malha, the southern half of this bank has been well sounded, and the survey completed as far as Latitude 9° 37' south. From this point to its extremity, in Latitude 8° 40', a space of about 90 miles, extending north-west, remains unsurveyed, which would take a vessel one month to complete."

Captain Moresby does not consider that the longitude of Saya de Malha has been well fixed. He recommends chronometric measurements to be taken from Diamond Islands, Peros Banhos, to Owen's Bank ; then to Saya de Malha, along the east edge of which bank he would run to fix that extremity, and afterwards to the Seychelles ; and after determining the geographical site of the landing place at Mahé, return to Peros Banhos, to verify measurements. This operation would take four or five months to execute correctly ; and Captain Moresby adds, that there still remains a large extent of unexplored space among the Seychelles Islands which requires to be surveyed.

The Maldives and Laccadives have been examined ; and for the former, copious sailing directions are given.   Of Ceylon there is not yet a complete chart on a large scale.   It was in contemplation, more than 20 years ago, to survey the Great and Little Basses on the south-east coast, when Captain Moresby had finished the Saya de Malha, but this intention was not fulfilled.   Mr. Twynam, the late Master Attendant at Point de Galle, has surveyed several detached portions of the Ceylon coast, and directions respecting it are given in Horsburgh.   What a valuable acquisition to the mariner and to science would be the delineation of the currents round Ceylon ! !

Mr. Franklin, the present Superintendent of Marine at Madras, has similarly examined some portions of the Tinnevelly, Madura, and Tanjore coasts ; but we have not yet a complete chart of the Coromandel Coast.   Lieutenant Sweny, for three years my most able assistant, was employed more than a year ago in executing the survey from Pulicat, near Madras, to Point Calymere ; but was lately, *I think*, diverted from that duty, and sent to examine some portions of the Andaman Islands, and the Gulf of Martaban.   I cannot, therefore, say for certain whether the south part of the Coromandel Coast be yet completed.   The northern part, and the seaboard up to Chicacole, and the Santapilly Rocks, were done several years ago, by the late Lieutenant Fell, I. N.   Coringa Bay, and the shifting banks of the Northern Godavery mouth, were re-examined by me two years ago.   I know of no recent survey to the north of Fell's work, as far as False Point Palmyras ; but from that Cape to the east, the whole sea-face and the deep sea, including the Sandheads and Sunderbunds, were twenty years ago carefully examined by Captain Lloyd, of the Indian Navy ;   nevertheless, the shifting nature of a delta such as that, demands for it an occasional examination.

Of the coast eastward of the Sunderbunds, and south of Chittagong, I cannot state with any certainty what is known ; in fact, my knowledge is very limited as to the late surveys on the Bengal side ; I can only state, in general terms, that there are not any complete charts of the Bay of Bengal.   The Andaman and Nicobar Islands are yet little known.   The only general chart I know of the coast of Chittagong, Arracan, Pegu, Martaban, and Tenasserim, is a compilation by an officer of the Bengal Marine, which, though containing the excellent surveys of Captains Ross, Crawford, and Lloyd, has much that was evidently the result of a flying survey.   Bengal, however, must have a large supply of fresh charts, for there have been officers of the

Indian Navy employed on that side for more than fifteen years. If the Society is anxious for a more detailed statement of the new surveys in the Bay of Bengal, Straits of Malacca, and elsewhere in that neighbourhood, the Secretary should write to some authority in Calcutta, not for a statement merely, but for copies of all their lately published charts, to reinforce our " Ross testimonial ;" for I believe that a promise of such periodical gifts was made by the Government of the day, when that useful and practical scheme, for bearing lasting testimony to the eminent services of one who had long been our President, was adopted.

Thus I have endeavoured to show what is wanting to complete our charts of the Eastern Seas. In the course of five years, if good use be made of time, we may hope to obtain sufficient information, to enable the Hydrographer to publish accurate navigating charts for these seas.

A supervision over the publications of chart-sellers is much to be desired, for even the Hydrographer of the East India Company, with all our Indian surveys at his command, could not apparently turn out a perfect general chart. Look at that one issued in 1852, which is the latest edition now saleable at the Bombay Observatory, and which leaves out the Byrangore reef and Kiltan Islands from the Laccadive group.

In the absence of any authorised control over such publications, could not our Society, in its capacity as an inquirer after geographical truth, undertake to review all Charts and Books of Directions which make their appearance in Bombay ? I see that such is the fashion of the Royal Geographical Society, and would be eminently useful at this seaport.

The object of such criticism should be merely the improvement of charts in the interest of commercial navigation, and in the interest of an impartial justice to the good and to the bad amongst both chart compilers, and the navigators who make use of compilations for the guidance of their vessels ; for how often we see judgment upon the careless mariner go by default, because existing charts, in their many fatal errors and omissions, afford him so many loopholes of escape.

Accurate charts must ever be the precursors to an extension of our commerce all over the world ; this fact seems to be at length recognised by superior authority, and it is to be hoped that we have now entered upon a new course on surveying matters, and that we shall soon see our charts of these seas brought to great perfection, and the commercial traffic of the country thereby much benefited.

Art. V.—NOTES ON THE ANDAMANS.—*By Lieutenant* T. M. Philbrick, *H. M. I. N.*

Read before the Society 15th March 1860.

The H. C. schooner *Charlotte* left Bombay on the 24th March 1858, bound for the Andamans. After the usual passage down the coast, touching at Cochin, we anchored at 7 P.M. on the 6th April, at the entrance of the sand-bank channel of the Paumben Pass.

Passage to Andamans.

The Pilot from Paumben came on board at daylight next morning, and at about 9 A.M. we weighed, stood through the channel, and worked up to the basin at the entrance of the pass.

Paumben Pass.

The wind not being fair, we were obliged to warp through the channel, a distance of 1,500 or 1,600 yards, the breadth being in some places only 70 feet. The warps and grapnels are provided at the Pilot station, as also are the requisite canoes and men.

The least water we had was 11 feet, and I heard from the Pilot that 12 feet, and sometimes even 13 feet of water, is found in the channel.

We occupied two hours warping through the whole distance, against a moderate breeze, which fell to a calm when we got through.

After waiting for a breeze till 10 P.M., weighed and stood out of Palk's Bay, and then along the Coromandel Coast, with a good south-easterly breeze to Madras, which place was reached on the 10th of April.

On the 11th of April, weighed and stood along the coast of Coromandel as far up as Vizagapatam, in order to preserve the breeze across the Bay towards the Andamans, which we should not have been able to do had we attempted to cross it more to the southward.

We had a fine south-east breeze all along the coast, making in one 24 hours 240 miles.

On the 13th April hauled to the wind, steering direct for the passage between the Little Coco and Landfall Island. The breeze decreased as we stood over to the eastward, and when within 150 miles of the Andamans, became very light and variable from N. E. to N. W. Sighted Landfall Island on the 20th April, at 4-30 A.M., and for two days we were becalmed between it and the Little Coco ; but a light air sprung up on the evening of the second day, which took us clear up the passage ; and after two days more of light north-easterly winds, we arrived off Port Blair on the morning of the 24th of April 1858.

The whole of the east coast of the Andamans is very steep to the sounding, being generally over 20 fathoms close East Coast An- to the shore, which is rocky, with small sandy damans. bays at close intervals. In many parts, coral banks extend a short distance from the shore, and small detached rocks are not uncommon ; but these dangers are mostly all visible in the daytime, when vessels can safely stand in close to the shore.

At night caution should be used to keep a vessel well out in about 40 fathoms or even more, there being no bottom at 100 fathoms in some places four or five miles off.

The Archipelago Islands are eight in number (named) and several other small islets ; the passages between them are generally safe, as also is the passage between the Archipelago and the mainland, called Diligent Straits. The soundings here are somewhat irregular, but there are no dangers but what are visible in the daytime.

Coming from the northward, it would not be prudent to attempt to enter the straits unless well up to the entrance before sunset, unless you are very well acquainted with the place ; but from the southward, a vessel can safely be navigated through, if the night be clear, and proper attention be paid to the chart.

The present chart by Lieutenant Blair and Captain Moorsom (Admi- ralty copy) is generally correct, so far as the Chart. east coast is concerned (I had not much opportunity of proving it on the western side), and is, in my opinion, quite sufficient for all the present purposes required ; but several of the large islets, which may eventually become settlements, have not been sufficiently examined, and in some cases not laid down at all. There is also a reef said to run off the north end of the Little Andaman, where the H. C. Bengal steamer *Sesostris* struck. With these exceptions, the chart, so far as my own observation goes, is very correct on both coasts.

On the western coast there are three coral banks, about fifteen miles
off shore, which have not been examined for many
years (I believe not since 1790). These banks are
said to have four fins on them, and probably less ;
and should the coast become frequented, it would be very necessary to
have them examined and carefully sounded.

West Coast An-
damans.

The Andaman Islands are named in the charts, Great and Little
Andamans. The Great Andaman is divided into three islands—North,
Middle, and South Andamans ; and off these are several smaller islands.
The only one of the adjacent islands I have landed on, are the
Archipelago Islands and Interior Island.

The general appearance of the Andamans is hilly, and densely covered
with jungle, which is quite impenetrable to Euro-
peans, except by clearing away as you advance. In
the inlets, the shores are covered with mangroves,
intersected by numerous creeks.

General appear-
ance.

The Natives seem to be very few, and to have no means of subsist-
ence, except wild pig, shell-fish, fish, and jungle
fruits. They will not allow the approach of Europeans, invariably retreating to the jungle when discovered, and
having time to do so ; but they have not much dread of our fire-arms,
for if they are come on suddenly by a small party, they generally attack.

Natives.

I have frequently, in the *Charlotte*, stood close in when we have seen
a party of them on the beach, and as long as we were standing broadside on to them, they would watch us most intently, and seemingly
without fear ; but when we were in stays, and the vessel's head end on
to them, they would retreat with great precipitation to the jungle,
reappearing, however, when we were trimmed on the other tack, and
gesticulating after the most approved savage manner.

Their canoes are of the most primitive fashion—a tree rounded off
at the ends, and scooped out with some instrument, very thin,
suffices for their wants ; their paddles they make of bamboo, by
splitting one end, and inserting crosswise split bamboos, and weaving
these again with grass.

They make fishing and turtle nets very neatly, and also baskets
and a kind of bamboo mat ; and these, with their bows and arrows,
are the only articles of manufacture I have seen. Of their habits
we know very little, the only source of information being a returned
convict, who resided thirteen months with them, and whose story was

printed some months back in the Indian papers, and which is, I presume, familiar to most people.

On reaching Port Blair, called Port Chatham on the chart, we found the settlement commenced by Dr. Walker, and the H. C. S. *Dalhousie* and surveying Brig *Mutlah* lying in the harbour, and two merchant vessels. The stores were landed on Chatham Island, and the vessels anchored in its vicinity.

Port Blair Settlement.

There were then between 300 and 400 convicts on the island, and, as a guard, 50 seamen of the Indian Navy, with the usual complement of officers. These, with an Assistant Surgeon in medical charge of the convicts, and an Apothecary, made up the Europeans of the settlement.

The convicts were at first landed on Chatham Island, and afterwards a party was placed on the mainland, and another on Ross Island, at the entrance of the harbour. The party on the mainland had, however, deserted *en masse* some days before we arrived, and a number had also gone from Ross Island on the evening preceding our arrival, by swimming over to the main. To prevent the further escape of the Ross Island party the *Charlotte* was the next day anchored off Ross Island.

Altogether, about 250 went in this first exodus. After a few days, however, one or two came down to the beach opposite Chatham Island, and were brought over, where they were tried, condemned, and hanged. Six men were hanged in this way, when they began to come in, in parties of 10 or 12, till, by the first week in May, 81 more had returned, as they could not exist in the jungles. They confessed that they had gone away with the intention of joining some Rajah, who they supposed resided at some distance from Port Blair, and with his assistance coming back and killing all the Europeans, and then making their escape by land to Hindostan. They thought this practicable, because they said the ship that brought them to Port Blair used to go back in the night the distance she went in the day, in order to deceive them as to the real distance.

These men were tried, and on the 18th of May, were all hanged on Chatham Island, in the presence of all the other convicts and the Europeans at the settlement.

At this time, the situation of the convicts was anything but pleasant; they had nothing to cover them but a few tarpaulins and blankets, with a few tents for the sick, and the rains were then

15 g

commencing. The best, however, was done for them that could be under the circumstances.

The European portion of the Settlement were lodged on board the *Edward*, which vessel was hired for the purpose by the Superintendent.

Great difficulty was experienced in obtaining provisions and stores of every kind at first, there being nothing to be procured at Port Blair ; and when the H. C. S. *Semiramis* arrived on the 31st of May, she was obliged to be despatched to Maulmain for these necessary supplies.

The convicts were employed in clearing away the jungle, cutting down the trees, and digging up the ground to get it under cultivation, in order to prevent the jungle from springing up again. On the 12th of June 1858, the H. C. Bengal Ship *Sesostris* arrived from China, to take up the *Edward's* duty as a store-ship and place of residence for the naval guard and Superintendent. On the 1st July, the Steamer *Italian* arrived from Bombay, with convicts. This vessel had been unable to find Port Blair, owing to the change of name, having in the first instance gone to Port Cornwallis, at the north-east end of the Andamans ; and finding nothing there, except a little coal (placed there some months previously, and of which they brought a specimen to us in a bucket), she steamed down the coast, looking into every inlet she came across, until she arrived off Port Blair, where, seeing the *Charlotte* at anchor at the entrance, she made towards us, and at last reached the desired port.

On the 6th July 1858, H.M.S. *Roebuck* arrived, and contributed to our amusement no little during her stay : we had the first regatta at Port Blair,—indeed, the first little amusement of any kind that took place at Port Blair.

The convicts by this time had got a little into the way of the place, and the jungle had all disappeared from Chatham Island, which was now given up to be a hospital only ; and the head quarters were about this time shifted to Ross Island, the *Sesostris* anchoring between it and the main, and the *Charlotte* taking her position off Chatham Island.

The clearance of Ross Island was now set about in earnest, and an office and storehouse erected there. The steamers now began to arrive a little more regularly, about once a month, and bringing additional convicts each time. The manner in which the convicts were worked has been already described in the book published by the Government of India. They were taught all kinds of trades, and seemed to get on in their calling very well. Ryots became boatmen, carpenters, sawyers, shoemakers,—anything they were required ; sepoys were transformed into agriculturists or shopkeepers, or perhaps oftener, into gangsmen, section, sub-division, and division gangsmen ; and matters now began to assume some shape and regularity. They were still very badly off for leaves to cover the convicts' huts ; but in October, a quantity was brought by the Steamer *Australian,* which sufficed for the present wants.

In the beginning of October 1858, a detachment of convicts were sent to Viper Island, to clear it and get it under cultivation ; and the *Charlotte* was then shifted from Chatham to Viper Island, to assist in guarding them from the aborigines, who, however, never made their appearance whilst we were there.

After remaining here until the 6th of December, we were at last

Cruise.   permitted to see the outside of Port Blair, and started, on the 9th of December 1858, for a cruise round the Andamans. Proceeding northwards from Port Blair, on the 13th December we reached Port Cornwallis, the harbour on the north-

Port Cornwallis.   east end of the Andamans, and the site of the former settlement, which was abandoned at the end of the last century, on account of its extreme unhealthiness. On anchoring off Long Island, we found the remains of a building still standing, in the shape of the part of the wall of a house with two windows. The sea has encroached on the land, and the wall nearest the sea has been demolished years ago.

We also saw the coal of which the *Italian* brought the specimens to Port Blair, and I questioned very much the story of the bucketful only having been taken away.

We landed, and found no other traces of the old settlement, except that the jungle was not quite so thick as usual.

The harbour of Port Cornwallis is very spacious and secure, with moderate depths of water from the entrance, and good holding ground at the upper part, near Long or Chatham Island. The shores, except near the entrance, are fringed by mangrove bushes and swamps, and there are several islands scattered about the harbour. As we entered, we saw a party of Natives on the beach, who seemed to regard us with some curiosity ; but as we advanced up the harbour, it gave one the idea of perfect loneliness,—one could hardly say desolation.

There was not a canoe, or hardly a stick, floating on the surface of all the expanse of water, and not a sound to be heard, save occasionally the screech of some feathered inhabitants of the jungle.

The old settlement, which was first at the present Port Blair, was removed here (Port Cornwallis), on account of the great superiority of the harbour.

There is a very accurate chart of Port Cornwallis by Lieutenant Blair; and with it, as the harbour is very easy of access, a ship would not find the least difficulty.

The only articles we found here were a few cocoanuts and a native bow, all on Chatham Island. The Natives had been there very lately, as we found remains of fires evidently recently left.

Leaving the harbour the next day, we came suddenly, after rounding the first point from Chatham Island, upon a Native in a canoe; but on seeing us, he made for the nearest jungle, and disappeared amongst the bushes. After clearing the mouth of the harbour, we proceeded northward again; and, keeping close in shore, saw occasional canoes, but seldom near.

Rounding the north end of the Islands, we stood down the west coast, and on the 16th December, came to off Interview Island with the kedge, at about 9 P. M. In the morning weighed the kedge, and worked up between Interview Island and the main. As we were working up, we saw two Natives on a little island to the south of Interview Island; and as I had directions to catch a Native, if possible, we bore away and anchored close to, dropped the boats, and landed on the small island; but so close did they lay, that although we traversed the island in all directions (it was very free from jungle), we were unable to find either of them; and after hunting about for some hours, we were compelled reluctantly to return. We found a good quantity of drift-wood, pieces of wreck, on this island. This harbour, called Port Andaman, is pretty well sheltered from all winds if a vessel is well up, and is easy of access; the shores are also tolerably free from swamps.

Port Andaman.

Proceeding southwards, we saw many canoes fishing, but were unable to catch any of them. From Port Andaman, southwards, there is no harbour until Port Campbell, about 50 miles from the former. I only looked into this place, not having any chart, and being pressed for time.

Port Campbell.

About 20 miles south of Port Campbell, there is another harbour, not laid down in the chart at all; the entrance is very narrow, and the water very shoal, and it is not at all adapted for vessels of any size, and it would be impossible to work in or out of it. It has been named Port Mouatt.

Port Mouatt.

Proceeding southward, we rounded Rutland Island; and, by means of cross-bearings, found all the islands thereabouts correctly laid down, and on the 20th December again anchored in Port Blair.

The harbour of Port Blair, formerly known as Port Chatham, and so named in the Admiralty chart, is formed by an irregular and deep indentation of the sea; it first proceeds in a westerly direction, and then turns down at nearly right angles to the south, forming several bays, with many creeks round their shores. Several of these are large enough to admit the largest ship's boats, having a good depth of water in them; they take very circuitous directions, and from the density of the jungle, it is almost impossible to ascertain, with any degree of accuracy, the position arrived at after pulling for miles. We have been for miles up several of these creeks, sometimes hauling the boats over large trees which have fallen across, and finding several old encampments of the Natives; but, strange to say, we have never found any canoes up them. We have often found pieces of chain and remains of other ships' furniture, human bones, skulls, &c.

Port Blair.

The harbour is easy of access by steamers or ships having a fair wind, but is very narrow for large ships to work in or out of, and too deep for kedging until abreast of Chatham Island, when the depths become moderate, and the holding ground remarkably good.

The passage between Ross Island and the main (the south passage) is safe for a steamer or a ship having a commanding breeze; but in using it, care should be taken not to stand too close to the land when to the southward of the passage, as there is a coral bank projecting from one of the points of land some distance out; but in light and baffling winds, it is decidedly dangerous for ships, it being so confined. The anchorage between Ross Island and the main is very bad, the bottom being hard sand and decayed coral, and there being no room to allow ships to get under weigh, except in light breezes, and then generally only by aid of a warp to spring them round.

The principal islands are Ross Island, at the entrance; Chatham Island, about 2½ miles from the former, and situated just where the harbour bends down to the southward, and quite close to the south shore ; and Viper Island, about 2½ miles from Chatham Island.   These islands were all occupied and cleared before they began on the mainland. The dangers are—a reef off the north-west end of Ross Island ; Blair's Reef, extending half-way across the harbour from the south shore, and about a mile to the eastward of Chatham Island ; and Ranger Reef, to the westward of Chatham Island, extending towards it from the opposite shore.

The harbour altogether is immeasurably inferior to Port Cornwallis, though I believe much more healthy, the shores not being so swampy.

On the 28th December, we started to take formal possession of the Archipelago Islands, and also to name them.   They were named as follows :—

Archipelago
Islands.

The largest and central island was called " Henry Lawrence" Island ; the next largest " Havelock" Island ; the north-most " Outram" Island ; the next northmost on west side " Wilson" Island ; the next " Nicholson" Island ; the south island " Neill" Island ; the small one to the southward of all " Rose" Island ; and the eastern island, East or " Inglis" Island.

These islands seems to be rather thickly inhabited for the Andamans, though very few canoes are to be seen.   Since October, we had had a steamer pretty regularly once a month from Calcutta, bringing us provisions and a supply of convicts ; and although the officers had always been pushed for supplies, the Europeans had never run short.   But from an increase to the strength of the Naval Brigade, in the end of January 1859, we ran rather short of provisions ; and not being certain when the steamer from Calcutta might come, the *Charlotte* was sent to Maulmain to send provisions over.   We left on the 5th of February, and having sent a supply over by a merchant vessel, returned to Port Blair, where we arrived on the 21st of March.

On our arrival, we found the convicts had been sent over to the mainland,—one party opposite to Chatham Island, and another on Atalanto Point, opposite to Ross Island.   The Natives had attacked them at the place near Ross Island, but had been driven back by the guard, after having wounded some of the convicts, and making off with a quantity of tools, &c.

The barracks for the Naval Brigade were also finished, and a portion of the men residing in them, the others still remaining on board the *Sesostris*.

On the 27th of March, the steamer *Fire Queen* towed the *Sesostris* from Ross Island to Chatham Island, as it was not considered safe to leave her at the former place during the change of the monsoon, and in the afternoon of that day left for Calcutta.

The *Charlotte* was left off Ross Island, and about 40 men in the barracks. Nothing unusual was remarked about the convicts, but on the morning of the 1st April, a convict informed the Superintendent he had overheard some convicts engaging in a plot to mutiny and destroy the Europeans. The Superintendent did not seem to put much faith in the report, and did not, in consequence, communicate it to any one, when, in the afternoon, the European sentry at the office was suddenly felled to the ground by an axe, his musket seized and presented at the Superintendent as he was sitting at his desk. The man, however, was unable to get the piece off, either from it being on half-cock or not being capped, and a well-disposed convict got behind the man and pulled his legs from under him ; and with the aid of the Darogah, the man was secured, and the signal given to the men at the barracks, who at once came down, and the affair was at an end.

The information turned out correct, and a very narrow escape we all had.

The plan was—they were first to kill Dr. Walker, then a party was to take possession of a decked lighter which was employed to take provisions and stores about, and with her to come alongside the *Charlotte* (the convicts being concealed under the deck) ; they were to take the *Charlotte*, and with her to proceed to Chatham Island and take the *Sesostris*, whilst another party were to surround the barracks, get the arms of the Europeans there, and then they imagined the game was their own. A captain was appointed to the *Charlotte* (whom I afterwards saw hanged), and all the other arrangements made.

The man who attacked the sentry first, was bayoneted by another of the guard, but lived some time, and offered, if his life were spared, to divulge the whole conspiracy ; but the Superintendent would not do that, and the man died without confessing any thing.

Four of the other ringleaders in this affair were tried and hanged, and matters went on quietly again.

A number of the convicts who were implicated were put in irons, and sent over to Atalanta Point, where most of them died, I believe.

On the night of the 16th of May, a man swam across to Ross

Island, who turned out to be one of the convicts who escaped about
13 months previously, and had been living amongst
Attack on Aberdeen. the savages ever since. He said that they intended
attacking the convicts at Atalanta Point the next
morning; that he was the leader, but that, not wishing to fight
against his countrymen, he had made his escape, and given the
information. Accordingly, next morning, a number of Andamanese
were seen from the vessels walking along the beach in the direction
of Atalanta Point or Aberdeen, as it has been named. We, on seeing
them, sent a shell in amongst them, which burst in their midst, and
they retreated precipitately into the jungle, and shortly afterwards
they were seen amongst the huts at Aberdeen : the convicts
immediately retreated into the water, and the Naval Brigade, landing,
frightened them off, not without carrying away with them most of the
convicts' implements, hatchets, pickaxes, cross-cut saws, and all kinds
of stores.

During this period, although there had been no desertions amongst
the convicts *en masse*, still men were frequently
Escapes. deserting ; but this was confined principally to the
new arrivals, and in nearly every instance they came back, after finding
they were unable to support themselves in the jungles. The punish-
ment was generally a flogging, but the convict who returned and gave
information of the attack by the Natives, was not punished at all ; and
ever after that, those individuals who returned made it a point to
concoct the wildest stories, in order to save themselves from punish-
ment.

The first instance of this occurred in the end of June 1859, when
an escaped convict returned, and brought information
Reports by returned convicts. that a large number of the aborigines were preparing
to attack the settlement. The place of rendezvous
was described to be the western coast of Rutland Island, and five or
six hundred canoes were said to be ranged on the beach, and the men
(stated at about 1,000) were daily employed in constructing others,
whilst the women were engaged in providing the commissariat stores
for the expedition ; and, besides all this, many of the minutest details
were supplied. The idea of these savages launching their frail canoes
from the western side of the islands, in the face of the strength of the
south-west monsoon! and the information that they were to reach
the settlement ten days after the convict returned, was rather opposed

to the view entertained by naval men, as far as regarded the possibility of the proceeding, but great preparations were made to resist the attack.

The *Charlotte* was anchored to the southward of Ross Island, and in a very unpleasant situation, and the launches of the Naval Brigade exercised every evening.

The Natives, however, did not make their appearance ; and on the 10th July, finding a gale setting in at south-eastward, and the schooner being in a critical position, we were obliged to slip our cable and run inside, and the alarm gradually subsided.

The next report brought in was, that an expedition was preparing, somewhere to the north of Port Blair, for the same purpose ; but this time, I think, there was not so much faith put in it, and no great preparations were made. I believe the runaways, however, escaped their rattaning.

The report of the convict who had been domesticated amongst the aborigines for thirteen months, has already been published, and it is unnecessary to allude to it here. It proved correct as far as the attack was concerned, and may, perhaps, be taken as *moderately* true in other respects.

On the 27th of June a company of Madras sepoys, called Sebundies, arrived, and were quartered on Ross Island ; they were used to furnish guards for working parties of convicts on the mainland, and as a guard for Chatham Island.

Nothing of interest occurred after this, until the 3rd of October, when the Bengal steamer *Pluto* arrived, bringing Captain Haughton from Maulmain to succeed Dr. Walker as Superintendent. On the 16th October, the late Superintendent left in the *Fire Queen* at daylight, and the *Charlotte* left also for Calcutta on the afternoon of the same day.

The climate of the Andamans, or, I should perhaps say, Port Blair, as far as the Europeans were concerned, has proved
Climate.   tolerably healthy, although, from the great exposure the seamen had to endure, many had to return to Calcutta on medical certificate.

The convicts were, in some instances, very sickly, and there was a great mortality amongst them ; but it must be remembered that many of them arrived in a bad state of health, from fatigue in marching down country, and the privations endured on the voyage from India.

16 *g*

The chief diseases were—fevers, bowel complaints, and ulcers, which were very difficult, and in some cases impossible to cure.

The productions of the Andamans are very few; at present there are valuable trees on the islands, the principal of which are the pedowk tree and the wood-oil tree.

Productions.

Trees suitable for spars are also to be obtained, but the labour required to transport the trees, after they have been felled, renders it almost impossible at present to put them to any use, unless they happen to be wanted near at hand.

Everything that has been sown or planted, however, has flourished, except, perhaps, the potato.

Plaintains, yams, sweet potatoes, pumpkins, Indian-corn, rice, millet, the sugar-cane, and most of the Indian vegetables, thrive exceedingly well; and the cleared islands, when we left, were producing large quantities of vegetables, &c.

Poultry and sheep were beginning to thrive, though, at the commencement, they could scarcely be kept alive; and altogether, when we left, matters had begun to assume a tolerably comfortable aspect. The Superintendent's house was approaching completion; the convicts were all as comfortable as they could be under the circumstances.

The Government of India have determined to send other than political offenders to the Andamans for transportation, and there seems to be no doubt but that it will become the penal settlement for India; whilst, from its position and capabilities, it bids fair to take its place as a very important part of the Indian possessions; but in order to take the fullest advantage of its natural capabilities, it is necessary that the islands should be re-surveyed, and the coasts and inlets fully explored; the latter particularly, for, though the general chart of the islands is good, the details have been filled in rather loosely, and I am not aware that there are any surveys, on any large scale, of harbours and inlets, &c., except those of Port Blair and Port Cornwallis, both of which are by Lieutenant Blair; though I believe that of the harbour which bears his name has not been published. It is much to be regretted, also, that the records of the former settlements, and those of Blair surveys, have been lost, therefore the information probably contained therein has to be again collected.

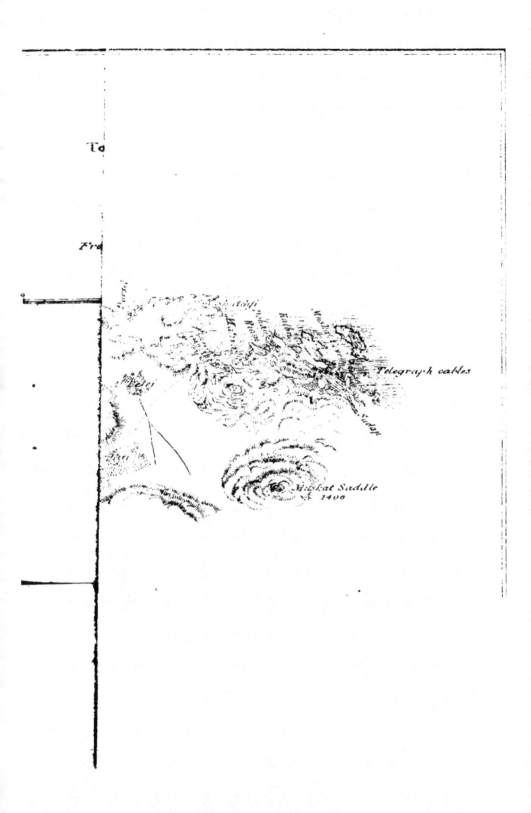

To

Fro

Telegraph cables

Meekat Saddle
1400

ART. VI.—A VISIT TO THE HOT SPRINGS OF BOSHER, NEAR MUSCAT, WITH A ROUTE MAP.—*By Lieutenant* A. W. STIFFE, *H. M. I. N.*

Read before the Society, April 19th, 1860.

LEFT Muscat for Muttrah in a canoe, or bellum, as the Arabs call it, the usual conveyance in fine weather, the pass through the hills being so rugged and winding, that it is only used in blowy weather, when the canoes cannot ply, or by those too poor to be able to afford the luxury of a conveyance.

These canoes are very large, many of them carrying twenty or thirty people comfortably ; they are made out of one tree, and all come from the Malabar Coast. The one I went in was three feet in breadth, and, perhaps, thirty-five feet long.

It being morning, we pass great numbers of canoes filled with well-dressed Arabs, most of the merchants of Muscat living at Muttrah, and going to Muscat every morning to carry on their business. As every body sits down in the bottom of the boat, with only the head above the gunwale, the bright-coloured head-dresses present a rather comical appearance.

The distance to Muttrah is about two miles, round a succession of bold rocky points, each with a fort on the top of the nearly perpendicular cliffs ; and the boatmen, who are as usual Sídís, salute each point, as we pass it, with the formal Mussulman salutation.

In the little bays between these points are a series of villages, which come in sight round one corner, and disappear round the next, like a shifting scene. The sea being deep, carries its blue colour close up to the little white sandy beaches, on which all these villages are built. I imagine this spot is unequalled for wild, romantic effect, the hills rising suddenly from the sea to twelve or fifteen hundred feet, with the most irregular, fantastic outline imaginable.

Before starting, the British Agent at Muscat had supplied two letters from His Highness Syud Thaweyni (commonly called by the English the

Imám), one to the Wálí, or Governor of Muttrah, the other to the authorities in the village near the hot spring.

The Wálí of Muttrah, Rasás-bin-Bakhín, is a Sídí, and, by descent at least, a slave; but, as not unusual in these countries, has risen to the post of governor of a town of about thirty thousand inhabitants. He is a middle-aged, dignified man, and, I believe, much respected by the Arabs.

This gentleman is to provide me with a horse, and donkeys to carry kit, as well as an escort of three Arab soldiers. I am afraid the wishes of the owners of the donkeys are not consulted. I did endeavour to remunerate them on my return, but doubt if the money ever came to the hands of the proper people.

We get away from Muttrah at about 2 P.M., and wind through a pass in the hills behind the town, the only road, I believe, into the interior. It follows the bed of a watercourse, which must discharge a large body of water during the rains, that must pass through the gate of Muttrah, and on through the town to the sea. About half a mile of the pass, and we come on a small plain between the hills, across which the road passes.

Half a mile on the right is the village of Al Felej, so called from an extensive subterranean aqueduct. These are very common in Arabia and Persia, and are too well known to require description. This one extended, with its branches, for two miles or more. There is here an imposing looking fortified residence, belonging to some relation of the Sultan, with a prodigious flagstaff.

No residence of any one connected with a reigning family in Arabia is complete without a flagstaff, with topmast, and sometimes a third or top-gallant mast, and always unpleasantly out of the perpendicular. On approach, the fort is found to be dilapidated, and the cannon in a state of rust and decay, which European artillerists would hardly credit. A fine grove of trees, the result of the water from the aqueduct, has, however, a singular beauty in the midst of so much barrenness.

Across the plain to Rúí, a small hamlet, at a point where we enter a gorge in the hills, inhabited by tillers of the soil. Here is plenty of good water in wells, which are about fifty feet deep: the first twenty feet is walled round, the soil being loose, but below that depth they appear cut through a coarse conglomerate rock. (The depths are only estimated). At least half a dozen water-drawing machines are creaking away. Here are grown nearly all the vegetables which come to

Muscat—onions, lettuce, radishes, brinjalls, sugar-cane, maize, &c. There are some fine mango and tamarind trees, and many dates; in fact, the valley for half a mile is a regular garden. Then the cultivation suddenly ceases, and we find ourselves in a barren watercourse, about two hundred yards wide, strewed with boulders and pebbles, while precipitous hills rise on either hand. Rúí lies at the entrance to this watercourse, which is called Wádí-al-Adai.

Following the Wádí to the north-westward, at a distance of half a mile from the cultivation, we come to the remains of a strong wall which has been built across the valley—a distance of about two hundred yards: nothing now remains beyond the foundation, the piers of a bridge which allowed the waters to pass, and an arched gate, which latter is in tolerable repair, the wall ends at the hills at each side being built as far up their side only as they are accessible.

On down the Wádí to north-westward, about two miles, to Watair. Having received several accessions, the valley is here about a quarter of a mile wide; the hills also on each side are much higher than at Rúí, where they were only from two to three hundred feet. It must be a grand stream in the rains, judging from the size of some of the boulders: now that it is dry, it much resembles a gigantic railway cutting.

At Watair is a fine building in the eastern style, with a date-grove. It is a summer residence of the Sultan, but out of repair and very dirty inside, with the usual carved-wood trellis work, stained glass-windows, &c. An aqueduct is in course of construction to this place, all the way from Rúí, with a branch extending to a great distance up another Wádí. This watercourse goes on in a north-west direction to the sea, but I could not make out its mouth. I imagine it to be somewhere in the bay westward of Ras Hamar.

Here we leave the valley, and up the hills on the west side, through a pass of no great height, called Akabat-ar-Hamaitha. Here the escort ought certainly to have come under "Martin's Act," for they insisted on riding up the hill two on one donkey, in heavy fighting order, with matchlocks, swords, and shields, &c., one of the proprietors of these useful animals having contrived to abscond at Rúí while watering.

The road now winds along the north face of the mountains, which here take an east and west direction, having low, rocky hills on the right hand, just sufficiently high to intercept the view of the sea. After about three miles of rough ground, we emerge from the pass, and get a view of the sea, distant about two miles, with the picturesque Island Al Fahil, and the great bay called Jubet Hail.   Here we halt, while the escort perform their afternoon devotions : they do not appear particularly attentive, stopping now and again to talk, or look after the donkeys, and then going on again with their prostrations, in ludicrous alternation.

From this point the road bends round to the south-westward, keeping close to the hills, which recede from the coast and increase in height as we proceed ; the ground also becomes sandy, and high sand hills shut out the view of the sea.

Three miles of this, and we reach a cultivated plain, dotted with forts and date-groves.   This is the district of Bósher, which it is satisfactory to hear, as the evening is closing in.   A great deal of drumming and firing of matchlocks is going on at one of these forts : some great man is being married, and there is a great concourse of guests.   As we pass, they are very anxious we should partake of the marriage feast, which is embarrassing, as presents would, of course, be expected, and I am unprovided for such a contingency.

We excuse ourselves on the plea of its being late, and go on across several watercourses.   Most of these villages seem to be called Al Felej, or, at any rate, the escort say so.

About three miles through this valley, and over a low ridge of hills, and we reach the village of Ghulla, where the springs are.   By this time it is nearly dark : we pass through the village, knock up the owner of the letter of credence, and are forthwith accommodated in a house belonging to the Sultan.   It is an agreeable place for hot weather, without doors or windows ; but the nights are now chilly—thermometer at 64° ; and the musketry and drums in the next village are distinctly audible all night.   A wood fire is found objectionable, there being no arrangements about smoke.

The hot springs, five in number, issue from fissures in the rock at the foot of a mountain about 3,000 feet high, chiefly of volcanic formation, all within a space of about two hundred yards.   Four of them are not much larger than can be stopped with the hand, and at these there is no perceptible deposit ; the fifth, however, which is considerably larger, deposits near its source a white earthy substance in a stalactitic form.   (I have shown a piece to Dr. Carter, who considers it to be sulphate of magnesia.)   The natives call this spring the " cow " from this circumstance.   This spring discharges about as much water as a five-inch pipe would. The temperature of the water at this spring was 100° Fahrenheit.

The spring most frequented, and the one considered to have such marvellous properties, is another and smaller one, but which has a temperature of 115°. It is drunk in large quantities by the sick and lame, who abound at the spring, and great quantities are carried away. The people have great faith in its virtue, but I could not detect any specific taste : it appeared simply hot water, and it is very limpid. I have, however, brought a bottle well sealed to Bombay, should the Society consider it desirable to have it analysed. It did not appear to contain any fixed air.

The other three springs range from 107° to 110° in temperature, and are not in any way remarkable.

The Aneroid barometer indicated an elevation of 380 feet above the sea.

The water runs from the springs into baths, enclosed within small buildings, of which some are roofed. The two springs described above have two baths each ; the others one. These baths were full of people all the time I was there, alternately parties of men and of women. Bathing seems the favourite form of benefiting by the waters.

After leaving the baths, the water is allowed to run into shallow reservoirs to cool, and is then used in irrigation.

The village is small, but is in a beautiful clump of trees and gardens ; it is the most fertile little spot conceivable—dates, mangoes, limes, pomegranates, plantains, and many other trees, and plenty of corn and vegetables.

The mountain rises quite over the village. On going a little way up, there is a fine view, over the trees, of the sea (distant about four miles), with the numerous groups of islets, called Jezirat Dehmányeh ; and nearer, the villages and forts seen through the date-groves along the shore, for near this place begins the fertile coast of Batneh, where, for near two hundred miles, the coast is one continuous date-grove. On the left, distant about 30 miles, rises the stupendous chain of mountains called Jebel Nakhl, of which some peaks are near 8,000 feet.

Art. VII.—IS THE HABAIAH OF BRUCE THE SOURCE OF THE WHITE NILE?—*By Assistant Surgeon* George Birdwood, *M. D.*

Read before the Society, Feb. 16th, 1860.

In Latitude 2° 30' S., and Longitude 32° 47' E., and at an elevation of 3,750 feet, Speke found the Victoria *Nyanza,* or lake—a vast sheet of water, 90 miles in breadth, and lengthened immeasurably due north. From its altitude, size, and bearing, from its being in the meridian of the river, and from the reports of the Arabs whose information had always hitherto proved correct, Speke justly concluded that the Victoria Lake communicated with, and in all likelihood originated the White Nile. The lake is known to the Arabs so high as 2° N., the parallel of Kibuga, the terminus of a caravan route between the Zanzibar coast and Central Africa. The trustworthiness of their evidence, regarding the length of the Nyanza, rests not only on Speke's experience of their truthfulness and intelligence, but is strikingly supported by the communications they had previously made to Livingstone on the same subject. That traveller, at page 476 of his book on Central Africa, writes—" From information derived from the Arabs of Zanzibar, whom I met at Narile (15° 30' S., and 23° 30' E.), *in the middle of the country,* the region to the east parts of Londa, over which we have travelled, resembles them in its conformation. They report swampy steppes, some of which have no trees, where the inhabitants use grass, and stalks of native corn, for fuel. A large, shallow lake is also pointed out in that direction, named Tanganyenka (*see* also page 506), which requires three days for crossing in canoes. It is connected with another named Kalagwe (Garaque ?), and may be the Nyanja* of the Maravim. From this lake (Tanganyenka) is derived, by numerous small streams, the river Loapula, the eastern branch of the Zambesi, which, coming from the north-east, flows past the town of Cazembe. The southern end of this lake is ten days north-east of Cazembe (10° 30' S., and 27° 27' E.) ; and, as that is probably five days from Shinte (12° 30' S., and 23° 15' E.), we cannot have been nearer to it than 150 miles. Probably this lake is the water-shed between the Zambesi and the Nile, as Lake Dilolo (11° 30' S., and 22° 30' E.) is that between the Leeba and Kassai."

* Or Nyassa.—G. B.

The White Nile was explored by the Egyptian Expedition in 1839-41 to 3° 22′ N.; a German Mission has for years been established on its banks, at Gondokoro, in 4° 44′ N.; and but a few years since, M. Ulivi penetrated its difficult channel to 3° N. From this point to Speke's station in 2° 30′ S., a tract of 330 miles, is just verge and room enough for the natural development of such a body of water as the Victoria Lake, and that the latter fully covers it might have been reasonably inferred, independently of all positive evidence of the fact. The White Nile, at Gondokoro, is 1,605 feet above the sea. If the Victoria Lake, therefore, extends to 2° North, in the short distance of 164 miles, between the head of the lake and Gondokoro, there is a fall of 2,145 feet. We know that the country rises east, south, and west of the lake; gradually on the south, the mere ground swell of the Victoria plateau, but abruptly in mountain ranges on the east and west. We know that on the north, also, the country rises towards the highlands of Abyssinia; that the Atlas chain, prolonged from these across the entire continent, subtends in common the great triangular table-land of Africa, and the yet loftier water-shed of the Nyanza, dividing them from the plains of Sahara and Soudan; and that the only gap in this barrier, leading to the north, gives passage to the White Nile, marked probably by those cataracts in 3° 22′ N., which stopped the Egyptian Expedition of 1841. If then the lake has any exit, must it not be by the White Nile? It is land-locked: at one spot, however, 164 miles from its northern extremity, there is a fissure in the rampart which surrounds it, depressed 2,145 feet below its surface. This gorge is the bed of the White Nile. Inevitably, therefore, the lake, in overflowing its basin, must discharge itself as the White Nile. The two must needs be connected. But while it is clear that the Nyanza is the most southern portion, and that it must be the main source of the Nile, it is not, I would venture to advance, the ultimate origin of that river. I would not, of course, look upon the streams which drain the Victoria plateau as the fountains of the Nile, in contradistinction to the Victoria Lake. To do so, would be to quibble. It must be some considerable river, a feeder either of the Victoria Nyanza, or of the White Nile direct, that can bear the palm from the lake of being the head of the immemorial Nile. The expedition of Mehemet Ali, when stopped by the cataracts in 3° 22′ north, found the White Nile there divided into two branches, one bearing due south a month's journey, or 300 miles, to

17 *g*

its reputed source, and from 1,300 to 1,700 feet broad, and from 9 to 12 feet deep, evidently the main current; the other flowing from the south-west, 60 feet broad, an affluent obviously of very near issue. Pethereck's journey from Gondokoro to Runga, on the Equator, in 26° East longitude, moreover, proved that the Nile was not supplied by any great river from that quarter. The explorations of Burton and Speke demonstrate that it receives no rivers from the south. No streams of any magnitude can find their way to it from that portion of the eastern ghauts of Africa which culminate in the peaks of Kenia and Kilimanjaro. No streams, indeed, from that direction could reach the Nile except through the Nyanza or the Habaiah, if that river empty into the Nyanza. If it does not, any river tending towards the Nile, north of the Nyanza, would be turned from its course by the Ganca hills, which lie between and parallel with the White Nile and the Habaiah, linking the Abyssinian highlands with the Atlas ranges and the Mountains of the Moon; the common point from which these three Alpine chains diverge being we may presume the cataracts of the Nile above Gondokoro; the Ganca hills towards Abyssinia, the Atlas range eastwards across the entire breadth of Africa, and the Mountains of the Moon southwards, separating the Nyanza and Tanganyka lakes, and forming, with the Atlas, the *Vallis Garamantica* of Ptolemy. If, then, the Nyanza is fed by any large river, it must come from the north and eastward of the Ganca hills. It must flow down through the elevated valley between these and the mountains of Andak, a valley in the direct meridian of the eastern shore of the Nyanza. This valley is the kingdom of Limmou, through which, in about longitude 34° 30' E., runs the Habaiah. It has been traced from its rise in the mountains of Kaffa 6° 4' North, to past Berry in 4° 40' North, beyond which its course has not been determined. Berry is, however, just in the latitude of Gondokoro; and, *mutatis mutandis*, the arguments which prove the connection of the White Nile with the Nyanza, prove that of the latter with the Habaiah. The mountains of Kaffa (Narea), writes Bruce at page 333 of Vol. III. of his travels (3rd Edition), are the highest land in the peninsula of Africa. The Habaiah at Berry is, therefore, in all probability, far more above the Nyanza than the White Nile at Gondokoro is below it. Like the Nyanza, the Habaiah too, is completely land-locked, except at one restricted spot: the Nyanza, as we have seen, in the meridian of the

White Nile, the Habaiah in that of the eastern side of the Nyanza. If, then, the Nyanza must empty itself into the White Nile, à fortiori the Habaiah must fall into the Nyanza. The Habaiah cannot be continuous with the Zebee river, as has been presumed, because the Andak Mountains intervene between them. It cannot be continuous with the Seboth, as Keith Johnston has represented (?), for the Ganca hills part them. I would observe, parenthetically, that the Seboth is a red river, draining a sandstone country ; the Habaiah is coloured white by the limestones of Narea and Limmou (?). Speke states that the Nyanza is so broad and deep towards its northern end, that the native craft navigating it there use sextants and logs. Does not this indicate that the lake stretches out to meet, as it were, some river entering it on the north-east, as it does towards the north-west to reach the Nile ? Does not this indicate that it is formed by some river from the north-east tumbling into a deep trough in its course, and that all of it, south of this broad crescentic depth, is mere marshy backwater, accumulated by the efforts of the Habaiah to overpower the natural dam interposed between the Nyanza and the ravine of the White Nile ? It is impossible that the Habaiah can end suddenly in a blind lake before it gains the Nyanza, as the neighbouring, but very differently circumstanced, Hawash does.

Considering the slope of the country it traverses, the Habaiah must, indeed, for very want of elbow room, pass into the Nyanza. Now this is the very river Bruce supposed to be the source of the White Nile. In Vol. VII., page 105 of his travels (3rd Edition), he states that the El Aice (White Nile) rises in the country south of Narea, supplied with perpetual rains ; and therefore the White Nile "never diminishes as the (Blue) Nile does, in the latitude of whose fountains the rains prevail only at stated seasons." In Vol. V., page 370, he accounts for certain appearances of the Nile inundation by the bursting of immense marshes in the country about Narea ; and further on, at page 384, in examining the account of the origin of the Nile given to Herodotus (lib. 11, sect. 28) by the secretary to Minerva, he remarks that, in latitude 9°, in the kingdom of Gingiro (east of Limmou), the Zebee runs south or south-east into the inner Ethiopia, as do also many other rivers ; and, " as I have heard from the natives of that country, empty themselves into a lake, as those on the north of the Line (Blue Nile, &c.) do into the lake Tzana." But, exclusive of the physical features of the country around the Victoria Lake, and of the authority of the sagacious Bruce, the phenomenon of the annual inundation of the Nile alone, would appear to force us to accept the Habaiah as a tributary of the Nyanza; while, added to the arguments already cited, no question of the fact can remain. The rains on the Victoria plateau fall from November 15th to May 15th. The inundation of the Nile through Egypt begins in June, and continues to the end of September. The phenomena seem quite unrelated. Sir Roderick Murchison has attempted to connect them as cause and effect, by representing the inundation of the Nile as the surplus drainage of the Victoria plateau. The Nyanza, when super-saturated with rain, must burst and flood the lowest land contiguous, the valley of the Nile; nevertheless, the annual overflow of the lake of itself does not I believe, completely account for the periodic rise of the Nile. Sir Roderick Murchison's hypothesis may be illustrated by the phenomenon formerly presented by the Nile in a lower part of its course. Between Nubia and Egypt, at Silsilis, the Nile was once interrupted by a natural granitic or basaltic barrier, behind which the river had to accumulate before falling over into Egypt. In fact, a lake was formed southward of Silsilis, the traces of which yet remain over a tract of 300 miles, and which delayed the inundation in Egypt until swollen to a level sufficient to overcome its own basin. Of course, therefore, the inundation was not only proportionably higher, but also earlier behind than before Silsilis. Now something of this sort must actually occur in the relations of the Nyanza and the Nile. Their communication must be crossed by a series of natural weirs permitting the free percolation of the Nyanza into the White Nile, while the current from the Victoria plateau is low, but effectually damming the lake back when it augments in volume during the rains; until, indeed, its gathered waters, welling up above every obstruction, discharge themselves with a rush on the country below, by a succession of cataracts—the cataracts, as we have presumed, which stopped the expedition of Mahomed Ali from further exploring the White Nile. From this, it is clear that some delay must take place before the effects of the super-saturation of the watery network of the Victoria plateau can be experienced in Egypt; yet, surely it is as clear that no division between the lake and the river can possibly cause the great distance in time which occurs between the season of precipitation on the Victoria Nyanza, and of the inundation of the Nile.   If the Nyanza only overflows on the 15th of May, how, if it be the sole cause of the inundation, explain that phenomenon continuing in Egypt to the end of September ?   If it overflow before May, why, if it be the sole cause of the inundation, is the fact not felt in Cairo until St. John's Day ?   The mean velocity of the Nile, when not in flood, is 2½ miles an hour : when not in flood, even a particle of Nyanza water should, therefore, be only 28 days in reaching Cairo.   Unmistakeably, then, we must look beyond the Nyanza, if we would find the complete elucidation of the yearly inundation of the valley of the Nile.   The Nyanza most certainly is an agent in the phenomenon under comment ;   I would only contend that it is not the sole agent.   We need take no account of tropical snows.   Sir Roderick Murchison altogether discredits the existence of snowy mountains in Central Africa—why, I ill understand.   So far back as 1842, that gifted geologist, with startling prescience, announced the hypothesis, " that South Africa certainly, and probably the whole of the Continent, is a vast trough or basin, encircled on all sides by higher ridges of primeval palæozoic rocks, for the most part crystalline," but enclosing lacustrine deposits ;   and that this vast table-land supported a system of lakes and marshes in which all the great rivers of Africa originated, these escaping to the sea by favouring depressions in the mountain chains which flanked the interior plateau.   We all know how wonderfully the discoveries of Livingstone demonstrated the truth of this supposition, and that the hypothesis of 1842 is now the established theory of the physical evolution of Africa ;—but is it in any way incompatible with the possible occurrence of snowy ranges in Central Africa ?   Still, Sir Roderick Murchison would seem to imply this, if I do not misunderstand his remarks on the subject in his address to the anniversary meeting of the Royal Geographical Society last May. Ptolemy (I quote him second-hand), Pausanias (I quote from Bruce), Bruce, and Krapf, all witness to the presence of such mountains about the sources of the Nile, and yet, and solely on the negative evidence of Speke and Burton, solely on the negative fact of these latter travellers not having determined whether Kenia and Kilimanjaro were snowcapped or not, Sir Roderick Murchison is sceptical of the assertions of all the former authorities cited ;   at least, so it would appear.   It is scarcely fair, I think, to condemn them thus simply by default.   But while we are not yet prepared to deny the existence of snowy mountains in Central Africa, I think we are fully entitled to repudiate the notion of the Nile flood being in any great degree owing to the melting of snows about the Equator. Speaking of the chain of Kenia and Kilimanjaro, Sir Roderick Murchison, in his address already referred to, observes—" Even if it be assumed that this is really a snowy range, the exact periodical rise of the Nile could never be caused by a periodical melting of its snows, since the power of the sun under the Equator is so nearly equable throughout the year, that it must operate in feeding the streams which descend from the mountains, with pretty much the same amount of water at all seasons." Without exactly agreeing to this—for might it not happen that with the rising of the temperature on the cessation of the rains on the Victoria plateau, the thawing of the assumed snows might, were they abundant enough, carry on the inundation commenced by the cataclysm of the Victoria Lake?—yet unquestionably we cannot reasonably hold that melting snows, if even granted, carry the solution of the problem of the regular freshening of the Nile one step beyond the point at which the data afforded by the physical circumstances of the Nyanza fail us. We are shut out, therefore, to the conclusion that the complete explanation of the inundation of the Nile necessitates the postulation of a feeder of the White Nile, the flooding of which is supplementary, or rather complementary, to the overflow of the Nyanza. It must be a river in the Tropic of Cancer ; and what other can it be if not the Habaiah ? We all know that in the Tropic of Cancer the season of precipitation, following the sun's course, is during the summer and autumn ; in the Tropic of Capricorn during the winter and spring. Now mark, in connection with this, the peculiar distribution of Africa on the face of the globe. Bruce, at page 337 of Vol. 5 (3rd Edition) of his travels, writes—" Supposing a meridian line drawn through the Cape of Good Hope till it meets the Mediterranean where it bounds Egypt, and that this meridian has a portion of latitude that will comprehend all Abyssinia, Nubia, and Egypt below it, this section of the Continent from south to north contains 64° divided equally by the equator, so that from the Line to the southernmost point of Africa is 32°, and northward to the edge of the Mediterranean is 32° also. Now, if on each side we set off 2°, these are the limits of the variable winds, and we have then 30° south and 30° north, within which space, on both sides, the trade winds are confined. Set off, again,.

16° from the 32°, that is, half the distance between the Cape of Good Hope and the Line, and 16° between the Line and the Mediterranean, and you have the limits of the tropical rains, 16 degrees on each side of the equator. Again, take half of 16 degrees, which is 8, and add it to the limit of the tropical rains, that is, to 16°, and you have 24, which is the situation of the tropics. "There is something," adds the sagacious philosopher of Kinnaird, " very remarkable in this distribution." Remarkable indeed ! It is the explanation of the inundation of every river in Africa, the differentiation of the inundations of the several rivers, and the peculiarity of that of the Nile, arising from the Atlas Mountains, unequally dividing Northern from Southern Africa ; so that the incline from the Atlas to the Cape is nearly 5° longer than from the Atlas to the Mediterranean. On this very point Bruce (page 384, Vol. 5, Edition 3), remarks :—" The periodic rains; from the Tropic of Capricorn to the Line, being in equal quantity with those that fall between the Line and the Tropic of Cancer, it is plain that if the land of Ethiopia sloped equally from the line southwards and northwards, half of the rains that fall on each side would go north and half south, but as the ground from 5° North declines all southward, it follows that the river which runs to the south-ward must be equal to those that run to the northward, *plus* the rain that falls in the 5° North latitude, where the ground begins to slope to the southward ; and there can be no doubt that this is at least one of the reasons why there are in the Southern continent so many rivers larger than the Nile that run both into the Indian and Atlantic Oceans."

Now this unequal division of Africa, which at first sight would seem opposed to the very existence of the Nile, owing to a special modification, is the efficient cause of that river. The rains which supply the Victoria Lake should drain off to the south, but the Victoria plateau counteracts the prevailing southward slope of Africa, and turns the waters northwards. The Habaiah, which, had Africa been equally bisected, would have flowed northward, flows southward; but, fortunate-ly, intercepted by the Victoria Lake, contributes its drainage to the Nile, which hence is perennial. The peculiarities of the Nile inundation depend on this same modification of the great table-land of Africa about the sources of the river. In his passage through the Tropic of Capricorn, the sun surcharges the Nyanza with the rains which fall from

November to May; in his passage through the Tropic of Cancer, the Habaiah in turn becomes swollen, and, descending into Egypt, on, as it were, the crest of the Nyanza flood, constitutes there the annual inundation.   The Nyanza, I believe, bursts before March.   "Before then," writes Bruce (Vol. 5, p. 332) "green boughs and leaves appear floating in the Bahr-el-Abiad ;" but alone it is no more than merely sufficient to sustain the Nile.   In June, however, on top of its waters come the northern rains carried down by the Habaiah, and we have the true inundation of Egypt.   That this is the real explanation of the inundation, is corroborated by the fact that, twice in the history of Egypt, once in the reign of Cleopatra, and again in 1737, the Nile, after the subsidence of the usual inundation, began to rise afresh in the December following.   For what does this indicate but unwonted rains south of the Equator? but an unwonted cataclysm of the Nyanza, and, by corollary, that the regular inundation of June results from rains north of the Line, superadded to those which fall on the Nyanza, and which can only reach the Nyanza, as we have seen, through the Habaiah.   Pococke has remarked that the Nile, when it first begins to rise in June, is green with putrid vegetable matter ; and Bruce, in commenting on this observation (Vol. 5, p. 370), writes :—"The true reason of this appearance is from those immense marshes spread over the country about Narea and Caffa * * * where the water accumulates, and is stagnant before it overflows into the river Abiad, which rises there."   This quotation clenches, in my opinion, the argument for the Habaiah being a great feeder of the Nyanza, and, therefore, the ultimate source of the Nile. It might be advanced that that portion of the White Nile which traverses the tropic of Cancer receives in sufficient quantity the rains of the northern tropic to render superfluous any reference to the Habaiah.   It must be remembered however, that the mere passage of the sun through Cancer does not precipitate rain—rain only falls in the sun's course in these regions, where the moisture he draws with him is condensed against mountain ranges ; and hence we find, that the further we travel westward of the highlands of Abyssinia, the limits of the summer rains of Africa lie more and more to the south.   It is clear, therefore, that it is not the White Nile in the plains of the Shellouks and Sennaar, but the Habaiah, encircled by the lofty mountains of Ganca, Andak, and Narea (the last the highest land in all Africa), and palpably emptying into the Nyanza, which must add the necessary supplement to the waters of the Nyanza, for the causation of the inundation of Egypt. If I have succeeded in satisfying you of this, I shall be truly happy, not on any scientific grounds, but happy simply to have added another proof to the many which have been collected in our days, of the rare truthfulness, wide knowledge, and wonderful sagacity of that philosopher whom the author of Baron Munchausen sneered to death—James Bruce of Kinnaird.*

* BRUCE THE ORIGINAL DISCOVERER OF THE TZETZE.

It is surprising that Bruce's notice of the *Tzetze* had never before attracted attention. In Vol. v., p. 304-306—Bruce writes.—

" Large swarms of flies appeared wherever that loamy earth was. * * *

This insect is called *zimb* in modern or vulgar Arabic : it has not been described by any naturalist. It is in size very little larger than a bee, of a thicker proportion, and the wings, which are broader than those of a bee, are placed separate, like those of a fly; they are of pure gauze, without colour or spot upon them. The head is large, the upper jaw or lip is short, and has at the end of it a strong pointed hair of about a quarter of an inch long ; the lower jaw has two of these pointed hairs, and this pencil of hairs, when joined together, makes a resistance to the finger nearly equal to that of a strong hog's bristle. Its legs are secreted on the inside, and the whole covered with brown hair or down. As soon as this plague appears, and its buzzing is heard, all the cattle forsake their food and run wildly about the plain, till they die, worn out with fatigue, fright, and hunger. * * * The camel even is not capable to sustain the violent punctures the fly makes with his pointed proboscis, * * * for when once attacked by this fly, his body, head, and legs swell out into large bosses, which break, and putrify to the certain destruction of the creature. Even the elephant and rhinoceros * * * are obliged to roll themselves in mud or mire * * * to enable them to stand against this winged assassin, and yet I have found some of these tubercles upon almost every elephant and rhinoceros I have seen. * * * Isaiah alone has given an account of this animal. * * Ch. VII., verse 18 and 19—" *And it shall come to pass in that day, that the Lord shall hiss for the fly that is in the uttermost parts of the rivers of Egypt, and they shall come and rest on all of them in the desolate valleys, and in the holes of the rocks, and upon all thorn and upon all bushes.*"

The Hebrew name, Bruce observes, is *tsaltsala*.

Art. VIII.—ON THE COMMERCE OF CENTRAL AFRICA.—
Contributed by Captain J. H. Speke.

Read before the Society by the Secretary on the 19th January 1860.

I was travelling in Africa about two and a-half years, from
1856 to 1859, both inclusive. I commenced work by making a cruising
trip up to Mombas, and in visiting the island of Pemba on the way.
Pemba is a very beautiful and interesting isle, called by the Arabs, very
appropriately, the Emerald Isle, in consequence of its lovely verdure.
Leaving Mombas, I coasted down to the mouth of the Pangani River,
touching at all the villages on the way, and thence proceeded inland,
westward, to a place called Fuja, the capital of Usambara, and paid the
King of that country, by name Kimwere, a visit. I then returned to
Zanzibar. Here, after some months, waiting for the monsoon to pass
away, I travelled with a caravan, commanded by Captain Burton, to
explore the interior. We first went inland westward to Unganyembe,
a distance of 400 miles or more. Here the Arabs have a depôt to
assist them in carrying on their traffic with the more distant interior
places, and here all caravans which are collected on the coast break up,
and again have to be created. This reconstructing process we effected
with the kind assistance of the Arabs residing there ; when again starting westwards, we travelled 200 miles or more, and discovered the
Tanganyika Lake, a sheet of water 300 miles long by 30 to 40 broad.
But we only navigated the northern half of it. This completed our
journeys westward. We now returned to Unganyembe with the same
men we had taken from that place. These porters now had done their
work, and a third new caravan had consequently to be formed. It was
here, in consequence of my companion being very ill, I had to travel
alone, and in six weeks, marching 450 miles, I then travelled to, discovered the Nyanza, and returned to join him again. Our leave of
absence from the Government having by this time expired, and the fund

advanced to us being long before exhausted, we proceeded homeward, and soon arrived at the sea coast. We now hired a sailing craft, called a Dhow in those regions, and coasted down shore to Kilwa, and back to Zanzibar, looking in at all the islands, towns, forts, and villages, as well as the rivers on the way.

Having now given you a brief notice of the country which I travelled over, a distance averaging from 2,000 to 3,000 miles, I will proceed with a description of the general nature of things existing there.

The principal rivers on this part of the coast are the Paugani, Kingani, and Lufiji ; the two latter of which are navigable by small crafts of 40 or 50 tons, to a distance of 30 miles or so, but large canoes could go up there, to at least 100 miles, without any difficulty, if the savages living on their banks were only friendly, which now unfortunately is not the case.

The islands about here are numerous, but only four—Zanzibar, Pemba, Morifia, and Kilwa, are of any size.

The population of Zanzibar is, I believe, nearly as great as that of Aberdeen, exceeding 60,000 souls. Sultan Majid resides there, and is Governor of all these regions. There are three Consuls—one English, one French, and one American. Besides them, the European community consists of several Mercantile houses of German, French, and Americans ; but I am sorry to say there are no English houses there at all, although Bombay is close at hand, and is not half the distance from it that any of these other countries are, which make large profits by its trade.

The population of coloured men consists in Hindi, Arab, and Sowahili merchants, besides the Negroes and slaves. These Asiatic merchants principally trade with Bombay, Cutch, Muskat, and the interior of Africa, and are the go-betweens for the Europeans and interior Negroes.

The European merchants have usually 5 or 6 square-rigged vessels lying in the harbour ; but how many come there annually I cannot say. The Native crafts are very numerous, but only sail, taking advantage of the monsoons, twice a year across the Indian Ocean to India, Arabia, Persia, or the Red Sea. The island of Zanzibar is entirely cultivated by slaves. The current money on this island is the Dollar, Indian Rupees, and Sovereigns ; this latter medium is solely required, I fear, for the purchase of slaves down in the Mozambique direction.

The following are the imports, as far as my knowledge extends :—
American sheeting, which constitutes the general wear of all the Africans,

blue indigo dyed stuff, very poor, and consequently not so much in use. This fabric comes, I believe, from India.   Then there are several descriptions of coloured cloths brought from Bombay, Cutch, and Muskat, these are in general use by the Native chiefs or elders, and by their wives and concubines ; in fact, by all who can afford to purchase them. Venetian beads come there by ship loads, of every quality, and variety of colour and shape.   Thin brass wire, from America, is an article of great consumption : this the Africans reform into bracelets, anclets, armlets, and other ornaments.   Arms and ammunition are also imported from America.   This concludes the principal imports.

Jackass Copal.   It is plucked off the tree like most other gums ; but this is very inferior, and consequently of little importance.   The copal tree grows on the island of Zanzibar as well as on the coast.   What quantity is exported from Zanzibar I cannot say ; but I was told, on good authority, that the 12 or 13 American ships (I believe) that trade there every year, take away as much as 19,000,000 lbs. of it ; what the Germans and Indians transport I cannot say.   The trade in copal, I am assured, might be increased to a very great extent beyond what it now makes, if the Negroes would only exert themselves in digging it.   But they dare not work, from fear of being robbed, and consequently content themselves in staying their appetites for the day.   Perhaps the next most important export of Zanzibar, and that most capable of extension, is its hides and horns.   These are brought in great quantities from the interior, where droves of cattle range in vast numbers.   Those nearest the coast belong to the Masai, a pastoral people, very savage and boisterous, who have, until lately, prevented the travelling merchants from penetrating that quarter of the Continent, but now it appears they are gradually becoming tamed : firstly, by the greater numbers of caravans which are daily increasing in that line ; and secondly, by the love they are now gaining for cloth and beads, produced, I imagine, by a competitive desire to equal in dignity and comfort those who they must now see are better off than they are.   Then, next, further inland, are the Wataturee, a set of robbing creatures, who do nothing but tend cattle and despoil their neighbours : they have nothing civilised about them ; in fact, they enjoy a supreme contempt for clothing or any other ordinary comfort.   This singular tribe bears a peculiarity which none of the others do — circumcision.   But in far greater numbers, as far as my experience goes, are the cattle of the far interior, extending from 34° to 29° East Longitude.   The whole of that country I know, from 5° South

Latitude to the Equator ; and, I hear, up to as far as 3° North Latitude, teems with cattle and goats.   Some of these cows are short-horned, of the hump breed, and all parts coloured : but others are large, even larger than any English oxen, and have horns of far superior size than the large Ceylon cattle ; but these are confined to the hilly districts in the mountains, which I consider are the Luna Mounts, formerly alluded to by Ptolemy, but of which no body hitherto has ever arrived at any satisfactory conclusion—save, of course, myself.

One other large article of export is the cowrie shell.

The Elephant abounds in the forests of these regions, as may be judged by the quantity of ivory annually exported.

This article (ivory) is considered to be very much finer here in these latitudes than in any other part of Africa, both in size and texture. The Arabs go half across the Continent, 150 miles west of the Tanganzik Lake, in search of it ; and also, starting from Unganzembe, go up round the western side of the Victoria Nyanza to 2° North Latitude.   The best description of ivory is, I believe, found about the Mountains of the Moon ; but tusks are said to be as abundant on the eastern side of the Nyanza, and are, very cheap, though the risk of going there, in consequence of the hostile character of the savage inhabitants, has hitherto precluded much business being done in that region.   Then, besides these places, Ubena, Uunza, and the country west of the Nyassa (lake) are well known to be abundant in ivory, Hippopotami teeth, and Rhinoceros horns, as well as of the skins of the Zebra, Giraffe, Wild Buffaloes, and Antelopes, and the Cows' skins, also numerous, that are found in those places are brought away by the Arab, Hindi, and Sowahili merchants.

On the construction of caravans.—Caravans are assembled on the coast by the different merchants and native headmen (or diwans), who live in villages on it.   There is now so much competition among these coast merchants, in consequence of the greatly increasing state of the trade, that they send procurers 150 miles or more into the interior to secure porters,—men who are bringing down ivory on behalf of the chiefs of the interior,—to form their own caravans with, as well as to secure to themselves the purchase of the ivory these men are bringing down country ; for all these commercial establishments on the Sowahili coast are simply branches of the Zanzibar ones, and these buy the ivory for transmission there, where the European merchants purchase it at their hand from the large Asiatic merchants living on the Island.

The Arabs travel in bodies, consisting of several caravans joined together, for mutual protection, of a number averaging from 200 to 800
men, of which a considerable portion, their own domestic slaves,
carry muskets, very often the condemned Indian Army ones,—whilst
the common porters, like all the natives of the interior, carry a bow and
spear.   Their loads are usually weighted before starting to 60 lbs.,
which consist chiefly of American sheetings, Indigo-dyed stuffs, some
coloured stuffs for chiefs, beads in every variety, and brass wire. This
is the stock for road expenses, and for bartering with the natives for
their ivories, skins, &c. &c.   The greatest porters in Africa are the
Wanzamuezis (people of the moon).   They go inland to Unganzembe,
where the Arabs, as I have said before, have a depôt ; indeed, Unganzembe may be said to be the emporium of east and central Africa. From
this place they, after exchanging the men they bring up from the coast
for a fresh set, diverge in all directions to the north, south, and west.
One porter's wages from the coast to Unganzembe is 9 to 10 loin cloths of
American sheeting, each of which measures 4 cubits. Caravans move
along in single file, by winding foot-paths, for they have no roads, in a
peristaltic kind of motion, as they circle in and out of the forest trees,
or wind round the jungle bushes.   They have no carts, horses, or
camels.   But, returning to Zanzibar, I will first enumerate the productions of that Island, and then proceed with the interior.   There the
clove grows well, and in great abundance.   This is an article imported
into England, and is quoted in price currents. Cocoanuts are in great
profusion. Sugar-cane is grown, and even a steam engine is used in
its manufacture. Pineapples are as easily raised as common turnips,
mangoes and oranges, as well as limes, are of a fine order, and all things
that are grown in India appear to be produceable there.   The other
Islands yield the same products, more or less limited; but being small are
comparatively of little account.   In the continent of Africa, from the
coast to the 28th degree of East Longitude, there are five distinctly different styles or features of country, which, for distinction sake, I will term
Zones. The 1st Zone, as I have said before, is the maritime plain, extending for 120 miles inland, to the base of a belt of mountains, which
average from 250 to 5,646 feet high, and is 90 miles broad. The range
extends longitudinally, I believe, from Abyssinia down to the Cape
of Good Hope, and is usually very fertile.   As far as this Zone the
people are well clad ; I think I may safely say, much better than our
Indian Ryots, for in place of the tiny, narrow, little lungotes, scarcely

two inches broad, which, passing between the legs, is twitched to a string or strap tied round the waist, which are those the Ryots use, these Negroes have a cloth to cover them, quite as decent, I may say, as the highlander's kilt.   Their villages, too, are very comfortable, consisting of groups of conical grass thatched huts, supported on a wooden framework of piles and sticks, cemented together with wattle and dab.   The people, besides tilling the ground, have cattle and goats in large quantities, and the aloe plant grows well ; its fibres are converted into cordage. The common domestic fowl, I must say, is a very general bird all over the Continent, and these Negroes are so refined in taste, we must suppose, though it is difficult to believe it, that they even have capons. This ends the second Zone, and now we may consider ourselves in the interior of the Continent.

The third Zone is a high, flattish table land or plateau, averaging from 3,000 to 4,000 feet, and extends from the 36° to 34° East Longitude, 120 miles of, unfortunately, badly watered country.   This misfortune, for the soil appears very good, is, I think, owing to the vicinity of the east coast range on the one side, and the Mountains of the Moon on the other, attracting and intercepting all the rains by their superior heights.   All the country from the sea coast to the east coast range, a distance of 200 miles, is well watered by the two monsoons ; that is, the South-western and North-east ones, which succeed each other in regular order every six months.   Again, the whole of the country, from the 34° to the 26° East Longitude, near these Luna Montes, has a rainy season of six months continuously, which renders those two regions very fertile in consequence.   All the soil of the interior appears to be the sand or disintegrated particles of the general granitic outcropping hills that are found more or less all over its surface.   The people who occupy this Zone are in most part called Wagogos ; they are considered rather a boisterous set, but they did us no harm.   Their huts, as well as the Wanzamuezis, are of a rather superior build, introduced, I suspect, by the Wanzamuezis, for they appear to be, from their travelling habits, the first men who, from the interior, paid visits to the coast, and learnt from there the way to build square huts.   All over this region the forests are composed of slender trees, amongst which there is a species of the frankincense, as well as other gum-producing trees.   The Acacia in varieties ; the Calabash or gouty-limbed tree, the Doune, and other palms, and the Sheeshum, or Indian blackwood, are all common in this section of Africa.

On the central meridional line of the 4th and next Zone lies the Nyanza, which I confidently believe will be found to be the true source of the White Nile, and will be a great convenience to the trader on the Nile when more fully known.

To return to the products of this Zone, which comprise Ungamuezi proper : it is certainly very rich. The Arabs, who live at Kazeh, in the Unganzembe, districts of it, grow a great quantity of rice (this the Ne-groes do not care about, as they consider it is poor food), and have onions, chillies, and other luxuries as well as the benghan and the rozelle ; from the fruit of this latter plant we made delicious jelly. The sur-face of this Zone is very uneven, being diversified by lines and groups of low, cropping, little, granite hills, separated from one another by flats and valleys. The sandstone, which forms a great feature in its geological structure, lying between 2° and 4° South Latitude, is so impregnated with iron ore, that many of the men residing there are smiths and smelters. These men form the metal into hoes, spear heads and other varieties of hardware. Indeed, the most of the iron used in this part of Africa comes from this quarter. The cotton plant which grows here, ap-parently, judging from its size and its difference from the plant usually cultivated in India, I judge to be a tree-cotton, and no perennial. The Negroes make this cotton into coarse fabrics in their looms : their potters, carpenters, and ropemakers, all do a little trade. The dress of the commonest men, in fact the negro working-dress, is simply a goat skin, which they fling, game-bag fashion, over one shoulder, and dangling by one side, covers but a small portion of the body at a time. Why they ever take the trouble to put it on I cannot say, since they take it off and put it away whenever any rain comes on, or they have a wet job to do ; such, for instance, as paddling in canoes. The further we go inland the more naked they become. In fact, from the well-clad damsel of the coast, we here find creatures going about with nothing more than a short head lappet, covering but a very small portion of the body ; this difference in the condition of the people of the coast and the far interior is illustrated in a very satisfactory manner in its beneficial effect even of the small commerce which now exists, and points at the greater benefits which would result from our more extended trade.

The fifth Zone, where we traversed it, has a remarkable fall of 2,200 feet in it from 4,000 feet, the altitude of Ungamuezi to the level of the Tanganzik lake, which is only 1,800 feet above the sea. This tract is a very peculiar feature in the geography of the country. In this place, the Tanganzik lake is not half the altitude of the surrounding plateau, yet it has high hills, double its own altitude, to the north; whilst, as far as I could ascertain, it has none at all on the south. Again, to the south, the Arabs say there is no exit for the waters of the lake ; but instead, affirm that water in a large volume runs into it by a river called Manunju. This lake is about 300 miles long, with a breadth of from 33 to 40 miles. I crossed it in the centre, and went to its northern extremity. The banks of it are well peopled in most places ; but although they are agriculturists, and produce magnificent crops, they are usually very turbulent. One of these tribes, the Wabombe, are said to be cannibals. There is a great variety of fish in this lake, many of which are very delicious ; the shrimp even is very numerous, and the eels very sweet and good. These are all brought to the markets which the negroes form at all the ports where canoes usually stop at. At the Ujiji market, for instance, where our camp was formed for several months, we had as good feeding as any one could wish for ; we obtained there besides, fish, goats, fowls, eggs, milk (from the Sultan only, as he was the only man who possessed cows at that place), spirits and oil from the palms that grow there, bananas of variety, pumpkins, melons, cucumbers, artichokes, manioc, maize, two species of millets, those most cultivated in a great variety of pulse, sugar-cane, and a great variety of pot herbs, as well as yams and sweet potatoes.

I may repeat that, in the meanwhile, the staple exports will consist of hides and horns, ivory and copal ; to these, I think, may be added, when there is a better security for life and property, some textile material, drawn from the banana, aloe, and pineapple ; with oleaginous plants, such as the ground-nut, the cocoa-nut, and a species of palm, which yields a concrete oil, which appears to me to resemble that which yields the palm oil of Western Africa. The coffee plant is a native of this part of Africa, and is consequently easily grown ; its produce ought, in time, to be a valuable article of export.

P. S.—I hope that the party being sent to Africa will not be a large one, or it will be found very difficult to move. Sickness and many other causes will arise to hinder progress, which a fewer number of members would, to a certain degree, obviate.

J. H. S.

19 g

ART. IX.—NARRATIVE OF SAID BIN HABEEB, AN ARAB INHABITANT OF ZANZIBAR. *Contributed by* GOVERNMENT.

Read before the Society by the Secretary on the 31st May 1860.

I left Zanzibar to travel in the interior of Africa about sixteen years ago. I went partly to trade in ivory, and partly for the purpose of visiting unexplored regions of that great country. I first travelled to Ugiji on the shore of the great lake of Tanganika. I then crossed the lake, and went twenty-seven days' journey down its western coast by boat to Umaroongoo, which is situated near the south end of the lake. A broad river, called the Maroongoo, flows into the lake near this place. From Umaroongoo, I travelled south, and visited the country of a powerful Chief whose title is 'the Casembe.' I first went seven days journey to Peto, thence seven days to Karembo Makoonga; in three days more to Karoongwesi, and thence in three days to Roonda, a large town, where the Casembe resides. Roonda is situated on the banks of a large river called the Ruapoora,—the stream flows North towards the Tanganika lake. The Casembe is a Negro, by name Sultan Chareka. The people are armed with muskets. There are plenty of sheep, goats, and poultry procurable at Roonda, but no horses, horned cattle, or camels. The markets of Roonda are well supplied with meat, fish, grain, and vegetables. There is no money : Venetian beads form the circulating medium. The people appear comfortable and contented, the country is everywhere cultivated, and the inhabitants are numerous. There are no stone buildings,—all the houses are constructed of wood or mud, with roofs of grass or leaves. The Casembe governs with mildness and justice, and the roads are quite safe for travellers. After residing for some time at Roonda, I went a journey of twenty-five days to the great copper-mines ; they are situated to the west of Roonda, and the country all forms part of the dominions of the Casembe ; it is well peopled and cultivated. The copper-mines are situated in a large range of mountains ; a great many people are employed at them, and the copper is taken for sale all over the country. After smelting, about seventy-five pounds weight of copper are sold for four cubits of American sheeting ; iron is everywhere abundant, and the miners' tools are made from iron procured in the neighbourhood. A large town called Katanza is situated near the copper-mines, it contains a greater population than Roonda. The bazars at Katanza are well supplied with rice, Indian corn, jowarree, bajree, vegetables of various sorts ; sheep and goats are plentiful ; cotton is abundant, and is made into cloth in the country. There are no horses or horned cattle. Around Katanza, the country is generally populous, and the land well cultivated ; but there are also extensive forests and mountains abounding in lions, elephants, and other wild animals. From the copper-mines, or "Maaden Safr," it is a journey of three days to Waramba, the country of an independent chief. The town of Katanza and the copper-mines are situated in the dominions of a chief, whose title is 'Manene.' A large river, called the Rafira, flows past Katanza, and joins the Ruapoora to the North. I remained two months at Katanza ; it is a quiet peaceable place, with very few robbers : the people always treated me in a friendly manner, and goods of all kinds were abundant. In payment of purchases in the markets, you break a few beads off a string, and give them in exchange. There is no coined money. I suffered but little inconvenience from my ignorance of the languages of the various countries through which I passed, because the Africans, who accompanied me from Zanzibar, acquired these languages with surprising rapidity, and always made themselves understood.

From Katanza, I travelled in a westerly direction, and, after two months, reached a country called Boira. The country through which I passed is divided into petty states, the chiefs treat travellers well, but it is necessary to stay amongst them and gain their goodwill. The country was generally thickly peopled, and grain, fowls, sheep, and vegetables, always procurable in abundance.

From Boira, I went a journey of seventeen days to " Warengeh :" the people of this country are the most barbarous I met with during all my travels ; they go entirely naked, and pull out all their upper front teeth. From Warengeh, I travelled in two months to a country called Ugengeh, not far from the river Zambesi ; the chief ruler of this country is named " Makororo :" the people are a handsome race, many are quite fair with long hair flowing over the neck, others are as black as negroes. In

Ugengeh, the people possess abundance of horned cattle, horses, sheep, and goats : they travel about, and carry on a considerable trade. From Ugengeh, I went in thirty days' journey through a fine rich country to Lui : there is very little forest in this part ; cattle, sheep, goats, and poultry are everywhere abundant. I reached the city of Loanda, on the shore of the great ocean in eighty-days' journey from Lui. I remained at Loanda twenty-five days, and then returned into the interior. I travelled about in various directions, trading in ivory, and visited the city of Loanda three times. I resided at various towns in the interior ; and, at length, having been absent from my own country for so many years, I resolved to return to Zanzibar. I travelled east until I reached the river Zambesi, and then proceeded north until I reached the great lake Nyassa. I travelled seventeen days along the shore of the lake towards its northern end, in order to cross it at a narrow point, and I then returned to the east coast through the country of the Miyan and Magindo tribes. The lake of Nyassa is of vast extent, a large frigate could manœuvre on it. The country all around is very rich ; cotton grows everywhere in great abundance, and the natives weave it into cloth.

During all my journeys, I met with hospitality and friendship, and I intend returning to the interior of Africa after arranging my affairs here. I met Dr. Livingstone near the Zambesi, and conveyed letters for him to Loanda. I have never written down anything I observed during my travels, because Arabs take no interest in the discovery of foreign countries, and do not care to hear of anything unconnected with the acquisition of riches.

INDEX.

INDEX.

BOMBAY : Printed at the EDUCATION SOCIETY'S PRESS, BYCULLA.